WHY THE JEWS REJECTED JESUS

THE TURNING POINT IN

WESTERN HISTORY

DAVID KLINGHOFFER

PUBLISHED BY DOUBLEDAY
a division of Random House, Inc.

DOUBLEDAY and the portrayal of an anchor with a dolphin
are registered trademarks of Random House, Inc.

Book design by Gretchen Achilles

Library of Congress Cataloging-in-Publication Data
Klinghoffer, David, 1965–
Why the Jews rejected Jesus : the turning point in
Western history / David Klinghoffer.— 1st ed.
p. cm.
Includes bibliographical references (p.) and index.
1. Jesus Christ—Jewish interpretations.   2. Jesus Christ—
Messiahship.   3. Christianity and other religions—Judaism.
4. Judaism—Relations—Christianity.   I. Title.
BM620.K55 2005
296.3'96—dc22
2004056174

ISBN 0-385-51021-7

PRINTED IN THE UNITED STATES OF AMERICA

March 2005

First Edition

1   3   5   7   9   10   8   6   4   2

For Naomi

CONTENTS

CONTENTS

THANK THE JEWS

One day not long ago, a pair of window washers came into my office in downtown Seattle. The older and brawnier of the two, a thoughtful guy about forty years old, noticed the Hebrew books piled around my laptop. He started a conversation. One topic led to another, and before I knew it he was giving me a scriptural proof of the virgin birth. I responded by pointing out that the verse in Isaiah he was referring to has been a matter of dispute between Jews and Christians for two millennia. He proceeded to speak of his relationship with Christ, and I spoke of knowing God through the medium of the Torah. Forty-five minutes later, the man shook my hand, looking puzzled and distraught, said, "Well, God bless you," and left.

The distress of sincere Christians at the thought of Jews rejecting Jesus is understandable. After all, in their system of beliefs, the eternal fate of a person's soul hinges on the relationship he has formed with the Christian Messiah. Jewish friends of mine who, like me, work and socialize with serious Christians are often asked, however the question may be phrased, "You seem like such a nice person. You know your Bible. How could it be that you don't see the need for Christ in your life?" The puzzlement is heightened when the Jew in question is a political conservative, also like me, speaking with conservative or Evangelical Christians.

That Jesus was a Jew is a point often made by such Christians.

What, then, accounts for the Jewish resistance to him? Wouldn't the world be a better place if Christ's people accepted their own Messiah?

A few days after my conversation with the missionary window washer, Mel Gibson's *The Passion of the Christ* was released. The film aroused tremendous hostility from leaders in the American Jewish community. The Anti-Defamation League (ADL), the country's most prominent Jewish group, feverishly prophesied that the film "could fuel latent anti-Semitism." In an article in the Jewish-owned and -edited weekly *The New Republic*, a Jewish professor of religious studies, Paula Fredriksen, in all earnestness gave it not as speculation but as a certainty that when the film appeared in countries like Poland, Spain, France, and Russia, savagery would erupt: "When violence breaks out, Mel Gibson will have a much higher authority than professors and bishops to answer to." The *Los Angeles Weekly* called Gibson's movie "a gasoline-soaked rag tossed on the already roaring flames of anti-Semitism." Rabbi Tovia Singer, a radio talk-show host, warned, "By the time the first nail is hammered into the cross, viewers in Germany will be passing around knife sharpeners in the theater. Israel may have to absorb a massive flight of European Jewry." Of course, none of this happened—despite the fact that, thanks to the ADL's widely publicized attacks, many more people saw Gibson's *Passion* than would otherwise have done so.

What was expected to bring on this tsunami of Jew hatred, not least from the very same Evangelical Christians who are among the state of Israel's most ardent supporters? The ADL specifically decried the movie's depiction of Jewish complicity in Jesus's death, recalling the history of medieval Passion plays that sparked anti-Semitic furies among Christians. As the New Testament tells the story, and as Gibson does, the Jewish leadership of Jesus's time not only rejected Jesus, but conspired to hand him over to the Romans for crucifixion. Or as the marquee of Denver's Lovingway United Pentecostal Church put it the day that *The Passion* was released, "JEWS KILLED THE LORD JESUS; SETTLED!"

A neutral observer might have come away from the whole episode thinking that the main point of dispute between Jews and Christians is over whether the Jews killed Jesus. The surprising truth, however, is that Jews have long acknowledged the role played by a few prominent ancestors in the events leading to the Crucifixion. Basing himself on the Talmud (before it was censored—of which more below), the twelfth-century sage Maimonides wrote of "Jesus of Nazareth, who imagined that he was the Messiah, but was put to death by the court." And again: "The sages, of blessed memory, having become aware of his plans before his reputation spread among our people, meted out fitting punishment to him." (Maimonides's comments were themselves later censored by Jews fearful of Christian reprisals. We'll see to what extent these passages can be taken as historically informative.)

What Jews in fact have disputed with Jesus's followers from the very beginning is not the circumstances of his death, but the question of his messiahship. It would not be accurate to say that the Jews who were alive in 28 CE actively and altogether rejected him. The vast majority had never heard of him. But it is also true that they did not accept whatever claim he made (or was made on his behalf) to being the promised Messiah. Later generations made a more conscious decision to reject Christian doctrine—though of course there were plenty of individual Jews who did accept that doctrine and became sincere Christians.

The disputation has been going on ever since, as I will show in this book—the first to tell the story of this ancient debate in the form of a historical narrative. Beginning with how Judaism looked in the year immediately before Jesus initiated his ministry, we will tell the story of how Jews reacted to him as a teacher and provocateur, what role they may have played in his death, how they violently rejected the apostle Paul, how the debate about Jesus developed in the Talmudic and medieval periods, and how the disagreement continues down to the present.

In our time, a strong current of opinion in the Jewish community is reluctant to engage the questions this book considers. As the reaction to Gibson's film dramatically illustrates, this is partly from fear of revealing the things traditional Jewish sources have said about Jesus, especially about his death; partly from the misconception that Judaism discourages Jews from exposing non-Jews to the Jewish faith where it contradicts other religions; partly, I'm afraid, because the leadership of the American Jewish community is not committed to the belief that their ancestral religion is even true and can be defended on rational grounds. There is a strong relativistic tendency among establishment groups like the Anti-Defamation League, which take it as a given that, as ADL national director Abraham Foxman has said, "it is pure arrogance for any one religion to assume that they hold 'the truth.' " Presumably this would apply to Judaism, too. For Gibson to assert the truth of his religion was therefore wrong, as it would be wrong to assert the truth of Judaism.

The release of *The Passion* was a cultural watershed in several ways. It demonstrated the untruths—about history, about Judaism—that much of the American Jewish community and many other well-meaning Americans have come to accept as dogma. According to one such untruth, Jews had nothing to do with Jesus's death. According to another, much more important for our purposes here, it is somehow un-Jewish to state unapologetically the case for Judaism as against other religions. Widespread misinformation poisons a culture. In our culture, the need to dispel the untruths has become urgent. That is why I have written this book.

I hear the objections: What good does it do, you might reasonably ask, to risk offending Christian friends with frank words about their savior? Who exactly benefits from a systematic exposition of the ways Jews have explained their decision to refuse the Christian "good news" about Jesus?

These objections can, arguably, even be substantiated from Jewish tradition itself. "I will give you treasures concealed in the darkness," the prophet Isaiah wrote.[1] There are indeed some things—hidden treasures, dark truths—we are better off leaving concealed. The Talmud recounts that when the Jews went into exile among the world's nations, God imposed on them a series of oaths. One of these forbade the Jews from exposing certain unspecified teachings, comprising a secret tradition (*ha'sod*), to their new gentile neighbors.[2] Could it be that one such secret concerns the reason, or reasons, behind the Jewish rejection of Jesus?

After all, other passages in the Talmud, that principal repository of

Jewish tradition, were long ago censored for fear of provoking Christian persecutors. Narrations concerning Jesus's life, death, and fate beyond the grave were all expunged. Is it possible that exposing them to the public would violate the oath? Even some friendly non-Jews have sought to hide the most explosive of these. In one book written by an English Christian scholar in 1903, collecting translations of Talmudic references to Jesus and early Christianity, the author decided that one passage in particular was so disturbing that it should not be rendered in English. Instead he translated it into Latin.

Yet I have decided to take the controversial step of gathering such material and using it to tell, for the first time from a Jewish perspective, the story of the two-thousand-year Jewish-Christian debate about Jesus. Besides the urgency of the present cultural moment, I have three reasons for believing that this is the right thing to do.

First, information technology has made the keeping of secrets increasingly untenable. Thanks to anti-Semitic hate groups, some of the material I have alluded to is already available on the Internet, if in a grossly distorted form and hedged around with hateful misinterpretations. I intend to provide the historical and spiritual context to make sense of this potentially dangerous information. Some of the same data is also available from entirely respectable, if scattered, sources. We live in a time when secrets of all kinds are being revealed, secrets that in the past spiritual teachers would never have dreamed of exposing to the world—not only Jewish mystical texts, but occult and otherwise obscure doctrines from many religions are nowadays to be found in any Barnes & Noble.

Second, the relationship of Jews to Christians has changed. In medieval Europe, Jews were forced to debate Christian evangelists, with sometimes tragic results, leaving to many of their descendants a general impression that such interactions are to be avoided. Yet other Jews, in the same perilous historical context, went out of their way to challenge the prevailing belief systems of the day—whether Christian, Muslim, or broadly philosophical. One of the chief instances of Jewish polemic, Judah Halevi's *Kuzari*, written in Spain in about 1140 and challenging both Christianity and Islam, was composed in the vernacular,

Arabic—an indication that Halevi was unafraid to place his book before the widest-possible audience. Had I lived in twelfth-century Spain, I don't know that I would have been so daring. Fortunately, I enjoy the gift of being an American, in a time when it is reasonable to hope that Jews and Christians have developed the maturity to honestly explore the main issue that separates us. Never and nowhere before has the affection of Christians for Jews been more in evidence. Only in America! We are ready, I think, to investigate the larger meaning of the Jewish rejection of Jesus, not to debate but to mutually inform each other, in a spirit of civility, friendliness, even love.

Third, I am drawing together and revealing this material because I have observed in our culture a unique coinciding of Jewish with Christian interests. Jews have always had an interest, or anyway a responsibility in which they should be interested, in illuminating the world with those truths of their faith that are most relevant to gentile lives. Christians, for their part, are more curious than ever before about what Judaism can teach. Sometimes this curiosity takes the form of a straightforward eagerness to know more about the roots of their religion in the Hebrew Bible. As the conversation with my friend the window washer makes clear, it can also take a more anxious, worried form.

In this book, I will deal mainly with the question of why the Jews rejected Jesus in his lifetime and continued to decline the Christian offer of salvation with what has often seemed to Christians like either stubbornness or malice.

Everyone accepts—both Christians and Jews—that the Jewish rejection of Jesus and of Christianity in general has had important spiritual consequences for both parties. Christians have been profoundly challenged by the Jewish refusal to acknowledge Jesus as the Messiah—the claim on which the authority of his revelation is based—while Jews and Judaism itself have been profoundly impacted by the reign of Christianity in Europe.

But what about the historical consequences? Would the world really be a better place if Jews had accepted Jesus? Christians naturally assume that it would, but allow me to propose a thought experiment, a "what if" scenario contrary to historical fact. Jesus began his preaching career in Roman Palestine about the year 28. Let's imagine that, right from the start, he had attracted not indifference and disavowals from his fellow Jew, but veneration and love. We have no record, in the New Testament, of Jesus in his preaching ever having directly, unambiguously, and publicly volunteered that he was the long-awaited scion of King David, the prophesied messianic king. But never mind that. Let's stipulate Jesus did teach that he was the Messiah. Let's say that his message included, as it did, an affirmation of the principal Jewish written teaching, the Torah, or five books of Moses. What if, in his lifetime, tens or hundreds of thousands of Jews rallied to him?

Since the Romans were assiduous in putting down messianic movements in Palestine, Jesus still would have died at the hands of the colonial authority. But imagine that his memory lived on. Let's say that stories circulated of a miracle: Jesus had been raised from the dead, then ascended to heaven! What would have been the outcome?

We need to recall that in historical fact, at a critical juncture and as a direct result of the Jewish rejection of the Christian message, the early church jettisoned the observance of Jewish law. The book of Acts recounts how the apostle Paul, in teaching about Jesus, was "contra-dicted" and "reviled" by fellow Jews, leading him to conclude that the future lay no longer with his own people: "Since you thrust [the message of Christ] from you," he said, "behold, we turn to the gentiles."[3] In this way, a split developed within the church. It could continue as it was, under the leadership of Jesus's brother James: within the bounds of Torah law, requiring all converts also to be observant Jews. Or it could take Paul's more radical view of Jesus's teachings. At a council meeting of elders held in Jerusalem in the year 49, Paul made his case for dropping Jewish law as a requirement for Christians. After much debate, James agreed—and the direction of Christian history was set.

Had the Jews embraced Jesus, therefore, followers of the church of James would have continued to be obligated in the biblical commandments of circumcision, Sabbath, *kashrut* (eating only kosher food), family purity (abstaining from sex with one's wife during and for a week after menstruation), and so on. Thus, in every key respect, the Jesus movement might have remained a Jewish sect.

The consequences of this outcome for Western history would be hard to overstate. Christianity would not have spread wildly across the Roman Empire and later across Europe, as it did. Though the Jewish religion in the first century had numerous gentile admirers, known as "God fearers" who prayed in synagogues without undertaking the Jewish program of study and action as described by the Torah, Judaism per se was never designed to be a mass religion. Its rewards ascend to the heavens, but its ways take careful meditation and definite commitment to appreciate their deeper joys. This is not to say that Christianity is undemanding or without its own later tradition of church law, but command of such things was never required except of its learned clergy. A "Jewish" Christianity would have stood as much chance of taking hold of huge numbers of people as a church nowadays that asks all members to earn a master's degree in theology.

Had the Jews not rejected Jesus, had Paul not turned the church leadership to a new course, the nascent faith would in all likelihood have perished along with all the other heterodox Jewish sects that disappeared after the destruction of Jerusalem and its Temple by the Romans in 70 CE, leaving only "rabbinic" Judaism—the traditional Judaism of today. There would be no Christianity, no Christian Europe, and no Western civilization as we know it.

Quite conceivably, Islam would have arisen more or less as it did, another offspring of Judaism that also dispensed with the complexities of Jewish religious practice. Even with Christianity as the European faith, Islam nearly did penetrate and spread across the continent. It was turned back only by force, 150 miles from Paris, at the battle of Tours in 732. Had Christianity died as a failed Jewish sect in the year 70, Europe today might very well be Muslim.

For Americans, no less than Europeans, the blessings of Christianity are clear. Our land was initially settled by Puritan Christians. As for the Founding Fathers, many were Deists but none were atheists, and they spoke and wrote passionately about the role of the biblical God in inspiring the birth of their nation. Today, the United States is the most enthusiastically Christian country on earth and the most tolerant and good-hearted in history. All this is the fruit of the Jewish rejection of

Jesus. If you value the great achievements of Western civilization and of American society, thank the Jews for their decision to cleave to their ancestral religion instead of embracing the rival teachings of Jesus and his followers.

The question posed by this book has been an interest of mine for more than twenty years. In 1983, I was a high school senior in Southern California, taking classes at UCLA. There I met a Jews for Jesus missionary called Sid who had set up a table with pamphlets on Bruin Walk. In a forty-five-minute conversation, he convinced me that I didn't really understand my own reasons for not being a Christian. There was a lot I didn't know about Judaism, being, as I was, the product of a very typical suburban-liberal Jewish upbringing. That was why he could so easily disturb me with his challenges from the famous Isaiah 53.

After college, I dated and considered marrying a very spiritually engaged Catholic girl. We had innumerable debates and discussions about Jesus, which again reminded me of how ignorant I was. Owing partly to her prodding, I started to learn about and practice traditional Judaism.

In 1998, I met my future wife, who like me had grown up Jewish but without a Jewish education. In college, she went through a period as a Catholic—was baptized, then felt the magnetic pull of Judaism and left the church shortly before we met, on a blind date at a New York bar called Fez. But she was still troubled by doubts: Could it be the Jews were wrong in rejecting Jesus as the Messiah? I started to fall in love with her that night as we earnestly discussed this question till four in the morning.

As my wife's perplexity illustrates, it is almost as if Jews and Christians occupy alternative realities. In one reality, the truth of Jesus's messiahship is obvious to anyone who takes an honest look at the biblical sources. In the other reality, Jesus as Messiah is a proposition that would be hard to take seriously were there not so many intelligent and earnest Christians who stake their lives on it.

I hope to bridge that massive chasm. I would hardly wish or seek to dissuade any of the world's two billion Christians from their faith, which I have no doubt helps them have a relationship with God. Nor do I think, if I did wish or seek that, I would have much success. We believe what we believe for reasons that mostly transcend argument. My intention, rather, is to tell a story of passionate disagreement.

But the story is about more than interfaith polemics. The reasons for the Jewish rejection of Jesus are many and have evolved and crystallized in confrontation with Christian polemics. We will find that the diversity of the Jewish response masks a single historical dynamic that requires it. The Jews, in remaining Jews, serve a purpose having to do with the spiritual advancement of the other nations, guided by providence.

So while the problem at hand has long been on my mind, it is also of much more than merely personal, or merely Jewish, interest. It is the question of how our world came to be as it is. Ours is a world the Jews made by rejecting Jesus, an act dictated by their conscience and, I hope to show, by their God. If Judaism emphasizes the responsibility not to disclose to the uninitiated more than he is ready to accept or understand, it also proposes that there is a time to reveal secrets, Isaiah's "treasures concealed in the darkness." As for the particular secret I am about to begin revealing, the right time is now.

CHAPTER ONE

BEFORE CHRIST
JUDAISM IN THE YEAR 27

One of the curious things about Mel Gibson's Jesus movie, *The Passion of the Christ*, is the part the Jewish priestly establishment, headquartered in the Jerusalem Temple, plays in arresting Jesus and turning him over to the Romans. As viewers, we are supposed to be moved by this to personal repentance, recognizing our own sinfulness in the act of betrayal and violence. But the villainy of Gibson's Jews is hard to recognize because it makes no obvious sense. We are intended to believe the Temple priests are after Jesus because of a big dangerous following that's going to crown him Messiah, but nowhere in the film do these massively numbered followers ever make an appearance. From all the evidence of *The Passion*, you would think Jesus had about ten disciples, twenty maximum. So why were certain Jews so intent on seeing him dead? Gibson leaves us with no clear idea.

Much the same difficulty is posed by the Gospels themselves. From a straightforward contemplation of the text, it is not immediately clear what gets the Jews who object to Jesus so worked up. If we try to read the Gospels together, imagining them as forming a single integrated story (to the extent possible, since they are marked by disagreements as to narrative detail), we find the Jews mounting an emotional staircase leading from initial warmth, to puzzlement and perplexity, to distress, to self-righteous annoyance, and finally to a murderous rage.

When Jesus begins his ministry around the year 28, teaching in the synagogue of his hometown, Nazareth, the congregation at first "spoke well of him, and wondered at the gracious words which proceeded from out of his mouth."[1] Then, on hearing more of his preaching, "all in the synagogue were filled with wrath."[2] Other Jews, however, were moved to follow him, and on one occasion his disciples and others stood about as he sat on a mountain—the Sermon on the Mount—at which "the crowds were astonished . . . for he taught them as one who had authority, and not as their scribes."[3] The Pharisees, a Jewish faction whom we'll meet shortly, get wind of the interest and controversy Jesus is stirring up. They "murmur against his disciples," who are judged to be morally unsuitable.[4] When these self-righteous Jews find him overseeing the disciples, who are plucking grain in seeming violation of the Sabbath, "the Pharisees went out and took counsel against him, how to destroy him."[5] When Jesus heals a man on a Sabbath, the same Jews again "went out, and immediately held counsel with the Herodians against him, how to destroy him."[6] When Jesus seeks to justify himself, citing the authority of God, his "Father," then "the Jews sought all the more to kill him, because he not only broke the Sabbath but also called God his own Father, making himself equal with God."[7]

We need to step back from our assumptions about the Gospel text. Through familiarity with the general story line—we all know Jesus had detractors among his fellow Jews—we tend to assume it was only natural that small-minded bigots would take offense at this spiritually uplifted, transcendent being. But if you try to imagine reading about the Jewish reaction to Jesus without bringing to bear the cultural background of Christianity, you'll see that, as one might say of characters in a novel, the outrage of Jesus's fellow Jews seems distinctly undermotivated. They want to kill him because he healed a man by faith on the Sabbath—something in itself that Jewish law does not forbid? Or because he called God his "Father"—when God is called "Father" of the Jewish people and of their kings many times in scripture and liturgy? What's the big deal?

In the next chapter, we'll see what reasons the Jews would really have had for turning away from, or against, Jesus. In the chapter after that, we'll address the question of whether or not they can be justly accused of having him killed. For now, we need to understand who those Jews actually were. Pharisees? Herodians? What do these names denote? When "the Jews" finally succeed in having Jesus arrested and brought to trial, his persecutors are described as priests and elders. It's impossible to understand how, at this initial stage, the Jews would actually have perceived Jesus without first having a sense of their context—historical and religious. We need to clarify how, historically, the Jewish people got to where they were in the year 27, the year before Jesus started his preaching career. And we need to know what their religion taught them to believe on four key points of special relevance to Jesus and his teachings.

THE OVERALL RECEPTION of Jesus among those who knew of him—doubt turning to outright hostility—was only in keeping with a general Jewish tendency evident in the nation's past. The Jews are an acidic people, inclined to debate and question. Their inherent, inherited skepticism may account for the fact that among ancient peoples they were the first to successfully critique and forever pull away from the dominant polytheism of their world. Jewish literature, preeminently the Bible, scorns the inadequate beliefs and customs of other peoples, though not limiting its thoroughgoing critique to non-Jews. On the contrary, in Hebrew scripture, the Jews themselves come in for the roughest treatment—their moral and other intellectual failings are held up for withering scrutiny. In short, as Jesus discovered if he didn't already know it, any claim you place before the Jews will be savagely critiqued. Of all the insults that their enemies through the millennia have leveled at the Jews, one thing they have never been accused of being is credulous.

Yet at the same time, they were not nihilists or cynics. With them, certain beliefs remained constants. It has been suggested that an indication of Judaism's plausibility as an account of God and man is this fact: that a skeptical people have nevertheless retained an unbroken tradition of faith in central doctrines. Strikingly, their belief system relied on an account of mass revelation. Jewish history begins at Mount Sinai, by traditional calculation in the year 1312 BCE. At Sinai, says the Bible, God spoke to some two million Jews. There is no record of dissent among the Jews, in any generation until very recently, on this basic point. The Jewish contemporaries of Jesus agreed that Torah—a word designating the first five books of the Bible but also a vast explanatory tradition—was received at Sinai by the children of the patriarchs Abraham, Isaac, and Jacob. It was this same "teaching" (which is what *Torah* literally means) that the Jews carried with them through history. They still possessed it in the year 27.

Let us, then, briefly review Jewish history from this perspective—as a narrative of the polarity between creed and critique, skepticism and secure knowledge.

Who were the people who gathered at Sinai to become the first Jews? Before the event of Sinai, there were no Jews per se. For it is the acceptance of the Torah that defines the Jewish people, in much the same way the publishing of the Declaration of Independence defines the American nation—so that before 1776, there were no Americans. Centuries before Sinai, God had made a covenant with Abraham, who by tradition was born in 1812 BCE. The patriarchal family under his grandson Jacob lived in the land of Canaan but went down to Pharaoh's kingdom initially to escape a famine and ended up dwelling there as slaves. After leaving Egypt and receiving the Torah at Sinai as free men, they resettled in Canaan.

There, Jacob's descendants finally established their own kingdom, that of King David and his son Solomon. The latter built God's Temple in the capital city, Jerusalem. But very quickly the kingdom split—around 900 BCE—into rival states: Israel in the north and Judah in the south, centered on Jerusalem. It was, right at the beginning of Jewish statecraft, one of the most painful instances of the people's factionalism, with both kingdoms arguing that they were the rightful inheritors of biblical tradition.

Hardly two centuries later, the northern kingdom was conquered and taken away to captivity in Assyria. These were the fabled ten lost tribes. Two centuries later, Judah was overthrown by Babylon, the Temple destroyed. The Judahites were themselves led off to captivity on the banks of the Euphrates River. Seventy years later, after Babylon was conquered by Persia under the Jewish-friendly king Cyrus, the Jews returned and built a second Temple.

In this period, from shortly before the exile of the ten tribes until shortly before the fall of the First Temple, from the eighth to the sixth century BCE, there arose the classical tradition of Hebrew prophecy. We may instinctively conceive of the prophets as men who foretold the future, but this is not really what prophecy is about. The prophets did limn future events, but they were much more concerned with self-critique: rooting out falsehood, demanding an adherence to religious truth. A modern writer, Norman Podhoretz, points out that Isaiah, Ezekiel, Jeremiah, and the rest had as their overriding goal to free the Jewish people from a tendency to revert to the paganism of their ancestors or of the peoples around them. While this may make them seem bound by time and place—certainly today no one worships Ashera trees or idols to the god Baal—Podhoretz makes clear that idolatry manifests itself in every age, in one form or another. The essence of idolatry is setting up spiritual authorities in competition with, or to the negation of, God. Today, we might identify it with a strain of secularism, which has all the elements of a religion but one, a deity. The other pagan hallmarks are there: relativism, nature worship, sexual corruption, and a willingness to sacrifice children to the cause.

Jews have been fighting idolatry in its guises since their inception as a people. Typically, it was other Jews who were the advocates of spiritual deviance, and sometimes it was not at all obvious that they advocated the worship of other gods. In Jeremiah's time, in the lead-up to the destruction of the First Temple, certain false prophets took it as their main theme to assure the people that despite moral turpitude, they would enjoy peace. But a "peace" that does not satisfy God's will to see evil rooted out is not true peace. They made phony promises, saying, "'Peace! Peace!' But," declared Jeremiah, "there is no peace . . . We may hope for peace, but there is no goodness; [we hope] for a time of healing, but behold, there is terror."[8]

Terror came, the Temple fell and was rebuilt. Later, through the conquests of Alexander the Great, the new Jewish land passed from Persian overlordship to Greek. At Alexander's death, in 323 BCE, his empire was divided. Initially the Jewish land was assigned to the Greek kingdom of the relatively easygoing Ptolemies. Subsequently it changed hands, coming under the power of another inheritor of Alexander's realm, the Seleucids.

Again we see the Jewish critical habit. The story is told in the biblical section called the Apocrypha, the first and second books of Maccabees (not found in Jewish Bibles). The Greek Seleucid kingdom was headquartered in Syria under the rule of the tyrant Antiochus IV Epiphanes. A Jewish elite in Jerusalem with social-climbing ambitions, wishing to emulate the Greeks with their cosmopolitan culture (Hellenism), began introducing elements of Greek secularism in the fields of athletics and education.

At first, the rewards of Hellenism were enjoyed only by an informally organized upper class. This self-consciously sophisticated smart set exercised in the new Greek gymnasium—naked discus throwing was the sport of choice. Jewish priests abandoned their sacerdotal duties and donned the latest Greek fashions. Embarrassed by the traditional ways of their ancestors, the chic urbanites even went so far as to have their circumcisions effaced through cosmetic surgery. They ended up opening Jerusalem's gates to Antiochus, who sacked the Temple treasury (where poor Jews had their money on deposit). To the applause of the radical Hellenizers, Antiochus outlawed Judaism altogether. Books of the Torah were burned, circumcision became a capital crime, and a pig was offered on a new pagan altar in the Temple itself.

The "critique" of Jewish Hellenism came from the party of the conservatives, the Maccabees, who revolted and initiated a civil war. The conflict pitted traditional religious values against secular values (the gymnasium, immodest dress or lack of dress, and other Greek fashions). While the progressives were driven as much by social ambition as by principle, the conservatives had numbers and passion on their side. They were ready to die in defense of their tradition. It is the victory of these religious fundamentalists, their establishment of the

Hasmonaean dynasty, that Judaism celebrates at the holiday of
Hanukkah.

The Jews kept on guard against departures from inherited truths.
The essential conservatism of the Jewish religion combined naturally
with the Jewish inclination to fierce ideological combat to produce frequent disturbances of the peace.

The rule of the Hasmoneans faded into that of the brutally dys-
functional Herod family, a client regime of the now dominant power in
the Mediterranean world: Rome. Gone murderously mad in his later
years, Herod slaughtered his wife and two male heirs. Altogether, it
would be hard to imagine a more mendacious, jealous, backbiting,
paranoid family. The acidic Jews objected to Herod on a variety of
grounds, one being that he wasn't, strictly speaking, considered to be a
Jew himself (his mother was an Arabian, his father an Idumaean, both
doubtful converts), another being that he sought to eviscerate the religious authority of the rabbis, or Pharisees, by having them all (or almost all, says the Talmud) murdered. But the Jewish critique of Herod
extended to more detailed matters, like the huge figure of a golden ea-
gle (possibly symbolizing the Roman Empire) he affixed above the
Great Gate to the Temple. A couple of rabbis encouraged their students to lower themselves by ropes and cut down the offending graven
image—which they did, only to be caught by the king's soldiers before
finishing the task and subsequently burned alive.

At his death, King Herod left upon the throne his son Aristobulus.
This king was too wicked to be tolerated even if the alternative was direct Roman rule, for which the Jews finally opted. Rome absorbed
Judea as part of the province of Syria, policed by Roman centurions
who kept an eye on the Jewish population, not least on their Temple,
from the sinister adjoining aerie of the fortress Antonia.

The Jews, not surprisingly, were restive with this situation. For the
Roman occupiers, supervising them was no easy job, not least on the
three yearly pilgrimage holidays when Jews from across the country
and everywhere in the Diaspora flocked to Jerusalem to offer their sacrifices in the Temple. Most of the pilgrims came armed and ready to
find offense in Roman conduct. The Romans obliged. On a certain un-

lucky Passover, an imperial soldier mooned the assembled worshippers, showing them his rear end and making an obscene noise. The crowd went wild with indignation, the procurator sent in troops to put down the possible uprising, and a reported thirty thousand Jews died in the crush.

Down to the fiery end with the Roman sacking of Jerusalem in 70, the people remained ferociously loyal to their biblical tradition. This is the context for the year immediately before the one we are focusing on here. In 26, Pontius Pilate came to Roman Judea as procurator, appointed by the emperor Tiberius (14–37 CE). As portrayed by Josephus, the first-century Jewish historian (born in 37, year of death unknown) who gives us the most complete and vivid portrait of the time, he appears as a very different character from the Pilate who makes a cameo in the Gospels and in Gibson's *Passion of the Christ*. In the New Testament, he is a weak personality who succumbs to Jewish pressure to crucify the obviously innocent Jesus. In Gibson's representation, he is world-weary, cosmopolitan, philosophical. In Josephus, he is simply a tyrant, callously indifferent to Jewish sentiment.

Soon after his arrival at the distant outpost, Pilate ordered military standards to be set up by night in the holy city. These were poles carrying circular plaques with the emperor's image, intended as objects of worship, for the Roman emperor was venerated as a god. Next morning, the people woke to discover the sacrilege. They formed an outraged mob. The mere presence of the standards so fired them up that they marched immediately to confront Pilate at his headquarters in the coastal city of Caesarea. Josephus recounts that the Jews, "casting themselves prostrate and baring their throats, declared that they had gladly welcomed death rather than make bold to transgress the wise provisions of the laws. Pilate, astonished at the strength of their devotion to the laws, straightway removed the images from Jerusalem and brought them back to Caesarea."[9]

Another time, Pilate inflamed the Jews by seizing treasure from the Temple: the yearly half-shekel tax paid by Jews around the world for upkeep of the great edifice. Pilate used the money for a public good, building a fifty-mile-long aqueduct. Nevertheless, when he next visited Jerusalem the crowd once again harangued him, but his soldiers massacred them horribly.

FROM THE VERY BEGINNING, Jews have been fighting with one another, and with other peoples, about the right way to serve God. It comes as little surprise, then, that one of the themes of Jewish history has been a constant reversion to factionalism. In Jesus's day, the factions included those Pharisees (the rabbis and their followers), Herodians (supporters of the royal family), and priests (broadly identified with the sect of the Sadducees) whom the Gospels identify as his persecutors. Understanding the reception Jesus got requires understanding what all these parties stood for.

For describing the fragmented religious beliefs of Jews at this time, Josephus, himself a priest and military leader, is one of our chief contemporary witnesses. Not that there is much competition. Literature written by Jews in this century is scarce. Today's professional scholars devote long careers to picking over the so-called intertestamental literature, including the Apocrypha found in the back of some Christian Bibles and still more so the books of the desert sect, the Essenes, that lived by the Dead Sea at Qumran, the monastic, cultish community that produced the Dead Sea Scrolls. The Qumran manifestation of Jewish spirituality in particular need not detain us long. Scholars today speak of there being not one "Judaism" at this time, but rather multiple "Judaisms." They are right, technically. However, by way of a modern analogy, it is also right technically to say that America has a multiparty political system. Besides Republicans and Democrats, we also have Libertarians and Greens and a host of other third parties, none of which has a major impact on the political decision-making process.

So it was in first-century Palestine. When the Gospel writers portray the religious scene they knew, they depict a Jewish establishment comprising two main groups: Pharisees and Sadducees. While there were other "Judaisms," evidently they were marginal. The intensity of modern scholarly attention paid to the Dead Sea Scrolls owes more to the intriguing spookiness of the name, and to the romance inherent in a discovery of ancient scrolls in desert caves, than it does to any genuine stature the sectarians possessed.

Josephus widens the field a little, describing four parties that were active in his day. One was the ascetic Essenes, whose headquarters may have been at Qumran while lay members lived in urban communes. He finds their customs exotic and goes into some detail about their communistic ways, pooling all property; their peculiar attitudes about women; their clothing and bathing habits, wearing white and going about with a special hatchet to cover over the remains of their passed wastes.

If the manuals and scriptural commentaries found in Qumran's caves belonged to the Essenes, then it would appear the group got its start as a breakaway from the priesthood of the Jerusalem Temple. The latter, dominated by the Sadducean sect, were the real power brokers of ancient Palestine. Sadducees were also the biblical fundamentalists of their day, insisting that all the faithful Jew needed to understand his Torah was the plain text itself. Because that text alludes only in cryptic fashion to certain matters that were close to many Jewish hearts, the Sadducees were distant from popular piety. They rejected the idea of a resurrection of the dead in the next world, and of any afterlife at all, because they found no clear indication of these in scripture.

Josephus notes that this priestly sect was ill-natured "even towards each other, show[ing] a . . . disagreeable spirit, and in their relations with men like themselves they are as harsh as they might be to foreigners."[10] Yet they controlled the Temple and worked closely with the Romans to keep the nation at peace.

Josephus has much the most negative things to say about a party of nationalists devoted to tax reform, whom he holds responsible for the disastrous revolt that broke out against Rome in 66. A rabbi with his own sect, called Judas, led this antitax movement, starting after 6 CE when Palestine came under direct Roman rule. A registration of property that year for tax assessment purposes is noted in Luke's Gospel as coinciding with Jesus's birth.

The "leading sect" in popular eyes, however, was the Pharisees. Their teachers were called rabbis, "held to be the most authoritative exponents of the Law," meaning the Torah. They "are friendly to one another and seek to promote concord with the general public.'" Josephus has them believing not only in resurrection, but in the transmigration of souls—rebirth in another body after one has passed from this life. They are "extremely influential among the townsfolk; and all prayers and sacred rites of divine worship are performed according to their expositions." Josephus writes, "The Pharisees simplify their standard of living, making no concession to luxury. They follow the guidance of that which their doctrine has selected and transmitted as good, attaching the chief importance to the observance of those commandments which it has seen fit to dictate to them.'" We shall return to the question of what this notable "doctrine" of the Pharisees actually was.

I have quoted from Josephus at length because his descriptions are so pungently clear, but also because his eyewitness account is hard to reconcile with that of New Testament, with its sweeping depiction of the Pharisees as fussy nitpickers. How such a narrowly circumscribed society of pious frauds could be so popular with ordinary Jews is hard to explain. Which of course isn't to say there were no such individuals on the Palestinian scene. Ancient rabbinic literature itself excoriates self-righteous hypocrites within the Pharisaic party, recounting their faults in amusing detail. But contrary to the portrayal in the Gospels, such "ruiners of the world" (as the most essential rabbinic document, the Mishnah, calls them) were a minority, not the whole of the rabbinic establishment.'"

Altogether the most rounded and fair view is that of the leading scholars of a couple of generations ago, notably George F. Moore and R. Travers Herford, supplemented in some respects by writings of some more recent historians, such as E. P. Sanders. They find a continuity joining the rabbis of Jesus's day with their students and their students' students, forming a grand tradition through the centuries seeking to explain all of the universe in terms of God's Torah, a tradition full of life and mystery.

This conception of "normative Judaism" is dismissed today in some scholarly circles, but it's in the nature of scholars to dismiss the work of their predecessors. Only this makes it possible to do work that can be hailed as new.

It was not so with the rabbis, who felt that to make up a doctrine of one's own was a betrayal, and this would be fundamental to the Jewish rejection of Pauline Christianity. Any authentic teaching had its origins not with the teacher who articulated it, but with his teachers starting with Moses at Mount Sinai, who learned from God.

Finally, to Josephus's four parties we may add a fifth, particularly active from about 44 onward: the mob, an ever shifting entity whose role was to lionize and follow a succession of false messiahs and pseudoprophets, whose careers as savior or seer each ended with disappointment and disaster. For a proud people irked at being under the thumb of a foreign occupation, however mild, as Rome's in fact was, and at the same time imbued with an ancient inherited literature with its cryptic messianic prophecies, it was only natural that such popular movements should spring up. In this time of religious and political ferment, there was a belief current that Hebrew scripture contained an "oracle" pointing to the imminent coming of a messianic deliverer, a world monarch who would emerge from the holy land. Then again, it might be not a messiah, but a prophet. It is unclear what the oracle actually was—though in Deuteronomy, Moses had promised, "A prophet from your midst, from your brethren, like me, shall the Lord, your God, establish for you—to him shall you hearken."[14] The fact that a deliverer was expected at this time does not mean that anything in the words of the prophets actually pointed to the first century as the foretold moment in history when the Jews would be redeemed. Just as in our own day when charismatic cults turn up, led by gurus who will show you evidence from the Bible that *now* is the long-ago prophesied time of redemption—the Reverend Sun Myung Moon, a self-styled messiah, comes to mind—so it was then. In the Bible, an imaginative person can "discover" proof of just about anything.

Thus, a man possessing the gifts of charisma, military prowess, or spiritual inspiration might easily get the idea in his mind that he was It: the promised Messiah. That the Messiah was supposed to be a descendant of King David wasn't necessarily a big problem for someone who, in fact, had no such distinguished lineage. Then as now, a family tree might be fudged a bit: a hopeful messiah could "remember" a family legend that one of the ancient ancestors was David himself. Or he might reason that since he was manifestly the Messiah, he *must* in reality possess Davidic lineage, but owing to poor memories or record keeping, this had been forgotten over time. The Messiah, some apparently thought, needn't even be a Jew. Josephus would later claim as the prophetically promised king the very same Roman, Vespasian, who as a general undertook the assignment of suppressing the Jewish rebellion that caught fire in 66. In the midst of the Jewish war, Vespasian was acclaimed as emperor—emerging from Palestine to the seat of world dominion, thus fulfilling the oracle in Josephus's estimation. This was not exactly the traditional picture of the Messiah, but never mind.

These mass movements might hope to attract as many as thirty thousand people—as did a man identified by Josephus only as "the Egyptian false prophet . . . a fraud who posed as a seer," leading his "dupes" from "the desert to the Mount of Olives, and from there was [he] ready to force an entry into Jerusalem, overwhelm the Roman garrison, and seize supreme power." He claimed that by his command he could make the walls of the city fall. They didn't. He was defeated by Roman heavy infantry, and most of the thirty thousand dupes were killed or captured.[15] Other prophets and messiahs met similar fates. The false prophet Theudas led four hundred to the Jordan River, which he promised would part at his word.[16] It didn't. The Roman procurator Fadus cut off his head.

The history of the Jewish people had been building toward this expectation of a future deliverer. And while messianic expectations could be quite free-floating, untethered to the actual writings of genuine prophets—as was Josephus's identification of Vespasian as the promised redeemer—any proposed messiah, to win popular approval, had to be measured against Judaism's biblical heritage. The Jews being the nation of self-appointed critics that they were, a messiah whose teaching seemed to depart too much from the inherited religion would meet with skepticism from his fellow Jews. Since Jesus was such a proposed messiah, we'll need to understand how he would have appeared *as a Jew* to his listeners. But that requires first grasping what the religion of Judaism meant in his time.

You might wonder to what degree the Jews of the time themselves had a firm grasp of their faith. Can we assume a high level of society-wide scriptural literacy—or of literacy in general? Probably so. Of all the peoples in the Mediterranean world, the Jews and the Greeks were the most intensively educated in their respective literatures—the Jews even to a greater degree, starting from young childhood. If you wanted to prove the authenticity of a religious claim, it was natural to do so by citing the Bible. When the Gospel writers sought to make their case for Jesus, they punctuated their stories with allusions to scripture—especially to prophecies that they believed he had fulfilled. Jesus himself said, "If you believed Moses, you would believe me, for he wrote of me. But if you do not believe his writings, how will you believe my words?"[17]

What are the key points that a reasonably informed Jew would have kept in mind in evaluating Jesus and, later, the early church? Judaism of the first century, where it is relevant to our subject, can be boiled down to four points: that scripture is cryptic, that God is One, that religious commandments are the eternal essence of Judaism, and that a Davidic messiah may be expected.

REVEALING TORAH. The basic source of Judaism, the five books of Moses, or Pentateuch, is quite unlike other holy works. The more you read it in its original language, the more you realize how in need of interpretation it is—and not just of any interpretation. Any new religious sect, like that of the earliest followers of Jesus, would have to explain where it stood in relationship to the inherited tradition of interpretation: the oral Torah.

The Pentateuch contained innumerable textual difficulties—syntax errors, spelling and grammatical anomalies, internal contradictions, narrative and other material repeated without apparent reason, persons abruptly introduced and then suddenly dropped, gaps of logic, key data left out, and so on. The rabbis taught that what looked like editing glitches in almost every verse were really allusions to esoteric teachings. This is the special "doctrine" of the Pharisees to which Josephus alludes.

The rabbis said they could trace the genealogy by which these meanings had been orally transmitted. So we find in the first chapter of the Mishnah's tractate *Avot* ("Fathers"). It begins, "Moses received Torah [the written and the oral] from Sinai and transmitted it to Joshua, and Joshua to the elders, and the elders to the prophets. The prophets transmitted it to the men of the Great Assembly . . ." There unfolds a listing of named authorities who received and passed on the tradition, down to Hillel and Shammai, and to Gamaliel the Elder, the leading rabbinic figure during Jesus's lifetime. The apostle Paul claimed to have been his disciple.

It was more than a century and a half after Jesus's death that the rabbis resolved that their tradition was in danger of being forgotten and so must be committed to writing. This was done about 200 CE in the Mishnah, which is almost as cryptic as the written Torah. Here, rabbis who had lived in earlier generations are quoted as ruling on a range of Jewish practices. Two centuries later, about 400 CE, more oral tradition was written down, explaining the Mishnah. This was the Palestinian Talmud. A century after that, a still more expansive rendition of the oral Torah was edited in the leading center of the Jewish Diaspora. This was the Babylonian Talmud.

Part of the tradition dealt with legal rulings, part with narrative embellishments on scriptural stories or tales about the rabbis themselves. Such narrative material, which can also encompass legal matters, is termed *midrash*. Rabbis active in the couple of centuries before the Mishnah was edited are called *tannaim* (individually, such a rabbi was a *tanna*). Their students, whose statements appear in the Talmuds, are *amoraim* (individually, an *amora*).

The important *tannaitic* text called *Sifra*, a *midrash* on the book of Leviticus, taught that all the commandments were revealed from Sinai, in every detail, whether in written or oral form.[18] Not only that, but God spoke to Moses *every word* that would be recorded in the ancient rabbinic sources, no matter in whose name any given teaching might be reported, no matter when it happened to be first written down.[19] Oral Torah was a special bond between God and the Jewish people, a secret link untrammeled by outsiders.

Whether or not you accept this rabbinic theory as a rendition of an actual historical transmission of data, it is impossible to understand Judaism of this period without at least appreciating the theory. It is also hard to think of another more plausible explanation for all the seeming glitches in the Pentateuch. Either the book really does seek to direct our attention to esoteric teachings, in which case the Torah is a code, a locked text, and everyone knows that neither a code nor a lock is ever made without a key; or it is the product of a unique editing process resulting in both the most ineptly edited book ever and at the same time the most brilliantly influential.

As an example of how oral tradition conveyed directives to be obeyed, the Mishnah lists thirty-nine forbidden Sabbath labors, which it finds only hinted at in scripture's story of the building of the Tabernacle, like a portable Temple, by the generation that left Egypt in the Exodus.[20] Yet it would have been regarded as the greatest mistake to understand Torah as merely a collection of rules. Rabbi Akiva, who lived a hundred years after Jesus, formulated the most sweeping assessment of what made Torah so precious. It was no less than the "desirable vessel through which the world was created."[21] The midrashic collection *Genesis Rabbah* clarifies this a little, quoting Rabbi Hoshiah, who said, "The Holy One Blessed Be He looked in the Torah and created the world."[22] Hoshiah draws an analogy to an architect (God) consulting his blueprint (Torah) before embarking on a building project. Is this supposed to mean that somewhere in the Pentateuch we should find a little map of the Middle East that the Lord was gazing at when He made Israel's Mediterranean coastline? No, the point seems to be that Torah gives its readers the key to understanding how the world works. In that sense it's a blueprint. If you understand Torah, you understand the world.

To what extent was this exalted evaluation of biblical and rabbinic tradition shared by the simple Jew who read his Bible? After all, in dealing with his fellow Jews, Jesus encountered not only sophisticated rabbis, but also—indeed, primarily—ordinary men and women who were not sages. Unfortunately, we cannot interview a typical "Jew in the street" from this period to find out what specific ideas he held about his religion. In investigating the Jewish reception of Jesus, we are limited to written sources, and these are invariably the work of an elite minority. Yet we may proceed by inference. What the popular party of the rabbis espoused, probably so did the people, if in a less expert fashion.

Even more so, what the biblical books said was held by them in high reverence. Rabbinic Judaism is an intellectually demanding religion, not quite like any other. Scripture, by contrast, speaks also at a simple level, hammering away at its primary messages, repeating them over and over in the clearest possible language, often in the very same words. The plainest Jew could not help but absorb the main points. Inevitably he would distrust anyone who misconstrued the Bible so as to contradict these basics.

From the vast corpus of the Hebrew Bible, three motifs are particularly important for understanding the Jewish rejection of Jesus. They are three criteria by which Jews would evaluate Christian assertions about him. We will now take up each in turn.

THE ONE GOD. The Jews repeatedly risked slaughter in defense of the idea that God can tolerate no competitors. As corollaries, He is also omnipresent yet invisible and for this reason affronted by any physical representation of divinity. On the first occasion when Rome took control of Jerusalem, in 63 BCE, the Roman general Pompey was amazed at the fanatical Jewish insistence on this point. He had fought his way into the Temple, butchering Jews around the altar itself. Josephus recounts that even during the Roman assault, the Jews kept up the observances of the cult: "Many of the priests, though they saw the enemy approach sword in hand, quietly went on with the sacred rites and were cut down as they poured libations and offered incense, putting the service of God before their own preservation." Not only priests, but a total of twelve thousand Jews died. When Pompey and his staff entered the Sanctuary, sending "a shudder through the nation [at] the exposure by aliens of the Holy Place, hitherto screened from all eyes," the Romans were astonished to find—nothing.[23] It was empty. For all the pomp and grandeur of the Temple, its heart, the holy of holies, was free of all statuary or other images, as befitting the universal, singular Deity who could not be seen.

All of which was simply in keeping with scripture. On this, no book in the Bible is clearer than Deuteronomy, altogether the single most important source for understanding what the ordinary Jew thought on the questions we are considering. It consists of Moses's farewell oration to the people, forty years after the Exodus from Egypt, as they stood in the plains of Moab ready to enter the land of Israel. During those forty years, the Israelites had received a thorough education in what it was going to mean to be a Jew. Now Moses, seeing his own death approaching, stood for five days and reviewed what they had learned.

As a centerpiece of the address, he recalls their experience at Sinai. "But you shall greatly beware for your souls, for you did not see any likeness on the day the Lord spoke to you . . . from the midst of fire, lest you act corruptly and make for yourselves a carved image, a likeness of any shape; a form of a male or a female . . ."[24] It was crucial not to imagine God as a visible being. Because the Lord never showed Himself in the "likeness of any shape," such an error could lead only to worshipping other gods who were imagined to have a physical manifestation. He was passionate about the exclusiveness of His relationship to the Jewish people. That basic fact was conveyed in the Second Commandment: "You shall not recognize the gods of others in My Presence . . . for I am the Lord, your God—a jealous God."[25] This was said over and over. "He is a consuming fire, a jealous God."[26] "For a jealous God is the Lord."[27] Anyone who worshipped other gods was warned, "The Lord will not be willing to forgive him, for then the Lord's anger and jealousy will smoke against that man."[28]

This was not because God had any divine companions in the heavens, with whom He competed for humanity's attention. "You have been shown [the miracles that accompanied the Exodus] in order to know that the Lord, He is *the* God! There is none beside Him!"[29] "There is none other."[30] "See, now, that I, I am He—and no god is with

Me."[31] "Hear, O Israel: the Lord is our God, the Lord is the One and Only."[32]

A RELIGION OF COMMANDMENTS. The last text cited immediately above, the opening verse of the *Shema*, the fundamental declaration of Jewish belief, continues: "You shall love the Lord, your God, with all your heart, with all your soul, and with all your resources. And these matters that I command you today shall be upon your heart."[33] Judaism doesn't get any more basic than these three sentences: The Lord is One. He desires the love of His people. This love is expressed through fulfilling commandments, which are the language in which the Jews act out their relationship with God.

In Deuteronomy, no idea is more strenuously emphasized than the binding nature of the commandments. Says Moses, "See, I have taught you decrees and ordinances . . . You shall safeguard and perform them."[34] "You shall observe His decrees and His commandments that I command you this day."[35] "Observe all His decrees and commandments."[36] "You shall observe the commandments of the Lord."[37] "So you shall observe the entire commandment that I command you today."[38] "This day, the Lord, your God, commands you to perform these decrees and the statutes, and you shall observe and perform them with all your heart and with all your soul." "You shall love the Lord, your God, and you shall safeguard His charge, His decrees, His ordinances, and His commandments, all the days."[39] God "show[s] kindness for thousands [of generations], to those who love Me and observe My commandments."[40]

"All the days," "for thousands" of generations—the eternality of the commandments was also stressed. "Not with you alone do I seal this covenant and this imprecation but with whoever is here, standing with us today before the Lord, our God, and with whoever is not here with us today."[41]

The covenant would stand unchanged in all its details: "You shall not add to the word that I command you, nor shall you subtract from it."[42] "You shall not add to it and you shall not subtract from it."[43]

What God asked was not beyond human capacity: "For this commandment that I command you today—it is not hidden from you and it is not distant. It is not in heaven . . . nor is it across the sea . . . Rather, the matter is very near to you—in your mouth and your heart—to perform it."[44]

The Jews would be tested. God would send the people true prophets, like Moses, to give advice and admonitions. But he would also send false ones, doing "wonders" and "signs" and urging Israel to worship another god and forsake the commandments. "Do not hearken to the words of that prophet . . . for the Lord, your God, is testing you to know whether you love the Lord, your God, with all your heart and with all your soul. The Lord, your God, shall you follow . . . ; His commandments shall you observe." The people must recognize the false prophet and eliminate the spiritual danger he poses, "destroy[ing] the evil in your midst." "And that prophet . . . shall be put to death."[45]

It was like a jealous lover that God set such tests. If enough of the Jews should depart from the true religion, the whole people would suffer chastisement: violence and exile from the land of Israel. "They provoked Me with a non-god, . . . so shall I provoke them with a non-people."[46] Moses presented this tragic outcome as a certainty, but there was a plan for recovery.

In the midst of their dispersion among the other nations, "you will return unto the Lord, your God, and listen to His voice, according to everything that I command you today, you and your children." The exile will end: "If your dispersed will be at the ends of heaven, from there the Lord, your God . . . will bring you to the Land that your forefathers possessed and you shall possess it."[47]

Moses uses the image of a heart whose barrier separating it from God has been cut away. We are to imagine a foreskin that, in intercourse, somehow fails to retract, so that the lovers are prevented from achieving the fullest intimacy. After this return from exile, "the Lord, your God, will circumcise your heart and the heart of your offspring, to love the Lord . . . that you may live." At that time, you will "perform all His commandments."[48]

All these themes are reiterated throughout the Hebrew Bible in its three major divisions: the Torah (Genesis, Exodus, Leviticus, Numbers, Deuteronomy), Prophets (from the book of Joshua through the major prophets, Isaiah, Jeremiah, Ezekiel, and the thirteen "minor" prophets), and the miscellaneous Writings (Psalms, Proverbs, Daniel, Chronicles, and so on). For instance, the often neglected two books of Chronicles, which recount history from Adam and Eve to the Babylonian exile, include a striking statement about the duration of the covenant. King David is cited as the author of a song of praise to God: "Remember His covenant forever, the word He commanded for a thousand generations . . . an everlasting covenant."[49] Taken literally, and figuring a generation as about twenty years, David is forecasting a relationship between God and Israel lasting some twenty thousand years. Says the book of Psalms, also attributed to King David, "He commanded His covenant for eternity."[50] Again, "He remembered His covenant forever—the Word He commanded for a thousand generations—that He made with Abraham and His vow to Isaac."[51]

The Psalms convey an ecstatic joy in the commandments, in doing and even simply studying and thinking about them. "Praiseworthy is the man [whose] desire is in the Torah of the Lord, and in His Torah he meditates day and night."[52] "The Torah of the Lord is perfect, restoring the soul . . . the orders of the Lord are upright, gladdening the heart; the command of the Lord is clear, enlightening the eyes . . . They are more desirable than gold, than even much fine gold; and sweeter than honey, and drippings from the combs."[53]

Psalm 119 in particular is an ecstatic love song to the Torah and its laws: "I will be preoccupied with Your commandments that I love, and I will lift my hands to Your commandments, which I love, and I will discuss Your statutes . . . Oh, how I love the Torah! All day long it is my conversation . . . I have loved your commandments more than gold, even more than fine gold."[54]

One motif that first appears in the prophetic books is God's complex attitude toward the subset of commandments having to do with the Temple service. In the Torah itself, the Temple is anticipated as the meeting place of God and man, where man will give thanks to God and seek reconciliation with Him through personal and communal offerings of animal flesh, wine, meal, and water. In the prophetic period, God expresses dissatisfactions.

Sometimes these are so sweeping as to suggest that He has lost interest in sacrifice altogether. In the prophecy of Jeremiah, who lived through the destruction of the First Temple, the Lord seems to deny ever having asked for sacrifices: "For I did not speak with your forefathers, nor did I command them, on the day I took them out of Egypt, concerning burnt- or peace-offerings." But He immediately clarifies. What's meant is that He asked for such offerings not per se, but only as an expression of obedience. The burnt flesh itself was of no interest to Him except insofar as it indicated a willingness to follow His commands in general, as He immediately says: "Rather, it was only this thing that I commanded them, saying: 'Hearken to My voice, that I will be your God and you will be My people; and you will go on the entire way that I command you . . .' "[55]

Everywhere else we find this motif, God qualifies His disgust at the Temple's services. It is not the sacrifices themselves that inflame Him, but that some people don't see them as integrated in the larger matrix of commandments. Certain Jews would sin and expect the burnt offerings to make amends with God, without realizing that offerings are only a kind of sensual aid to accompany and enhance personal repentance.

From Isaiah, who prophesied in the eighth century BCE, before the destruction of the northern kingdom: "Why do I need your numerous sacrifices? says the Lord. I am sated with elevation-offerings of rams and the fat of fatlings; the blood of bulls, sheep and goats I do not desire . . . Bring your worthless meal-offerings no longer, it is incense of abomination to Me. [As for] the New Moon and Sabbath, and your convocations, I cannot abide mendacity with solemn assembly."[56]

These and similar verses have been taken by Christians to mean that God rejected not only sacrifice, but the Jewish sacred days of the new moon, the Sabbath, and festivals, all mandated in the Torah. But the reply is given in the words I have just quoted: "I cannot abide mendacity with solemn assembly." God simply detests hypocrisy, the pious attendance to ritual *without* an accompanying attention to ethical values. Isaiah continues, "When you spread your hands"—in the posture of prayer—"I will not listen; your hands are replete with blood."[57] In other words, someone who has shed blood without repenting should not expect God to listen to his prayers. If we say God wants no more sacrifices, we are compelled to say He also wants no prayers—something that nobody suggests Isaiah means to convey.

THE MESSIAH AND THE END OF HISTORY. The commandments were eternal, the very grammar of God's relationship with the Jews. That relationship would continue down to and beyond the climax of history, the coming of the Messiah.

The word *Messiah* or *mashiach,* "anointed," has a complex history. While occurring some thirty-nine times in the Hebrew Bible, it never does so unambiguously in the sense of "*the* Messiah." Rather, there are various personalities identified as "anointed," specially chosen, for some task or another. In Isaiah, the gentile king of Persia, Cyrus, is God's "anointed" in the sense that he receives the task of returning the Jewish exiles from Babylon.[58] In Habakkuk, the Jewish people are called the Lord's "anointed."[59] In the book of Daniel, attributed to one of the Jews exiled to Babylon, a prophecy appears concerning an "anointed" who will be "cut off" before the destruction of "the city and the Sanctuary," meaning the Second Temple.[60] This "messiah" was a morally corrupt individual: being "cut off" (*yi'karet*) is the common Hebrew designation for spiritual excision (*karet*), visited by heaven on egregious sinners.[61]

Yet in the Bible there is unmistakably a role given to a Davidic king with a destiny of cosmic importance, even if he is not yet called "the Messiah." Long before the prophets, the book of Genesis gives an inkling of such a personality. On his deathbed, the patriarch Jacob blesses each of his sons, who will go on to found the twelve tribes of Israel. Judah would rule over the others. Says Jacob, "The scepter shall not depart from Judah . . . until Shiloh comes, and his will be an assemblage of nations."[62] In the first century, "Shiloh" was already understood as an esoteric reference to the Messiah, a Judahite ruler and a Davidic one, David having come from the tribe of Judah.

God's promise to King David himself carried the same significance. David wished to build a Temple, as the Pentateuch directed, but God said no: David's son Solomon would do this. The old king's hands were too stained with the blood of war. However, God promised that David would lay the foundation of something longer lasting, a dynasty. "I shall raise up after you your offspring who will issue from your loins, and I shall make his kingdom firm . . . I shall be a Father unto him and he shall be a son unto Me, so that when he sins I will chastise him with the rod of men and with the afflictions of human beings . . . Your dynasty and your kingdom will remain steadfast before you for all time; your throne will remain firm forever."[63]

These verses spoke powerfully of the promise that the Davidic throne would be restored. It was to be occupied by a "son" of God, but this Messiah is distinctly a human personality, "chastised" for his "sin" with "the rod of men."

Humanity was moving toward the appearance of a new order, starting with the birth of the Messiah. Being of Davidic lineage, he would in that sense "emerge" from the humble town of Bethlehem, birthplace of King David, without necessarily being born there himself. This is according to the prophet Micah, a contemporary of Isaiah's: "Bethlehem . . . from you someone will emerge for Me to be a ruler over Israel; and his origins will be from early times, from days of old. Therefore, he will deliver [Israel to its enemies] until the time that a woman in childbirth gives birth; then the rest of his brothers will return with the Children of Israel. He will stand up and lead with the strength of the Lord, with the majesty of the Name of the Lord his God. They will settle [in peace], for at that time he will be great to the ends of the earth, and this will [assure] peace."[64]

Notice the order of events: 1) the Messiah's emergence, by royal lineage, from David; 2) his birth; 3) "then," soon after, the return of the exiles of Israel to their land; 4) reign of the Messiah over all the earth; 5) establishment of peace. Micah seems to understand this sequence as part of one sweeping process of redemption.

The ultimate goal, facilitated by world peace, is universal recognition of Israel's God, to be worshipped at the Temple in Jerusalem from which the teaching of Torah will extend over all the peoples. Isaiah prophesied: "It will happen in the end of days: The mountain of the Temple of the Lord will be firmly established as the head of the mountains, and it will be exalted above the hills, and the nations will stream to it. Many peoples will go and say, 'Come, let us go up to the Mountain of the Lord, to the Temple of the God of Jacob, and He will teach us of His ways and we will walk in His paths.' For from Zion will the Torah come forth, and the word of the Lord from Jerusalem. He will judge among the nations, and will settle the arguments of many peoples. They shall beat their swords into plowshares and their spears into pruning hooks; nation will not lift sword against nation and they will no longer study warfare."[65]

Of all the prophets, Ezekiel is the most lucid in depicting the shape of things to come. Ezekiel, who was among the Jews exiled to Babylon, clarifies that there will first take place a gathering in of the exiles. Then, "on that day," the ruined land will be rebuilt. "I will take you from [among] the nations and gather you from all the lands, and I will bring you to your own soil. Then I will sprinkle pure water upon you, that you may become cleansed . . . I will give you a new heart and put a new spirit within you . . . I will make it so that you will follow My decrees and guard My ordinances and fulfill them . . . On that day when I cleanse you from all your iniquities, I will cause the cities to be inhabited and the ruins will be built."[66] The prophets' frequent use of the phrase *on that day* must have led Jews to suppose that all this would take place in one great swoop. There is no indication anywhere in the prophets of distantly separated stages in the redemption.

Ezekiel's final chapter describes the building of a new Temple on a new design, different from either the First or the Second Temple, as Jews of Jesus's time surely recognized. To anyone who took these visions seriously, it must have been evident that the Second Temple would be destroyed, to be replaced by a wonderful structure distinguished by supernatural features. These included a swollen, mighty river flowing from underneath it, giving life to the desert on either side as it descended to sweeten the Dead Sea.[67]

Once this architectural marvel is in place, the non-Jewish people will come to know God: "Then the nations will know that I am the Lord Who sanctifies Israel, when My sanctuary will be among them forever."[68] Here Ezekiel gives another rendition of the course that history will take: "Behold, I am taking the Children of Israel from among the nations to which they have gone . . . My servant David will be king over them, and there will be one shepherd for all of them; they will follow My ordinances and keep My decrees and fulfill them . . . I will seal a covenant of peace with them; it will be an eternal covenant with them . . . and I will place My sanctuary among them forever."[69]

Let's review. In Ezekiel's presentation, the stages are 1) gathering of exiles; 2) reign of the messianic king; 3) a new covenant characterized by scrupulous observance of the commandments; 4) eternal peace; 5) a new Temple; 6) the nations recognize God.

If we condense the foregoing into a few criteria for recognizing when the redemption process is unfolding, we arrive at three. While one finds apparent disagreements among the prophets, there does seem to be a generally defined sequence, certain things happening before others can occur, all of it transpiring rapidly: 1) The ingathering precedes the other major redemptive events. 2) The reign of a messianic king precedes the new covenant with the Jews, based on a renewed commitment to Torah observance. 3) A new Temple precedes the recognition of God by the non-Jews.

All had been foreseen. The prophet Amos, an ordinary herdsman who saw visions in the classical prophetic period of Isaiah, had said, "For the Lord God will not do anything unless He has revealed His secret to His servants the prophets."[70]

Was it one of God's secrets that the terms of His relationship with the Jews, spelled out in the Torah, would be changed, with new commandments given or old ones eliminated? Might it have entered the consciousness of a Jewish reader of the Hebrew scriptures, in 26 CE, that the following year or a few years hence God would rewrite the terms of the relationship? This concept, the new covenant, or new testament, has been subject to misunderstanding.

The prophet Jeremiah voiced the Lord's promise: "Behold, days are coming . . . when I will seal a new covenant with the House of Israel and with the House of Judah: not like the covenant that I sealed with their forefathers on the day that I took hold of their hand to take them out of the land of Egypt, for they abrogated My covenant . . . For this is the covenant that I shall seal with the House of Israel after those days—the word of the Lord—I will place My Torah within them and I will write it onto their heart."[71]

Two points need to be absorbed about this *brit hadashah,* this "new covenant." First, it is placed in a future where the return of the world's dispersed Jews has already taken place. Jeremiah wrote two centuries after the conquest of the northern kingdom and the exile of the ten tribes of Israel. Those Jews were lost, seemingly forever. Yet here he portrays God as forging a new relationship with the "House of Israel" as well as with the "House of Judah." In the year 27, there had been no return of the lost tribes of Israel.

Second, this new covenant will differ only in the attitude of the Jews toward God's laws—they will no longer be tempted to transgress—not in the laws themselves. Jeremiah continued: "If these laws could be removed from before Me—the word of the Lord—so could the seed of Israel cease from being a people before Me forever . . . If the heavens above could be measured or the foundation of the earth plumbed below, so too would I reject the entire seed of Israel . . ."[72] Ezekiel speaks of the new heart Israel will receive. Says God to the prophet, again linking the ingathering with the new covenant: "I will assemble you from the nations and gather you in from the land where you have been scattered, and give you the Land of Israel . . . I will give them an undivided heart and I will place a new spirit in them; I will remove the heart of stone from their flesh and give them a heart of flesh, so that they may walk in My decrees and observe My laws and fulfill them."[73]

Far from signaling the obsolescence of the commandments, the prophets everywhere affirm their ongoing validity. These include not only general ethical imperatives—"Learn to do good, seek justice, vindicate the victim, render justice to the orphan, take up the grievance of the widow"[74]—but much more specific obligations called for by Jewish law: Sabbath observance, including details like not carrying objects in a public space,[75] abstaining from sexual intimacy during a woman's menstrual period,[76] choosing a mate only from among other Jews,[77] and making the pilgrimage to Jerusalem for Jewish festivals.[78]

Malachi, considered to be the last of prophets, concludes his vision: "Remember the Torah of Moses My servant, which I commanded him at Horeb [another name for Sinai] for all of Israel—[its] decrees and [its] statutes."[79] He meant, evidently, *all* its decrees and statutes.

THE SCRIPTURES THEMSELVES encouraged the native Jewish skepticism toward any claims a visionary individual might make for himself as the prophet of a new vision of God's relationship with the Jews. Daniel foresaw that "sons of the lawless men of your people will exalt themselves to establish a vision, but they will stumble."[80] The Psalms warned, "Do not rely on nobles, nor on a son of man, for he holds no salvation."[81]

At the coming of the Messiah, our first-century Jew must have felt certain there would be few big surprises. In the book of Numbers, Moses had long before recorded the prophecy of the gentile seer Balaam: "God is not a man that he should be deceitful, nor a son of man that He should relent. Would He say and not do, or speak and not confirm?"[82]

Meanwhile, a certain son of man from Nazareth would soon open his ministry in Galilee. Did he fit the messianic prophecies? His followers thought that he did, and they could point to statements of the very same prophets just cited that seemed to turn everything we have said so far on its head. He steps from the pages of the Gospels with uncanny vividness. As even a Jew reading the New Testament is forced to admit, there was something extraordinary about this man. So much so that he was able to overcome the skepticism of some number of Jews in his day, enough of them that in the end, say historians, this was what got him killed. It's time to meet Jesus, called Christ.

CHAPTER TWO

FIRST ENCOUNTER

WAS JESUS THE MESSIAH?

If Jesus was the Messiah, then the Jews today are in big trouble, as all their ancestors have been for the past two millennia, along with a lot of gentiles who haven't grasped what a vital truth the Christian idea is. Even setting aside the belief that the disposition of one's immortal soul depends on recognizing him in this role, if Christians are right about Jesus, then many generations of Jews and other peoples have missed out on the very climax of history, the ministry and death of Jesus Christ. It happened, but we weren't paying attention.

So what about this, the central question that divides Jews from Christians? Did Jesus truly merit the title "Christ," meaning "Messiah"?

We might do well here to back up a moment and ask, as some skeptics and a lot of village atheists have done over the years, whether Jesus existed at all. Modern secular Bible scholars tend to doubt the existence of other key figures from the scriptural past—from Abraham, Isaac, and Jacob to Moses and even a relatively late personage like King David. The answer is, there seems little reason to doubt that there was a Jesus. We'll see that Jews have always, in their tradition, assumed that he was a genuine actor in the drama of Jewish history. They have even assumed that, just as the Gospels say, their ancestors had a hand in his death. But that's getting ahead of our story.

As we have seen, an important non-Christian Jewish witness to key events in first-century Palestine is the historian Josephus. In printed editions of his *Jewish Antiquities*, he gives a brief and famous summary of the life and death of Jesus. As Josephus bluntly states, he "was the Messiah," besides being "a wise man, if indeed he was a man." He "won over many Jews and many of the Greeks . . . When Pilate, upon hearing him accused by men of the highest standing amongst us, had condemned him to be crucified, those who had in the first place come to love him did not give up their affection for him. On the third day he appeared to them restored to life."[1] Held up by Christians down to today as proof that even a wise and scholarly Jew like Josephus could come to accept his near contemporary Jesus as the Messiah, this paragraph has attracted controversy for centuries. Did Josephus really write it this way? There is general agreement among scholars that he wrote not all but probably some of it, giving us strong evidence that Jesus was a genuine historical figure known outside the church.

But accepting the whole passage as genuine poses insurmountable problems. In all the twenty books of his *Antiquities*, Josephus devotes no more than these few words to describing Jesus, and none in his other important work, *The Jewish War*.[2] For this reason alone, it seems the paragraph is probably not entirely from the hand of Josephus, but is rather, in part, a later Christian insertion. It would be very strange for a Jew who believed Jesus was the Messiah to mention this in such a passing, offhand sort of way.

This much modern scholars have made clear. I'm not aware of any scholar, however, who has pointed out a curious and pregnant parallel between the story of Jesus of Nazareth and another tale that Josephus chooses to tell in the *Antiquities* immediately after the paragraph about Jesus: the story of Decius Mundus. The juxtaposition is worth contemplating.

During Jesus's lifetime, a Roman knight called Decius Mundus wished to seduce Paulina, a married pagan woman. The would-be lover tried every stratagem. Finally his servant gave him a brilliant idea: Pay the priests of the local temple to tell the pious Paulina that the god

Anubis had fallen in love with her. Accepting a sizable bribe, the priests convinced the lady that it would be an honor to spend a night with the god. She agreed. When she was sealed in the god's chamber, there appeared to her "Anubis" in the form of a man. It was really Mundus in disguise. Next morning, she boasted of the sexual services she had performed all night long for the god-man. However, Mundus let slip what he had done. When Paulina's husband told the emperor Tiberius of the crime, the parties involved were all crucified—except Mundus, who escaped, having been exonerated because he acted out of passion.

Josephus tells the story of Decius Mundus at far greater length than that of Jesus: seven times the length, to be precise, another reason to be suspicious of the Jesus paragraph. In its immediate context in Josephus's history, the tale of adultery and deceit apparently has nothing to do with the events the historian is narrating—a listing of the outrages committed against the Jews in Palestine by the Roman procurator Pontius Pilate.

We can only speculate about how the paragraph about Jesus came to be in the *Antiquities* and how the story of Mundus came to be placed where it is. The way the mind of a Jew worked, at least the mind of a Jew steeped in rabbinic tradition as Josephus described himself, was to think of strangely juxtaposed stories as commenting upon one another. Is Mundus the Jewish historian's comment on Jesus? In countless places in the Hebrew Bible, when the Jews are seduced to worship another deity, we are given the image of a woman committing adultery, betraying her faithful husband, God. "How the faithful city has become a harlot!"[3] "You have committed adultery with many lovers and would now return to Me—the word of the Lord. Lift your eyes to the hilltops and see; where have you not been lain with?"[4]

To whatever extent Josephus was aware of the earliest movement surrounding Jesus, if he noted it in some way only to be amended by a later Christian hand, he as a Jew would surely have regarded it as an outrage. A man, Jesus, had presented himself to Israel and been rejected by most of his countrymen. He then put on the guise of a deity; or rather others—who later would come to be called "priests"—put it upon him, attributing divinity to him. As a god, he succeeded in seducing some number of Jews. The story of Jesus also included a crucifixion, overseen by the emperor's representative Pilate. Perhaps it too was ultimately triggered by the betrayed husband, God.

WHO, EXACTLY, WAS JESUS? Modern scholars have portrayed him variously as a wandering cynic philosopher, a peasant revolutionary for democratic socialism, and a campaigner against the supposedly class-based system of ritual purity necessitated by worship in the Temple.

Professor Paula Fredriksen has crystallized the problem confronting historians today. In essence, given the internally contradictory nature of the evidence in the Gospels, scholars are faced with a choice between an "ethical" and an "apocalyptic" Jesus. The former is a holdover from nineteenth-century Protestant analyses, which emphasized the Christian savior as a prophet of the brotherhood of man. In this view, the "kingdom of God" was not to be something you could see or touch, hardly the end of history, as the Hebrew prophets seemed to predict. Rather, God's kingdom would be in the hearts of men. Jesus came to free his followers from the limitations of rabbinic Judaism, which—it is said by advocates of this interpretation—possessed no such grand, sweeping, universal ethical vision. This picture of Jesus is derived primarily from his sayings, as recorded in the Gospels. Not all the sayings, however. Those that seem to give the impression of a different sort of man are dismissed as inauthentic.

The other Jesus, the apocalyptic one—favored by scholars like Fredriksen and E. P. Sanders—is a prophet of the end of the world, literally, just as the ancient prophets said would occur. This view pays less attention to the sayings of Jesus and focuses instead on the few known facts about him, about his *actions*, and, even more so, about his *death*.

For now I will simply state, and then, as we go along, defend, my own view, which is that Jesus was a most complicated person. We can, as scholars do, interpret his life by ignoring what he said or by ignoring what he did. Either of these approaches can yield a picture of a man with a unified program or ideology. But such an exercise is circular.

Some historians sculpt the Gospels like topiary animals, pruning away branches and leaves until the desired shape emerges.

Scholars do this, I imagine, because a man whose deeds contradict his words is deeply conflicted, and such a person must seem less plausible to the historian than does a man with a definite plan. But very charismatic people are, in fact, often very conflicted. You can't pin them down. They are protean, none too concerned with whether or not their sayings and doings fit well together. It is precisely their charisma that allows them to get away with this, whereas less personally compelling individuals are forced to say what they mean clearly, to state a program of action or belief and stick to it. Such a *complicated* Jesus, the Jesus portrayed when we try to accept as much of the Gospel record as possible, is entirely plausible. Thus, I present neither an ethical nor an apocalyptic but instead a foxy, ambiguous Jesus. It is this Jesus whom the Jews of his time rejected, to the extent they could understand him.

THE FACT THAT JESUS first presented himself to Israel in the Galilee, opening his ministry there in the fertile northern end of Palestine, distant from the intense urban and religious life of Jerusalem, is of interest for our purposes. If you were going to set up a new Jewish charismatic movement that departed in certain key ways from biblical authenticity, the Galilee was the place to do it. It would be much easier to pull off such a thing there, among the relatively simple folk, than in the south, in Judea and its metropolis, Jerusalem, with its rabbis, its priests, who would know better.

Jesus's fellow Galileans, the first to hear his message, were famous for being on average less knowledgeable about the Torah than their fellows to the south in Judea. Given the geographic distance from the center of learning, the holy city, this is not surprising. Viewed as rustics, they were recognizable by a countrified way of pronouncing their Aramaic. The better-informed Jews assumed that Galileans would be unfamiliar with the fine points of Jewish religious observance. Rabbinic literature even hints at a strain of hostility to tradition in the Galilee. A leading sage, Yochanan ben Zakkai, during the first century spent eighteen years in the town of Arabah, twelve miles north of Jesus's hometown of Nazareth. He was frustrated by a lack of receptivity to his teaching, causing him to cry out, "Galilee, Galilee, you hate the Torah!"[5] It is possible that his time there coincided with Jesus's ministry. Given the lack of confidence one might have that they shared the traditional Jewish religious value system, there was some doubt among the rabbis whether it was advisable to marry such peasants (*amei ha'aretz*), despite their being Jews by birth and thus not posing any problem of forbidden intermarriage per se. The New Testament, specifically John's Gospel, provides a confirmation that Galileans, and Jesus himself, were seen this way. Jesus would preach in Galilee, but on the occasion of a Jewish festival, *Sukkoth* (Tabernacles), he went to the Temple in hostile Judea to speak to the crowds gathered there. His followers were putting out the word that he was the Messiah, but others who heard him responded incredulously, "Is the Messiah to come from Galilee?" The Pharisees, aware of his preaching, were disdainful of his followers, "who do not know the Torah" (literally, "the law"). Others were surprised that Jesus spoke with the apparent erudition he did, seeing that "he has never studied."[6]

However, let's not exaggerate. The image persists of the typical Galilean as a hayseed, but even he could not have been totally unacquainted with scripture. In the context of a synagogue service at Nazareth, Jesus is portrayed in Luke's Gospel as standing up to give a lesson from the prophets—evidently a common practice at worship.

How many of the Jews of his day did Jesus draw to himself, in the Galilee and elsewhere? What are the numbers, the percentages? The evidence is scant and contradictory. In the first century, there were about a million residents of Jewish Palestine, with another five million Jews in the Diaspora—spread across the Mediterranean and the Middle East from Rome to Antioch (now in Syria) to Alexandria (Egypt) to Babylonia (now Iraq). It seems doubtful that anyone outside Palestine knew about Jesus before he died—though the Christian historian Eusebius (260–339?) recounts a tantalizing legend. The prince of Edessa (now in southeastern Turkey) was afflicted with an ailment and, says Eusebius, he had heard of Jesus's miraculous cures. He wrote a letter requesting that Jesus come for a visit to heal him—to which the latter politely replied (Eusebius gives the supposed text of Jesus's letter) that he must not be distracted from his present business, which was to die and be resurrected, but he would later send a disciple in his place.

A comparison is in order to Jesus's forerunner, John, the size of whose following was such as to alarm the local government. Josephus in the *Antiquities* has a passage about John the Baptist, the desert preacher who baptized Jesus as early as the year 27. This passage is longer than the one about Jesus: John "was a good man and had exhorted the Jews to lead righteous lives, to practice justice toward their fellows and piety towards God, and so doing to join in baptism"—that is, a ritual immersion. "In his view this [repentance] was a necessary preliminary if baptism was to be acceptable to God." The Jewish ruler (tetrarch) of Galilee, Herod Antipas (a son of Herod the Great), became troubled by the size and passion of John's following: "Eloquence that had so great an effect on mankind might lead to some form of sedition, for it looked as if they would be guided by John in everything that they did."[7] Herod's tetrarchy included the side of the Jordan where John was doing his baptizing, so he fell under the king's jurisdiction and was accordingly beheaded.

What's significant about Josephus's account is that whereas John, with his crowds, attracted the attention of Herod, evidently Jesus while he was still in Galilee, also under Herod's rule, did not. The Gospels portray Jesus as being harassed incessantly by rabbis questioning his religious teachings. A reference in Mark to "Herodians"—"The Pharisees went out, and immediately held counsel with the Herodians against [Jesus], how to destroy him"—is overwhelmed by all the other Gospel references to Jesus's persecutors representing other parties, not Herod.[8] If Josephus and the Gospels are right on these points, it would seem evident that Jesus's following, before he left Galilee, must have been smaller than John's.

Or consider the size of the mobs that followed later messianic figures on the Jerusalem scene, such as the Egyptian seer with his thirty thousand "dupes," according to Josephus, most of whom the Romans slaughtered. Admittedly, Josephus happens to be a notorious exaggerator. He describes Israel's Mount Tabor as standing 20,000 feet high, when it is in fact only 1,300 feet high.

In any event, this information sets in a certain light the Gospels' wide-eyed accounts of the huge mobs Jesus was bringing in: gathering five thousand, "besides women and children," on one occasion and four thousand on another, chasing him from town to town.[9] In Jerusalem, too, "many of the people believed in him," to the point where the Pharisees say to one another, "Look, the world has gone after him."[10] If this were so, however, we should have expected it to register in Josephus's description of the four parties that made up the leading forces in Jewish society: Pharisees, Sadducees, Essenes, and the "fourth philosophy," the nationalist, antitax faction. To put matters in perspective, it seems that for the Jews in Palestine, belonging to a religious party of any kind was not typical. Of the million or so inhabitants, Josephus says that only six thousand were Pharisees, four thousand were Essenes, and far fewer than either were Sadducees. Evidently, the party of the Christians did not seem of enough significance as a population group to register as a fifth philosophy.

Assuming that if he had attracted a bigger crowd than five thousand the Gospels would have given us the more impressive figure, we can conclude that Jesus's core following was small—smaller than five thousand, since that number obviously includes merely curious onlookers who never committed themselves to his teachings. Compared with the followers of the Egyptian, the supporters of Jews were distinctly modest in number.

On the other hand, it appears likely that many Jews reacted to him with distaste. The Gospels are full of accounts of Jesus's speaking and teaching in synagogues. While at first the people listen to him open-mindedly, after a certain point the tide of public opinion shifts. The Jews profess themselves to be "astonished," which could be good or bad.[11] We are given the names of some Jewish towns that have shown no enthusiasm: "Woe to you, Chorazin! Woe to you, Beth-saida . . . And you, Capernaum, will you be exalted to heaven? You shall be brought down to Hades."[12] Jesus warns his disciples they will be "beaten in synagogues."[13] In John's Gospel, the Jews repeatedly try to stone him—in the Temple, no less.[14] They cry, "Crucify him, crucify him!"[15]

We need not accept the historical truth of all this. The Gospels were written down anywhere from thirty (in the case of Mark) to seventy years after the Crucifixion, and they clearly reflect Jewish-Christian tensions of a much later date than the lifetime of Jesus. Still, they are all we have to go on. As we shall see presently, it is not surprising that Jews should have greeted this man with skepticism at best. I cannot find any reason to deny the basic tenor of the Gospels' depiction of the reception Jesus got from many of his fellow Jews.

BY SAYING THAT the Jews "rejected" him, however, we are in a sense already speaking in Christian language. Only a tiny fraction of the Jews alive at the time were aware of his existence. His public ministry lasted only a year or so, from the arrest of John the Baptist in 28 or 29 to the Crucifixion in 30; and we have already seen the modest numbers of people who, even according to the New Testament itself, attended his discourses. Remember, we are talking about the first century CE, when information traveled only by foot, hoof, wagon, or boat. Today a personality in the news can become well-known to millions or billions of people within a matter of days or weeks. Obviously this was not the case with Jesus's contemporaries. Of those who did have some familiarity with him, some secondhand, only a minority would have felt they had enough information to make a judgment one way or the other. If the Jews comprised 6 million people across the Mediterranean and the Middle East, and if—estimating liberally—60,000 heard him teach in that year, and if half of those formed a definite opinion about the great man, then we are talking about 0.5 percent of the Jewish people then alive who either "accepted" or "rejected" Jesus—that is, 1 out of every 200 Jews. To speak of "the Jews" corporately taking any position vis-à-vis the Christian savior is, then, quite a stretch.

Even from the perspective of those who personally heard him preach, what exactly was there to "reject"? Such language presupposes that Jewish people of Jesus's day were faced with a definite choice, whose gravity they must have been aware of, because to "accept" or "reject" this man was so obviously a matter of ultimate importance. Jesus himself is quoted as placing the embrace of himself—not his teaching, but *himself*—front and center before his audience: "So every one who acknowledges me before men, I also will acknowledge before my Father who is in heaven; but whoever denies me before men, I also will deny before my Father who is in heaven."[16] "He who rejects me rejects him who sent me."[17] "He who believes in [the Son] is not condemned; he who does not believe is condemned already."[18]

This emphasis is taken for granted—as normal, to be expected—by those who already believe in the New Testament, but if Jesus said these things, they would have sounded very strange to his contemporaries. There was nothing in Jewish tradition that laid such tremendous importance on whether or not one "acknowledged" any person apart from "our Father who is in heaven." In the prophetic writings, there is no concept of "accepting" or "denying" the promised Davidic king.

In Jesus's lifetime, if the Jews did reject him, that was only so, *in effect*, passively: Their "rejection" of him arose not from a definite decision, but from a combination of simple unawareness of his activities and skepticism about the roles he was casting himself into. To be precise, among those who knew of him, rather than an outright denial, it was more a turning away, a questioning of the authenticity or even the importance of the personas he adopted. Matthew, Mark, and Luke give us Jesus's career from his immersion in the Jordan River by John the Baptist to Jesus's arrest, crucifixion, and reported resurrection—a narrative framework of about one year. John's Gospel starts a couple of years earlier, filling us in on Jesus's activities before the meeting with the Baptist. The Jesus who emerges from the portrait given by the evangelists is a many-faceted character. What must the Jews have thought of his quite different roles and personas? He was an exorcist. He had a reputation as a miracle worker. He was called a "rabbi" by some followers, though it was known that "he [had] never studied." Either in his lifetime or shortly afterward, he was understood by his followers to be the "Christ"—that is, the Messiah—and more than that: a being partaking of divinity itself.

The Christian case for Jesus, before his death, would have rested on seeking to impress us with Jesus as exorcist, miracle worker, rabbi, Messiah, and divine being. There is reason to doubt that in historical reality he presented himself in these last two roles, as Messiah and divinity, but for the sake of argument let's entertain the maximalist position of faithful Christians who find it hard to believe Jesus did not somehow convey all these vital truths about himself to his followers. Let us take up each of these roles in turn. We shall find that the first two, even if conceded in their entirety, would not necessarily have turned the heads of Jesus's Jewish contemporaries. Of the other three, an informed Jew would have been skeptical, to say the least: They constitute the chief reasons why, at this early stage, those relatively few Jews who did actively reject Jesus would have done so.

JESUS THE EXORCIST. In the Gospels, Jesus's principal occupation is casting out demons—and healing, which to the ancient mind amounted to the same activity, since illnesses were held to be demonic in causation.[19] Did this not prove that he had special divine powers?

In antiquity, the Near East crawled with demons. Speaking specifically of Mesopotamia, the psychologist and anthropologist Julian Jaynes wrote, "The very air . . . became darkened with them," a "decaying civilization as black with demons as a piece of rotting meat with flies."[20]

As the Gospel record shows, the people "brought [Jesus] all the sick, those afflicted with various diseases and pains, demoniacs, epileptics, and paralytics, and he healed them."[21] A "demoniac" was someone whose body and soul had been seized by a demon: Imagine Linda Blair in *The Exorcist*. In the spookiest tale recounted in the Gospels, a man living among tombs suffers from possession. Even chains can't hold him down. Saying, "Come out of the man, you unclean spirit!" Jesus cast the demon, called "Legion" ("for we are many"), into a herd of swine. The pigs then rushed into the sea like lemmings and drowned.[22]

We're told that Jesus's Pharisaic opponents distrusted him for his power to exorcise. "But when the Pharisees heard it they said, 'It is only by Beelzebul, the prince of demons, that this man casts out demons.' "[23] This is hard to credit as what Jews would actually have said. Against the background of first-century Palestine, there is no reason to think Jesus the exorcist would have stood out so much at all, to be overly revered or censured.

Certainly the belief in demons was not out of the ordinary. The Hebrew Bible is rife with references to them. However, determining what sort of image the prophet Isaiah had in mind when he alludes, for example, to the figure of Lilith—a demoness—is difficult to say.

More to the point, demons and the challenge of neutralizing them were nothing new to the rabbis. Possession per se is not much discussed in the ancient Jewish sources—though one rabbi is said to have had his face turned clear around to the back of his body, à la Linda Blair, by a demon. He was able to quickly set things straight.[24] Demons were said to have been created during the twilight before the seventh day of Creation.[25] They have always been around but function more as an annoyance than a grave threat, dangerous only if left unchecked.

Seeing them was held to be a frightening experience. In a *tannaitic* teaching, the sage Abba Binyamin passed on the information that, normally invisible, they fill the air around us: "If the eye were to be granted permission to see [them], no creature would be able to stand in the face of the demons [around him]."[26] The rabbis knew of a procedure for temporarily making them visible, but a certain Rav Bivi bar Abaye tried it and was "harmed": "The rabbis prayed for mercy on him and he recovered."[27] Not a big deal. This seems to refer to a case not of possession, but of mere "harm" or "damage." In the Talmud, getting rid of a demon is put on the same level of seriousness as getting rid of blisters.[28] Therapeutic incantations are given for both.

Still, one would naturally be impressed by an ability to control demonic forces—as, for that matter, one would be impressed by the ability to control blisters. Josephus in his *Jewish Antiquities* tells of a Jewish exorcist named Eleazar who, witnessed by the emperor Vespasian himself during the Roman reconquest of rebellious Judea, extracted a demon through a man's nostrils. This was accomplished by holding a kind of root native to Transjordan under the nose of the suffering demoniac, who promptly passed out. "Reciting incantations which he had composed," Eleazar "adjured the demon never to come back into him."[29] It worked.

Some Christian commentators argue that what was unique about Jesus was that he could command demons without resorting to spells or magic. If it's true he had this power, it was not unique, at least if you are also prepared to credit reports of rabbinic wonderworkers. Such was the first-century rabbi Hanina ben Dosa, a Galilean like Jesus whose deeds have been compared with the Christian savior's. The Talmud reports that before Hanina's time demons were quite commonly encountered, especially at night. On one occasion he bumped into a demon called Agras bas Machlas. She said, "Were it not that they proclaim in Heaven about you, 'Beware of Rabbi Hanina and his Torah learning,' I would menace you!"

He replied, "If I am so highly regarded in Heaven, I decree upon you [and all demons] that you must never again pass through places where people live." She begged for mercy, and—unaccountably—he showed it to her, agreeing to allow demons some free rein a couple of nights each week.[30]

Admittedly, there is no record of a rabbi spending as much time tackling demons as Jesus did, but then they would not have regarded the problem as severe enough to merit such acute attention. It is hard to see why a Jew would follow or reject Jesus because of his powers as an exorcist.

JESUS THE MIRACLE WORKER. We needn't spend time retelling the stories of Jesus's miracles, which are well-known. Apart from those having to do with healing and exorcism, they include feeding five thousand people with five loaves of bread and two fish; feeding four thousand with seven loaves and a few fish; turning water to wine; calming the wind and sea; walking on water; and giving life to a dead man, Lazarus, and to a dead girl, the synagogue president's daughter. Again, did these not show Jesus was a unique person with a very special relationship to God, perhaps that he was God incarnate?

The catalog of miracles is impressive—if brief when listed in this way, item by item. However, a Jew who believed in the Hebrew scriptures would know that not all such acts, causing nature to depart from her course, came from God. In the book of Exodus, when Moses confronts Pharaoh, demanding that the Jews be allowed to leave Egypt and doing some wonders of his own, the Egyptian king's magicians at first match the Jewish leader miracle for miracle. To ascribe magical powers to forces apart from God would not have strained the imagination of a Jew in Jesus's day.

Even if we take all these deeds at face value, as having actually occurred as the New Testament describes them, they would not have made Jesus unique. A Jew at the time, upon hearing of such things, might well be expected to seek out this man and see what he was about. But no more than that.

As Professor Geza Vermes has shown, the Galilee in particular was famous for producing a species of charismatic sages and healers known as *Hasidim* (literally, "Pious Ones"), whose most prominent representatives included the aforementioned Hanina ben Dosa, along with his counterpart of a century earlier, Honi the Circle Maker. As the Mishnah relates, Honi got his name by bringing down miraculously huge quantities of rain during a time of drought. He first prayed to God, but when his prayer went unanswered he drew a circle on the ground and swore he would stand in it until rain fell. It immediately did so, but in miserly fashion, not the volume he had in mind. He said, "I have not asked for this, but for rain to fill the cisterns, the pits and rock-cavities." God then sent a cloudburst so heavy that the people were compelled to petition Honi to make it stop.[31] Josephus relates a brief version of this story in the *Antiquities*.

Honi had two grandsons who continued the tradition of miracle working. One was called Hanan the Hidden, whom when rain was scarce the children would follow around, tugging on his clothing and begging, "Father, Father, give us rain!"

For his part, Hanina was one of a category of wonderworkers called "men of deeds." He apparently lived through the destruction of the Second Temple, because the Mishnah states that from the time of the destruction, the power of the "men of deeds" (*anshe ma'aseh*) was weakened, and with Hanina's death they ceased altogether.[32] Professor Vermes points out that Jesus in the New Testament is also characterized as a man of "deeds."[33]

Hanina was a healer, deriving his gift from a special relationship with God, likened in the Talmud to a household servant who is always passing everywhere through the king's household. Such a personality, humble like a slave, nevertheless has the king's trust in every matter. He can gain entrance to the sovereign's presence anytime he chooses, so if he makes a petition, it is sure to be heard. Thus, Hanina intervened with God on behalf of the deathly ill daughter of his teacher. While the teacher, a far greater scholar, could do nothing for the girl, Hanina healed her, casting himself down with his face between his knees. His power operated even at long distances: He was able to heal his master's son without leaving his home to visit the boy.[34]

A story is told about Hanina and a serpent. There was a dangerous snake known to live in a hole nearby a town. Local residents complained to the rabbi that the creature was menacing them and had killed or injured many. Hanina proceeded to the mouth of the viper's hole and calmly stuck his heel down into it. On this provocation the snake bit him—and died. With the animal wrapped around his neck as a trophy, Hanina made his way to the town's study hall and displayed it to the crowd. He explained, "It is not the viper that kills. It is sin that kills"[35]—meaning that in the long run, while nature may take its toll on human longevity, a much graver threat is the wages of wrongdoing, which deprive a person of eternal life.

I am not trying to instigate a spitting contest between Jesus and the rabbis—just making the point that a Jew would not have been overawed by tales of Jesus's wonderful deeds. Admittedly I don't know of a sage of this century to whom the rabbinic sources attribute the power of resurrection. However, such is not lacking from a little later in Jewish history. The Talmud tells of a certain Purim feast—celebrated to mark the anniversary of the redemption of the Jewish people recounted in the biblical book of Esther, where by custom it was obligatory to engage in prodigious drinking. One revered rabbi, Rabbah, got so carried away with his observances that, in a heavily drunken state, he killed another sage, Rav Zeira. The next day he prayed and raised his colleague from the dead.[36]

Unlike the Gospel writers, the Talmud doesn't make a fuss about this. Indeed, a sage of the Mishnaic period, Rabbi Pinchas ben Yair, presents the power to resurrect as a goal toward which a person of extraordinary spiritual ambition may direct his energies. He alludes to a program for developing one's soul, apparently known at the time in more detail, comprising ten steps leading finally to the capacity to give life to the dead.[37] The Jews, whose religious consciousness was formed by the spiritual system later embodied in the Talmud, would thus have seen miracles, even if witnessed with their own eyes, as a proof of spiritual potency, but nothing more than that.

JESUS THE RABBI. Centuries of Christian understanding of the New Testament saw that document as having set the Jews and everyone else free from the rigors of Jewish religious observance. In this traditional view, Jesus stands opposed to Judaism. On the other hand, if you read almost any book nowadays by a professor, rabbi, or Christian clergyman who cares deeply about Jewish-Christian relations, about interfaith dialogue and mutual understanding, you are likely to encounter the notion of Jesus the rabbi or Jesus the Pharisee. In this view, Jesus was a faithful Jew of the rabbinic persuasion, a believer in Pharisaic doctrine. After all, he spoke forcefully about the importance of the religious commandments written in the Torah. Yes, some of these writers may admit, he differed with the rabbis on certain points of belief or practice, but then the rabbis in their discussions among themselves differed on such questions! Jesus is presented as a uniting figure rather than a dividing one.

A pleasing notion, but is it accurate? Did Jesus stand for or against the only Judaism of his day that survived into our own—namely, the Judaism of the rabbis? The question is crucial because if, apart from the country bumpkins of the Galilee, the mainstream of religious Jewry found him to be an inauthentic spokesman for their faith, we can well see why they would turn away from him.

The advocates of a fully Jewish Jesus are persistent, if not necessarily consistent with the evidence. Take a well-meaning Christian, Professor Marvin R. Wilson, who locates Jesus in the "Pharisaic" tradition: "It would appear . . . that the teachings of Jesus shows closest affinity to that of the Pharisees."[38] This is a sentiment one hears often from Evangelical Christians today, who wish, in all their wonderful earnestness, to reclaim some of the Jewish background to their faith: Jesus was a Jew, he was circumcised on the eighth day, he observed Passover, in his lifetime all his followers were Jews, he frequented and taught in synagogues. So the Gospels make clear.

Looking at the bigger scholarly picture, Professor E. P. Sanders scolds old-fashioned Christian theologians who emphasize Jesus's differences with his rabbinic contemporaries. As Sanders points out, as more Jews who apparently know something about rabbinic tradition have entered the field of New Testament studies, they have shown how close Jesus was to the rabbis, how far he was from repudiating Pharisaic tradition.

"The situation seems to be this: those who presumably know the most about Judaism, and about the law in particular—Jewish scholars—do not find any substantial points of disagreement between Jesus and his contemporaries."[39]

One naturally wonders what it was Jesus taught in those Galilean synagogues, starting in Nazareth, that the more they listened to him preach, the more the congregation became outraged. So says Luke's Gospel, which portrays the worshippers at the Nazareth synagogue as becoming so upset with his message that in the end they hustle him out of the town and up to the top of a hill. They intend to throw him off the brow of the hill, but he gets away.

Yes, Jesus is repeatedly quoted in the Gospels as embracing Torah observance. In the Sermon on the Mount, he says, "Think not that I have come to abolish the law and the prophets; I have come not to abolish them but to fulfill them. For truly, I say to you, till heaven and earth pass away, not an iota, not a dot, will pass from the law until all is accomplished. Whoever then relaxes one of the least of these commandments and teaches men so, shall be called least in the kingdom of heaven; but he who does them and teaches them shall be called great in the kingdom of heaven."[40] He must have accepted certain broadly defined commandments like eating only kosher food and offering sacrifices at the Temple, because just after his death his followers were still practicing them.

What Jesus rejected was the oral Torah that explains the written Torah. Essential to rabbinic Judaism, this concept of an oral Torah recognizes the Pentateuch as a cryptic document, a coded text. It posits that the Bible's first five books were revealed to Moses along with a key to unlock the code. Jesus derides this orally transmitted interpretation on matters including the details of Sabbath observance (no carrying objects in a public space, no harvesting produce or use of healing salves except to save a life), praying with a quorum, burying the dead, refraining from bathing and anointing on fast days like Yom Kippur, donating a yearly half-shekel to the Temple, and hand washing before eating bread.

Stated laundry-list fashion, such commandments from the oral tradition may seem like trivialities. But from the constellation of such discrete teachings there emerges the gorgeous pointillist masterpiece of Torah—not merely "the Torah," the finite text of the Pentateuch that the Christian founder accepted, but the infinite tradition of Judaism as a whole, reflecting God's mind as applied to human affairs.

Consider the Sabbath, that most distinctive of all Jewish institutions. The Hebrew scriptures offer only the scantiest idea of what constitutes a departure from the practice of Sabbath rest. Nowhere is the category of forbidden creative activities, reminding the Jew of God's creation of the world and mistranslated as "work" (*melachah*), ever defined. Only the oral Torah does this, and in great detail.

The Mishnah was a first attempt to write down the traditions that the rabbis believed they had received from Moses. In its tractate *Shabbat*, the very first paragraph deals with the prohibition of carrying. It would be left to later sages to explain what was so creative about carrying: Put simply, it increases value, hence wealth.[41] For example, foodstuffs in my house, where everyone has just eaten dinner, are less valuable than if I carry them to your house, where someone forgot to do the Sabbath shopping and the family's stomachs are grumbling. Move my food to your house and suddenly it's worth a lot more than it was five minutes ago. This is why people are paid for transporting goods to market. By doing so, they have increased the value of the goods.

The rabbis took such matters seriously. Jesus didn't. On one Sabbath in Jerusalem, says John's Gospel, he healed a man who had been sick for thirty-eight years, then told him, "Rise, take up your pallet, and walk." His listeners remarked, "It is the Sabbath, it is not lawful for you to carry your pallet."[42]

Healing on the Sabbath is a topic on which Jesus and his fellow Jews reportedly disagreed. In Jewish tradition, there is no problem with faith healing on the Sabbath since it involves no preparing of medications, which would be a problem. When Jesus healed a blind man by making a salve and touching it to his eyes, the Pharisees again objected: "This man is not from God, for he does not keep the Sabbath."[43] By the light of tradition, they were right. While the written Torah says nothing about using a medical salve, the oral Torah rules it out except in case of an emergency, which this clearly was not.[44]

An emergency, the possibility of starvation, would also permit another labor, harvesting on the Sabbath. Otherwise the tradition forbids it.[45] In the absence of any apparent extreme contingency, Jesus allowed his followers to pluck grain on the Sabbath.[46] Again the Pharisees objected. Whether or not there were actually rabbis hanging around the grain fields of Galilee isn't important. Had there been, and had he asked their opinion, they would have said what the Gospels quote them as saying.

So it goes, on point after point. The oral Torah values sociability and thus calls upon the individual to pray in company with a minimum of ten men (a *minyan*, or quorum).[47] Jesus advised his followers, "when you pray," to pray by yourself, "in secret."[48]

On the day of repentance, Yom Kippur, the oral Torah instructs the Jew to engage in acts of abstention from certain physical pleasures—not only fasting, but also anointing and washing. This was meant as an aid to repentance.[49] Jesus rejected the teaching. On fast days, he said, "anoint your head and wash your face."[50]

The oral Torah laid great stress on honoring life by showing reverence to those who have passed away, not allowing their bodies to lie out like carrion but rather burying them immediately. The duty was to come before every other religious obligation in the entire Torah.[51] Jesus had no patience for it. To a man who had just lost his father and hadn't yet attended to the burial, he said, "Follow me, and leave the dead to bury their own dead."[52]

The written Torah commanded that every Israelite of the generation of the Exodus contribute a half-shekel for the maintenance of the desert Tabernacle, but it said nothing about extending the practice to all future generations. The rabbis possessed a tradition that, to make sure the Temple offerings were genuinely communal, every Jew was obliged to contribute his yearly half-shekel as long as the Temple stood. When the Mishnah was put together, the editor, Rabbi Judah the Prince, saw fit to devote an entire tractate, *Shekalim*, to the subject. Jesus disparaged it. As Matthew's Gospel recounts, he judged that the people by rights should be "free" of the tax. "However," he told his disciple Peter, "not to give offense to [the collectors], go to the sea and cast a hook, and take the first fish that comes up, and when you open its mouth you will find a shekel; take and give it to them for me and for yourself."[53]

Again, the written Torah said nothing about an obligation to ritually wash one's hands before eating bread. This commandment was likewise entirely a matter of tradition, the intent being to elevate in holiness the act of eating above the crude animal need to feed the body. Here once more Jesus belittled "the tradition of the elders," as Mark phrases it in his Gospel. Jesus goes on the attack against the Pharisees, who question his followers' neglect of hand washing: "You leave the commandment of God and hold fast the tradition of men."[54]

It won't do to argue that Jesus was unaware of the points of orally transmitted legislation he was busy dismissing or that because the Mishnah was written down only around 200 CE, maybe the tradition had not yet been formulated at all. We know that Jesus was aware of the oral tradition and of rabbinic authority because he argued with them, as in, for example, his discussion of circumcising on the Sabbath. Normally, on that day, performing a surgery not required to save life or limb—such as a circumcision—would be forbidden. However, the Pentateuch states that the procedure is to take place on the eighth day, and the rabbis understood—only as a matter of oral tradition—that this overrode the Sabbath.[55] Jesus asked why, if this was the case, other sorts of healings did not also override the commandment to rest: "If on the Sabbath a man receives circumcision . . . are you angry with me because on the Sabbath I made a man's whole body well?"[56]

For Jesus, oral Torah was a man-made accretion without transcendent authority. He tells a group of Pharisees, "So, for the sake of your tradition, you have made void the word of God," citing Isaiah, "In vain do they worship me, teaching as doctrines the precepts of men."[57] Elsewhere, "Woe to you lawyers also! For you load men with burdens hard to bear."[58]

This explains why he felt it was appropriate to teach solely on his own authority, rather than by citing previous sages, which is how the rabbis taught: "And when Jesus finished these sayings, the crowds were astonished at his teaching, for he taught them as one who had authority, and not as their scribes."[59] There could be only one reason for this: Jesus did not see himself as a link in the chain of tradition. This was a repudiation of the very heart of rabbinic faith. Without tradition, either the cryptic text of the Pentateuch was locked forever, its true meaning indiscernible, or it was open to all to guess as their intellect or whim directed them—a free-for-all of scriptural interpretation where the Torah means whatever the reader wants it to mean.

A phenomenally charismatic person, Jesus mocked the Jewish establishment of his day and was adulated by a following from Galilee, the region where he conducted his brief ministry, famous in this period (says Professor Geza Vermes) for the ignorance of the local populace. Knowing no better, loathing Pharisees as their own teacher did, they thought Jesus uniquely had Judaism all figured out.

What Jesus apparently didn't appreciate is that there is an integrity to the written and oral traditions. From his position, it was a logical next step to that of the apostle Paul, whose still more radical attitude to Torah observance we'll see in chapter 4. To the extent Jesus's better-informed listeners understood this, it was unsurprising that they should regard his approach to Torah with suspicion.

It is also unsurprising that some Jews of the time might have chosen to confront and debate with him, much as the New Testament depicts. Rabbinic literature has a term for a Jew who knowingly rejects the oral tradition, not from ignorance but from willfulness: he is an *apicuros*. The term, entering Hebrew by way of Greek, originally meant "Epicurean," a follower of the pagan philosopher Epicurus. The Mishnah records a first-century teaching that one must know how to rebut the *apicuros* even as one disdains the philosophy.[60] For rabbis to argue with Jesus would have been entirely in line with this idea.

JESUS THE MESSIAH. In moving from Rabbi Jesus to Jesus Christ, the anointed Messiah, we proceed from an honor he likely claimed for himself in some form—teaching in such a way as to imply he possessed an authority comparable or superior to the rabbis'—to a rather more speculative one. The very name "Jesus Christ" contains the affirmation that he was "the Christ," which is to say the Messiah. How credible a candidate for the role would his contemporaries have adjudged him? I pose the question specifically regarding Jesus in his own lifetime rather than in death. The latter question we'll consider in the next chapter.

Before evaluating his claim to messiahship, we need to know if he actually made such a claim. This is jumping ahead of our story, but it is interesting to note that the rabbis, in passing along their own traditions about Jesus, critique him on other grounds, but not on this one. Nowhere in the Talmud or other classical rabbinic literature is there any reference to Jesus's saying he was the Messiah.

Maybe that's because he didn't. In the traditions that later were written down as the Gospels, Jesus is cagey. Never in a public setting does he volunteer to identify himself as "the Christ"—not even in John's Gospel, where he is most forthcoming. Scholars have expended much time at their typewriters and word processors trying to figure out which of the Gospel writers, and on which discrete narrative elements, is the most likely to have preserved orally transmitted data before it was shaped and added to by the early church. I don't propose to enter that quagmire. But let us note the scenes where Jesus comes closest to disclosing a messianic identity.

At Caesarea Philippi, he meets with his circle of disciples. Jesus asks Simon Peter who he thinks Jesus is. Peter replies, "You are the Christ, the Son of the Living God." To which Jesus answers, "Blessed are you, Simon bar-Jona! For flesh and blood has not revealed this to you, but my

Father who is in heaven."[61] So Matthew records the conversation. However, in the versions of Mark and Luke, Jesus replies to Simon Peter by telling him to say nothing further about the matter to anyone.

On another, more sinister occasion, his interview with the high priest immediately prior to the Crucifixion, Caiaphas asks him, "Are you the Messiah?" In Matthew and Luke, Jesus answers without answering: "You have said so" (but Caiaphas had ventured no opinion!); or "You say that I am," which again Caiaphas had not done.[62] Only in Mark does he give a forthright rejoinder: "I am."[63]

If the early church was going to shape or edit these scenes for the purpose of educating Christians, then most likely it would do so in the direction of attributing to Jesus more, not less, clarity on the question of his messiahship. Hence, if there is any historical truth at all to any version of the two conversations, Jesus probably gave the more ambiguous replies.

In a scene in John's narrative, Jesus is by himself at a well in Samaria, the district immediately north of Judea and south of Galilee. A woman approaches him and, in the course of the conversation, says that she has heard "the Messiah is coming." Jesus says, "I who speak to you am he."[64] Even if we credit John with preserving a genuine incident, it still remains true that with his own disciples Jesus was never so direct, much less in his public preaching. Why?

If he ever preached his messiahship openly, why did none of the Gospels record this? It stands to reason that he did not. But then remember what we said earlier about the idea, stressed in the Gospels, that to reject Jesus, in his lifetime or after, was to condemn oneself as an unbeliever. This hardly seems fair. You were supposed to acknowledge Jesus in a role he refused publicly to claim?

However, as the dialogue with Peter shows, there were certainly those among his followers who saw him as the promised Messiah. This was natural. The first century produced messiahs the way our own time produces movie stars. There was always a hot new candidate for the role emerging from obscurity, whose glory faded either as he was slaughtered by the Romans or as his followers lost interest when he failed to produce the goods promised by the prophets. Josephus wrote of "an ambiguous oracle, likewise found in their sacred scriptures, to the effect that at that time one from their country would become ruler of the world."[65] When Jesus started his ministry, exorcising and healing and telling people they could dispense with the requirements of oral tradition, and when he gathered a modest-size following of modestly educated Galileans, it's unsurprising that Peter and other disciples should have got the idea into their heads that this was the Messiah.

One reason the Jews who heard of him before he died would have shied from such an identification should be clear. To begin with, Jesus never told them that's who he was. Probably he entertained the possibility that Peter was right, that his messiahship would be revealed clearly to him, by God, at a later date that never came. Hence the foxiness, the reluctance to go public. He was pleased by the idea, but not entirely confident that it was true.

Since the most impressive of the later Christian proofs of Jesus's messiahship (from the Hebrew prophets) have to do with the circumstances of his death, and since we are here dealing with the question of why Jews would have rejected such a claim in his lifetime, these proofs needn't concern us yet. There is, of course, a certain irony in the old Christian notion of holding the Jews of his time responsible for not seeing the "truth" about Jesus, when Christians themselves place heaviest emphasis on prophecies that they say prefigure the Crucifixion, which hadn't happened yet.

Even if a Jew were to reflect to himself, Well, Jesus hasn't said anything about being the Messiah, but some of his top followers say that's who he is and they must know what he thinks, our hypothetical Jew would also be skeptical for another reason. The first century was a time when Jews habitually thought in terms of the fulfillment of scriptural prophecies. Contemporary happenings were instinctively run through such an analysis, the question being: Does this event, does this person, match those scriptural passages where the prophets describe the coming of the promised Davidic king?

As we found in chapter 1, the Hebrew prophets describe the elements of a messianic scenario that could not easily be overlooked: an ingathering of the Jewish exiles, the reign of a messianic king, a new

covenant with the Jews based on a restored commitment to observance of the commandments, a new Temple, the recognition of God by
the world's peoples. The future Davidic king was expected to radically
change the world.

For the faithful Jew, this was constantly reinforced in the form of
liturgy. Every day, a Jew prayed the *Shemoneh Esrei*, the Eighteen Bene-
dictions, the most basic of all petitions to God. The benediction beseeching God to bring the Messiah was unambiguous in confirming
the royal identity of this figure. The version recited in the first century
by Palestinian Jews asked for graciousness and mercy on "the kingdom
of the house of David, your righteous Messiah."[66]

In communities ranging from the monkish Essenes at Qumran to
the urbane, philosophical Diaspora Jews who followed a great Alexandrian scholar, Philo, the plain meaning of the prayer and of the prophecies was accepted. The Messiah would be a military and political leader.
Philo, whose views have sometimes been taken as foreshadowing
Christian teachings, is clear on this: "For 'there shall come forth a man'
(Num. 24:7), says the oracle, and leading his host of war he will subdue
great and populous nations."[67]

The Gospel writers thus faced the challenge that Jesus never raised
an army, fought the Romans, returned any Jewish exiles, ruled over any
population, or did anything else a king messiah would do. In some of
his sayings, Jesus appeared to locate his kingdom not on any visible
earthly stage, but in the human heart. In John's Gospel he says, "My
kingdom is not of this world; if my kingship were of this world, my servants would fight, that I might not be handed over to the Jews; but my
kingship is not from the world."[68] This was not what the Hebrew Bible
had promised for the messianic future.

Elsewhere it appears Jesus expected a dramatically changed world.
And soon: "Truly, I say to you, there are some standing here who will not
taste death before they see the Son of man coming in his kingdom."[69]
Meaning, the kingdom would somehow burst forth, or in, during the
lifetimes of some of his listeners. Modern scholars point out that the
earlier the Christian source, the more "this worldly" its apocalyptic vision tends to be, suggesting that Jesus himself likely saw future events in

such literal terms.[70] But then we find other sayings that depict the future kingdom as a purely interior phenomenon. In Luke, he says that the kingdom "is not coming with signs to be observed" but rather "the kingdom of God is in the midst of you"—yet four chapters later he says that observable signs will indeed be seen, such as "the Son of man coming in a cloud with power and great glory."[71] Which is it? Perhaps the Gospel writers are true to Jesus's own teachings, which had a tendency to walk both sides of the street simultaneously. Heads I win, tails you lose.

Hearing Jesus preach, a Jew might reasonably have crossed his arms upon his chest and muttered, "Hm, intriguing, but let's see what happens." After all, the scriptures themselves commonsensically defined a false prophet as someone whose prophecies fail to come true. According to Deuteronomy, this was the chief test of a prophet—though the converse did not apply: Predictions that happen to come true (lucky guesses) were no proof of a genuine prophet.[72] While nothing yet had transpired along the lines Jesus foretold, our Jew would have little reason to embrace him as the foremost figure in the coming kingdom.

To overcome such skepticism, Matthew works harder than any of the other Gospels, paying energetic homage to the Jewish preoccupation with prophecy fulfillment. In chapter after chapter, the narrator either himself quotes ("This was to fulfill what the Lord had spoken by the prophet") or has Jesus quote from prophecy, demonstrating how remarkably Joseph's son confirms the visionary ideas of Isaiah, Micah, Zechariah, and the rest. Anyway, the Gospel writer finds the confirmation remarkable.

Christians over the centuries have been getting better and better at finding ancient prophecies to match the life and death of Jesus. However, in the first century, Christian proof texting was still in its infancy. As they pertain to the life of Jesus, Matthew's attempts fall well short of being definitive.

The very first sentence of Matthew's narrative invokes what everyone knew about the Messiah: As the prophets made perfectly clear, he would be a descendant of King David. Matthew gives as a heading to his chapter 1, "The book of the genealogy of Jesus Christ, the son of David, the son of Abraham." The obvious problem is that in Matthew's own account, only the man's adoptive father, Joseph, is the parent with the Davidic lineage, so that even if the genealogy is accepted as true, it says only that Joseph was a "son of David," not Jesus.[73] Maybe this is why John's Gospel admits that neither Jesus's Davidic descent nor his birth at Bethlehem, another messianic prerequisite, was accepted as fact in his lifetime.[74]

Of course, it is also possible that Jesus really was Joseph's son, in the full biological sense. That would seem to be the implication of the earliest Gospel, Mark's, which gives no hint that God sired Jesus in the manner that the later Gospels contend. But then what to do with Matthew's first explicit citation from a Hebrew prophet, Isaiah, with its doctrine of the virgin birth?

This is a famous mistranslation: "Behold, a virgin [Greek: *parthenos*] shall conceive and bear a son, and his name shall be called Emmanuel."[75] The "virgin" whom the Gospel has in mind, Mary, "had been betrothed to Joseph, [but] before they came together she was found to be with child by the Holy Spirit."[76] The writer was working from his text of the Greek scriptures, the Septuagint. However, the Hebrew original calls the lady in question not a "virgin," but merely a "young woman" (*almah*), who—as the word is used in Hebrew scripture—could be married or single, sexually experienced or not. In Isaiah's words, there is no intimation of a virgin birth. If this prophecy was ever cited in Jesus's lifetime, any biblically literate Jew would quickly have seen the problem. Parenthetically, one might also mention that Jesus's name was not "Emmanuel."

Matthew proceeds to quote the prophet Micah's statement that the Davidic king would be a Bethlehem native—again a problem if, as John hints, Jesus wasn't from Bethlehem.

Next Matthew tells the story of the slaughter of the innocents. In this tale, Herod got word that a savior had been born in Bethlehem, so he killed all the male children there—Jesus having already escaped with his family to Egypt. This was to fulfill Jeremiah's prophecy about the biblical matriarch Rachel, who was buried in Bethlehem, "weeping for her children; she refused to be consoled, because they were no more."[77] Problem is, the context makes clear that Rachel is weeping for the whole exiled Jewish people. As Jeremiah writes in the two immediately following verses, "They will return from the enemy's land . . . and your children will return to their border," that is, the border of the land of Israel.

The flight to Egypt and the return from there when the coast was clear were also meant to fulfill a prophecy, this one in the book of Hosea, given by Matthew as "Out of Egypt have I called my son."[78] However, the "son" was not Jesus or the Messiah, but Israel, as the rest of the verse from the prophet makes clear: "When Israel was a lad I loved him, and from Egypt I called forth my son"—a reference to the Exodus.

Matthew then offers another apparent citation of Isaiah. The Gospel says, "And [Jesus] went and dwelt in a city called Nazareth, that what was spoken by the prophets might be fulfilled, 'He shall be called a Nazarene.' "[79] The prophets say no such thing. Perhaps, as scholars suggest, Matthew had in mind Isaiah's reference to the Messiah: "A staff will emerge from [King David's father] Jesse and a shoot will sprout from his roots."[80] The Gospel writer evidently finds it significant that the Hebrew for "shoot," *netzer*, sounds kind of like "Nazareth." If so, the substitution yields, "A staff will emerge from Jesse and Nazareth will spout from his roots," which makes no sense.

And so on. Pointing out the imprecision of proof texts like these, one feels almost unsporting. It's too easy. Yet it is with these that the New Testament begins its first attempt at a narration of the life of the Christian Messiah. Whoever the first educated Jews were to have these prophetic verses cited to them, whether in Jesus's lifetime or later, they could have reacted only with puzzlement and disbelief. As the song says, "Is that all there is?" In fact, there are much more plausible proofs associated with the events surrounding Jesus's death.

JESUS THE DIVINE PERSON. There is every reason to think Jesus entertained some extravagant notions about himself. Most secular scholars are inclined to rule out, as axiomatically impossible, that a Jew of the period under discussion thought he was God, or a divine being, or a person who in any way could be set alongside God. As the Jesus biographer A. N. Wilson writes of his own intellectual development, having previously embraced the Christian faith, he ultimately "found it impossible to believe that a first-century Galilean holy man had at any time of his life believed himself to be the Second Person of the Trinity. It was such an inherently improbable thing for a monotheistic Jew to believe."[81] However, to say that no other contemporary Palestinian Jew could have imagined such a thing of himself is only to point out that Jesus was a unique personality, to which everyone agrees anyway. If he did suggest to his listeners that he partook of divinity, then the Jews of the time would have had to grapple with the enormousness of the claim. Is it remotely plausible that some might have believed him?

Yes, it is. The same historians who find it impossible to think a first-century Palestinian Jew regarded himself in some sense as divine also say that no one in his audience could have believed such a thing. Yet whether it was Jesus himself or one of the early Jewish Christians who took his presumed message to the gentiles of the Mediterranean world, there was a Jew who was the first member of his people to preach the supernatural personhood of Jesus. Such a doctrine was certainly being taught by some Jews before the end of the first century, so the doubts of A. N. Wilson can be laid to rest.

The idea that Jesus thought he was God is indeed thinkable. Yet it is pointed out that the very earliest layers of Christian literature show the greatest reluctance to attribute anything like divinity to Jesus. Presumably these reflect most accurately what was said by and about the man in his own lifetime. Later texts show an increasing boldness, ratcheting up the claims made about his relationship to the Almighty. This suggests that the equation of Jesus with God is an artifact of decades long after Jesus died.

Thus the three synoptic Gospels portray men, demons, and heavenly voices all proclaiming Jesus as the "son of God." But how would a first-century Jew, not a Christian but someone who had just encountered him in the flesh for the first time, have interpreted that phrase? Without the background of Christianity, it's not at all obvious how the title would be understood. Paul goes a step beyond this in the direction of clarity, depicting Jesus as "the likeness of God," "the image of the invisible God, the first-born of all creation"—but still not directly equating him with the Divine.[82] John's Gospel advances another step with its magisterial opening sentence, giving us Jesus as God's divine "Word," or *Logos*, somehow identical with Him: "In the beginning was the Word, and the Word was with God, and the Word was God." It is generally thought that a lone statement of the resurrected Jesus laying out the Trinitarian doctrine, at the end of Matthew, reflects relatively advanced Christian thinking and was not part of the original Gospel text: "Go therefore and make disciples of all nations, baptizing them in the name of the Father and of the Son and of the Holy Spirit."[83] From these expressions it's a long leap to the Nicene Creed (325 CE), still accepted today: "Jesus Christ, the only-begotten Son of God . . . God of God . . . being of one substance with the Father."

Clearly the idea of the divine Jesus is the product of an intellectual evolution. It did not spring ready-made from his lips. However, if Jesus never so much as hinted that he possessed a unique, semidivine relationship to the Father, it is hard to see how such a notion could ever have taken hold so quickly after his death, as it did. Already in Paul's first letter to the Thessalonians, the earliest extant Christian document, we find the apostle in his introductory words setting Jesus alongside the Father: "Paul, and Silvanus, and Timothy, Unto the church of the Thessalonians which is in God the Father and in the Lord Jesus Christ . . ." That was written barely twenty years after Jesus died.

As to the title that most concerns us in this chapter, "son of God," evidently used in Jesus's lifetime, Geza Vermes points out that in Palestine during this period, "sonship" in relation to God was attributed to those wonderworking Jewish charismatic sages, the *Hasidim*, and not only to them. The Talmud has God fondly calling both the *Hasid* Hanina ben Dosa and the second-century Rabbi Meir "my son."[84] This conveyed nothing more than that the person was particularly beloved by the Almighty. If Jesus accepted the title "son of God," argues Vermes, he did so only in his role as a first-century Galilean *Hasid*, not as someone wishing to be recognized as a heavenly being.

Yet somehow this doesn't ring true. The emphasis in the Gospels on Jesus's sonship, the veneration he receives from others on the basis of it, goes far beyond anything associated with Jewish sages like Hanina and Meir. Demons and men alike fall at his feet, exclaiming, "You are the son of God!"[85] If we are prepared to accept the Gospels' word for it that he was called "son of God," it makes sense also to take seriously the downright worshipful contexts in which the title was invoked. This may fall short of what he says about himself in John's Gospel—"I and the Father are one"—which, if in fact he had said it, would no doubt have provoked Jewish listeners to throw rocks at him, just as John says they did.[86] It is hard to believe that he did say that, however, because if so, how could Matthew, Mark, and Luke forget to mention such a momentous fact as that God Himself had walked the earth in human form? If Jesus made it known, how could the information fail to be noted and publicized?

We can't hope to recover the exact meaning of the phrase *son of God* as Jesus's contemporaries applied it to him. It may not have had a precisely definable meaning. One must judge it likely, however, that while not attributing to himself divinity per se, Jesus was not averse to being thought of as a man quite beyond the category of other men, in a relation to the Father without parallel in previous Jewish thinking.

A teacher holding such an opinion of himself would have had to overcome some heavy skepticism from those of his listeners with a secure grounding in Jewish thought. The tradition of the sages of this period, which as Josephus indicates was also the popular way of understanding Judaism, was about nothing if not precedent. If there was no precedent among the rabbis themselves for the honor Jesus's immediate disciples claimed for him, there was such, if of an ambiguous nature, in the Bible. The Davidic kings were certainly human—in many cases (sinners, idolaters, rebels against God) altogether too human. Yet the promised royal scion of David, the Messiah, would surely inspire veneration and awe beyond that accorded even to David himself.

This scion, the Messiah, could indeed claim the title "son of God." God had promised David, concerning Solomon: "I shall be a Father unto him and he shall be a son unto Me."[87] The messianic king would declare, "The Lord said to me, 'You are My son, I have begotten you this day.' "[88] The nations will "prostrate" themselves before God, says one psalm; but so will they "prostrate" themselves (same Hebrew verb) before the Davidic king, says another psalm.[89] It is apparently this same messianic figure who, according to the book of Daniel, will come "with the clouds of heaven." As Daniel puts it in describing his vision, "like a son of man"—another title given to Jesus in the Gospels—"he came up to the One of Ancient Days, and they brought him before Him. He was given dominion, honor, and kingship, so that all peoples, nations and languages would *serve* him; his dominion would be an everlasting dominion that would never pass, and his kingship would never be destroyed."[90] Note the word in the previous sentence that I've put in italics.

The future Davidic king was expected to receive honor that could fairly be called unprecedented. The Hebrew word translated in the previous quotation as "serve," *yifl'chun*, may also be rendered as "worship." However, such a translation would grossly violate everything else Jews believed about worshipping only one God (remember the book of Deuteronomy?). Nor did the fact that nations would bow to him indicate a divine nature. This was simply the Oriental manner of showing obeisance, which is why, for example, the patriarch Jacob "prostrated" himself no fewer than seven times to his wicked brother, Esau, when they met after a long separation.[91] What was unprecedented was the scope of the power he would wield: "all peoples, nations and languages would serve him; his dominion would be an everlasting dominion that would never pass, and his kingship would never be destroyed."

The Gospel writers, as well as Paul, latched on to Daniel's image of the Messiah coming in the clouds. There is obviously something heavenly, if not necessarily superhuman, much less divine, about such a person. Jesus is quoted as saying that the world would see "the Son of man coming on the clouds of heaven with power and great glory."[92] It would happen very soon, he assured his listeners: "Truly, I say to you, this generation will not pass away till all these things take place."[93]

While such wondrous things still hadn't happened, while Jesus's followers waited expectantly, this "son of God" or "son of man" carried on his shoulders a heavy burden of proof. A teacher cannot say such things about himself, nor a student about his teacher, without producing some kind of spectacle beyond what Jesus is actually said to have accomplished in his life—not if he wants to escape mockery.

You can easily imagine his contemporaries dismissing him with characteristic Jewish irony: So Jesus gathered crowds of five thousand. So he performed magical feats like producing food for a multitude from a few loaves or fishes. So he performed faith healings. So he's even reported to have revived two individuals thought to have died. Very nice! But let him do what the "son of man," the promised Messiah, had been advertised as being destined to do from Daniel back through Ezekiel and Isaiah and the rest of the prophets. Let him rule as a monarch, his kingship extending over "all peoples, nations and languages." Let him return the exiles and rebuild the Temple and defeat the oppressors and establish universal peace, as the prophets also said.

His followers could go on citing curious parallels between presumed biographical facts about him and certain sayings of the prophets. But let Jesus come up with the real messianic goods—visible to all rather than requiring us to accept someone's assurance that, for example, he was born in Bethlehem—and then we'll take him seriously.

As the New Testament recounts, there *were* Jews who took Jesus very seriously indeed, though not as a candidate to sit on the Davidic throne. The Gospels place the blame for his death very firmly on Jewish leaders and, in the case of Matthew's Gospel, on the Jewish people as a whole. In that great crime, the Romans are held to be mere accessories. Only after clarifying the circumstances of the Christian savior's execution can we consider how Jews might have reacted to the new proofs that Christians began discovering, not long after the Crucifixion, that the man on the cross had been the Messiah.

CHAPTER THREE

FATAL ATTRACTION

DID THE JEWS KILL JESUS?

The question of who was responsible for Jesus's death still
haunts our civilization. Mel Gibson's *The Passion of the Christ*,
dramatizing the last twelve hours of Jesus's life, was hotly denounced for allegedly stirring anti-Semitism. Jewish and other organizations objected to its depiction of Jewish crowds egging on the
Romans to kill him. A devout Christian, Gibson was merely following
the Gospels. In John's telling, the Jews cry, "Crucify him, crucify him!"[1]
In Matthew's, Pilate washes his hands and tells them, "I am innocent
of this man's blood; see to it yourself"—to which the Jewish mob re-
sponds with a howl, "His blood be on us and on our children!"[2]

In the New Testament, every Gospel writer has his own version of
the story, but essentially it's this: By this point, Jesus's accustomed opponents, the rabbis, have dropped away, to be replaced in the role of
archvillains by the "chief priests." They sit on the Jewish high court,
the Sanhedrin. Upon their order, Jesus is arrested. After a travesty of a
trial or perhaps just a hearing with the high priest, Caiaphas, the Jews
hand him over to Pontius Pilate. Roman soldiers then whip, humiliate,
and crucify him.

One thing is clear. To say that Jewish leaders were instrumental in
getting Jesus killed is *not* anti-Semitic. Otherwise we would have to call

the medieval Jewish sage Moses Maimonides anti-Semitic and the rabbis of the Talmud as well. In his authoritative *Mishneh Torah*, Maimonides accepts as historically accurate the version of the Crucifixion given in the Talmud's tractate *Sanhedrin*. The Talmudic text was long ago censored and excised for fear of Christian anger, along with the related passage in the *Mishneh Torah*, but can now be found in very small Hebrew type in the back of some editions of the Talmud. Understandably, the Jewish community has sought to keep texts like this out of the public awareness for fear of inciting Jew haters. But since the latter already know about it, as a quick check of the Internet will reveal, there is no reason to keep denying what the early Jewish sages stated plainly.

The Talmud gives it as a tradition of approximately the same period as the Mishnah, that "on the eve of Passover they hung Yeshu ha'Notzri [Jesus of Nazareth]." His sentence was that he should be stoned to death, then hung up briefly on a wooden scaffold, a punishment given in Deuteronomy.[3] The passage goes on to list the charges against him. He "performed magic, enticed, and led astray [the people] Israel."[4] The last two of these three items on his rap sheet, stating that Jesus "enticed, and led astray" his fellow Jews, are actually technical terms from biblical law for an individual who influenced others to worship alien gods, a crime punishable by stoning.[5] In the Mishnah, Rabbi Eliezer (c. 100 CE) explains that anyone who was stoned to death would then be hung up by his hands from a cross, shaped like a T.[6]

I don't mean to swear by this as a piece of historical reporting. I do want to suggest that it may be unfair to denounce someone as an anti-Jewish bigot for saying something that the Talmud and Maimonides also say. Yet it does seem that the Romans, in bringing about Jesus's death, were not acting alone.

Oddly, one of the Jewish scholars who denounced Mel Gibson is also the author of an outstanding book that gives a plausible answer to the "who killed Jesus?" question. In a controversial article in *The New Republic*, Professor Paula Fredriksen, a leading scholar in New Testament studies, promised that Gibson's film would inspire anti-Semitic violence. But in *Jesus of Nazareth*, she indeed implicates the chief Temple priests. So does another impeccably serious modern historian, E. P.

Sanders, who has done important work to rescue first-century Judaism from the nasty reputation given to it by centuries of traditional Christian scholars.

Pilate killed Jesus. But even Fredriksen allows that it was the priests who tipped him off to the threat posed by the Christian savior—or rather, by those who followed him. Jesus himself preached a coming apocalypse, to be accomplished only by supernatural means. His was no message of rebellion against Rome. But on the days leading up to Passover of about the year 30, his movement suddenly exploded in numbers and enthusiasm. It spun out of Jesus's control. Perhaps he had announced that this would be the last Passover before the End. We don't know.

This tremendously alarmed the Temple hierophants. Their role was to maintain order in the holy city, not least on festival days, which were always powder kegs with everyone milling around armed to the teeth.[7] They knew that if they failed and riots broke out, Pilate would hold them responsible and the people would be made to suffer along with them. What was needed was to eliminate the lightning rod— Jesus. His immediate disciples posed no risk, which is why they were all allowed to live. Writes Fredriksen: "As the highest Jewish leader responsible for preserving the peace, [Caiaphas] would have alerted Pilate."[8] That's all he could do. As the Talmud and John's Gospel agree, the Jews had lost their right to impose the capital penalty.[9] Nor, as Josephus makes clear in his portrait of the Roman governor, would Pilate give in to Jewish pressure or demands unless, for his own reasons, he wanted to do so.

The form of the penalty was the usual Roman one given to rebels against the state, crucifixion, meant to scare off anyone else who might think of encouraging sedition. It was a Roman punishment for a political crime against Rome—though as we saw, the Sanhedrin earlier had the power to impose a kind of crucifixion, minus the torture, hanging up the corpse of the executed criminal as a punishment for religious offenses.

However, was Jesus's "crime" really of an entirely political nature? In connection with his execution, we may mention a motif in the New

Testament that has greatly puzzled scholars. According to the witness of the Gospels, his death was not essentially political. At this "trial" before the high priest, Caiaphas, Jesus is denounced for committing "blasphemy." In an apparently realistic detail, on rendering this decision, Caiaphas tears his garments—just as the Mishnah says that Jewish judges must do on condemning a man to death for blaspheming God. The trouble is, nothing in Jesus's words would actually, in the Jewish legal definition, count as blasphemy. In Matthew's Gospel, the high priest is set off when Jesus speaks of himself as the "Son of man, seated at the right hand of Power, and coming on the clouds of heaven"—an allusion to a prophecy in the book of Daniel referring to the Messiah.[10] In Mark's version, the priestly explosion comes at Jesus's answer to the question "Are you the Christ, Son of the Blessed?"—in other words, the Messiah, Son of God. Jesus says, "I am."[11]

But there was nothing blasphemous about claiming to be the Messiah, even if you were incorrect in identifying yourself this way, or about claiming the title "Son of the Blessed" or "Son of God." To us, as readers who are familiar with the history of Christianity, the latter appellation possesses associations of divinity. To a Jew in 30 CE, it needn't have possessed any such association. In biblical terms, the Davidic king was defined as a son of God. As the Lord had said to David, regarding David's son Solomon, "I will be his father, and he shall be my son."[12]

In the Jewish legal understanding, "blasphemy" meant, very specifically, abusing God's name—pronouncing the ineffable four-letter name, the tetragrammaton, to some forbidden purpose.[13] Scholars are puzzled because nowhere in Christian sources is there a reference to Jesus doing anything like this or to anyone accusing him of doing so. Why, then, the charge of "blasphemy"?

We may never know, but it is at least worth mentioning a Jewish tradition that is customarily dismissed as being far too late in origin to preserve any historically reliable data. Early or late, it is the only theory I know of that would make sense of the blasphemy charge. In those Talmudic passages we mentioned earlier, censored for fear of Christian persecution from about the sixteenth century on, the rabbis speak of a "Jesus of Nazareth" who practiced magic and thereby "led astray and deceived" his fellow Jews.[14] One thread of tradition alleges that he acquired his magical skills in Egypt, a land associated in the Jewish mind, above all other places, with the occult. There the Gospel of Matthew says his stepfather, Joseph, took the boy immediately after his birth to hide from the wrath of King Herod, who sought the child's life.[15]

Another strand of ancient tradition hints at a different origin of Jesus's powers. In the Talmud's tractate *Sanhedrin*, there appears an extended examination of the biblical character Bilam. In the Pentateuch's book of Numbers, he is a wicked gentile prophet who seeks to curse the Jewish people during their forty-year sojourn in the desert. As the scholar R. Travers Herford has intriguingly argued, the rabbis apparently also used Balaam as a coded figure for Jesus. Matters that were too sensitive to be stated openly they wrapped into their exegesis of the scriptural passages about Balaam.

In the course of the discussion, Rabbi Shimon ben Lakish says about Balaam, "Woe to him who makes him to live with the name 'god,' " or "with the name of God."[16] Or words to that effect: The rabbi's statement is cryptic. Its meaning has been debated down through the centuries. Some have understood him to mean that Balaam claimed to be a god or to be God, others that Balaam gave himself life—that is, resurrected himself—by pronouncing the ineffable name of God. For using God's name can bring about wonders and miracles, to malign purposes if the person using the name—blaspheming it, you might say—is not motivated by good intentions.

In the biblical narrative, Balaam does nothing like this. We may wonder if something is being covertly communicated about the other "Balaam"—namely, Jesus. That's the way later Jewish interpreters understood it. A fairly vicious Jewish retelling of the Gospel story "*Toledot Yeshu*"—its text generally dated to the Middle Ages but containing material going back to the sixth century or even earlier—states that Jesus (Yeshu) performed wonders by abusing the power of God's name:

"In the Temple was to be found the Foundation Stone on which were engraved the letters of God's Ineffable Name. Whoever learned the secret of the Name and its use would be able to do whatever he wished. Therefore the Sages took measures so that no one should gain its knowledge. Lions of brass were bound to two iron pillars at the [Temple] gate . . . Should anyone enter and learn the Name, when he left the lions would roar at him and immediately the valuable secrets would be forgotten.

"Yeshu came and learned the letters of the Name; he wrote them upon the parchment which he placed in an open cut on his thigh and then drew the flesh over the parchment. As he left, the lions roared and he forgot the secret. But when he came to his house he reopened the cut in his flesh with a knife and lifted out the writing. Then he remembered and obtained the use of the letters."[17]

I wouldn't vouch for the historical accuracy of any of this, but it does offer a solution to a problem that no modern scholar has adequately addressed. If his contemporaries believed that Jesus worked his miracles by misapplication of the power of God's name—by "blasphemy"—we can imagine why they would not object to seeing him killed.

Whatever the cause, he was executed. Sometime after Jesus's death, which was probably on the day before Passover, as the Talmud and John's Gospel once more agree, rumors spread that his body had disappeared from the rock-cut tomb in which he had been laid to rest. These were followed by rumors that Jesus himself had been seen alive, resurrected. We possess no reliable record of how Jews who had not become followers of Jesus reacted to such tales. Perhaps the tomb wasn't sealed as tightly as the Gospels say. Perhaps, like historians today, the Jews speculated that the ubiquitous wild dogs that haunted the city had got to the body. This would explain why archeologists have recovered almost no remains of crucified bodies from this time and place: They were torn apart and consumed by the dogs. Perhaps the "resurrected" Jesus who had been seen by witnesses wasn't Jesus at all but his brother James, who would quickly assume the top leadership role in the Jesus movement. We don't know.

NOR CAN WE SAY EXACTLY how contemporary Jews would have responded to the further and more substantial proofs offered by his followers that Jesus was the Messiah, proofs eventually incorporated in the Gospels, pointing to prophetic texts that seemed to hint at the events of Jesus's last days on earth. These centered on three motifs: the triumphal entrance into Jerusalem that preceded his death, the trial and execution, and the resurrection story. We don't know what the Jews would have said, but we can guess.

Regarding Jesus's entry into Jerusalem, to cries from the crowd of "Hosanna to the Son of David!" Matthew has him riding through the city gates on two animals, a colt and an ass.[18] Says the Gospel writer, this was "to fulfill what was spoken by the prophet," namely: "Tell the daughter of Zion, Behold, your king is coming to you, humble, and mounted on an ass, and on a colt, the foal of an ass."[19] The proof text is confused on two counts. First, in what's presented as a saying of "the prophet," there are actually the sayings of two prophets. "Tell the daughter of Zion" is a phrase from Isaiah; the rest is from Zechariah.[20] Second, in Hebrew, Zechariah speaks not of two animals, but one, "a donkey, a foal, a calf of she-donkeys." The colt thrown in there by the Gospel is extraneous.

Still, what we have here is the Christian attempt, and not a bad one, to resolve an apparent contradiction among the prophets. When the Messiah showed himself to the world, it was obviously going to be a dramatic moment. Zechariah emphasizes the humility of the Davidic king, who, it is said in the very next verse, would also rule "from sea to sea" and bring peace, eliminating the "bow of warfare."[21] However, in a text we have already looked at, Daniel's vision, the Messiah would come with "the clouds of heaven"—a much more exalted kind of entry.

Which was it? Not both at once, unless he came on a flying donkey. The rabbis solved the problem with their tradition that the Messiah would come in one of two ways. If the Jews deserved to be redeemed, the king would come as Daniel indicated, on the clouds. If the Jews did not deserve to be redeemed, God would send the Messiah anyway, but he would come as Zechariah said, humbly upon a donkey.

At first glance, the Christian rejoinder was no less plausible. The Messiah would come twice: the first time on an ass (and a colt—why not?); then the second, following his death and resurrection, on the clouds. The Gospels as well as the apostle Paul and the book of Revelation all give this solution. Christians, like Jews, are still waiting to see their interpretation borne out by events.

Meanwhile, back in Jerusalem, the adulation around Jesus was short-lived. Not only did "all the chief priests and the elders of the people [take] counsel against Jesus to put him to death," say the Gospels, but the people themselves, "the crowd," now did an about-face and called for him to be crucified even when Pilate offered to release him.[22] The Gospels hold that this rejection of Jesus had been prophesied and was itself a proof that he was the Messiah.

His having been judged unfit for the office of Davidic king is a strange kind of qualification to advance on behalf of a would-be Messiah, since it hardly makes Jesus unique. There were plenty of other failed messiahs. But once he indeed had been rejected, executed with the connivance of his people's highest leadership, the earliest Christians searched the Hebrew prophets and found some sayings of Isaiah that could be put to use, retrospectively salvaging Jesus's aborted career as messiah.

Matthew has Jesus quoting the prophet to show that it was foreseen that the Jews would fail to understand his message: "With them indeed is fulfilled the prophecy of Isaiah which says: 'You shall indeed hear but never understand and you shall indeed see but never perceive. For this people's heart has grown dull, and their ears are heavy of hearing, and their eyes they have closed, lest they should perceive with their eyes, and hear with their ears, and understand with their heart, and turn for me to heal them.' "[23] The problem is that the text is here describing Isaiah's being called by God to prophecy and God's lamentation that in Isaiah's time the people refused to listen to divine teaching. The prophet then asks, "How long, my Lord?"—meaning, how long will his fellow Jews refuse to hear?

God replies with a description of the land of Israel laid waste: "Until the cities become desolate without inhabitant, the houses without a person," and so on.[24] Isaiah says his vision took place in the year of the death of King Uzziah, or about 742 BCE—in other words, before the fall of the northern kingdom in 721 BCE and the destruction of the

First Temple and the depopulation of the land by Babylon in 586. It was until *then* that the Lord said the people would fail to understand; but after that, presumably including in Jesus's day, they *would* understand. Hence, any biblically literate Jew in 30 CE would know that the prophecy in question had been "fulfilled" long ago and could prove nothing about Jesus.

John's Gospel cites the same passage from Isaiah, along with the first verse of that prophet's fifty-third chapter. Taken as a whole, Isaiah 53 would become the most famous Christian proof text of all. Reports the author of John: "Though [Jesus] had done so many signs before them, yet they did not believe in him; it was that the word spoken by the prophet Isaiah might be fulfilled: 'Lord, who has believed our report, and to whom has the arm of the Lord been revealed?' Therefore they could not believe."[25]

John understands this as a reference to the Jews and their spiritual blindness: *Who has believed our report*, that is, the report about Jesus the Messiah? *Not the Jews!*

Some ancient manuscripts of Mark and Luke also deploy Isaiah 53 to show it was prophesied that Jesus not only would be rejected by the Jews, but also would be crucified among criminals, which is what the Gospels say happened. He is sitting at the Last Supper before his execution, explaining to his disciples that "this scripture must be fulfilled in me, 'And he was reckoned with transgressors'; for what is written about me has its fulfillment."[26] Jesus here lays down a principle that in life and death what he experiences is so significant as to have been foretold in detail hundreds of years earlier. However, does Isaiah 53 really refer to Jesus?

We shall return to this question in coming chapters, for, interestingly, Isaiah 53—so central a text for Christians who have sought to prove to Jews that Jesus was the Messiah—is hardly made use of at all in the New Testament's own narratives of his life. For now we shall merely note that Isaiah's most famous and controversial chapter speaks of a "servant" of God who will endure great suffering because of the sins of other people: "He was despised and isolated from men, a man of pains and accustomed to illness . . . But in truth, it was our ills that he bore, and our pains that he carried—though we had regarded him diseased, stricken by God, and afflicted. He was pained because of our rebellious sins and oppressed through our iniquities; the chastisement upon him was for our benefit, and through his wounds we were healed."[27] And: "With his knowledge My servant will vindicate the Righteous One to multitudes; it is their iniquities that he will carry. Therefore, I will assign him a portion from the multitudes and he will divide the mighty as spoils—in return for having poured out his soul for death and being counted among the wicked, for he bore the sin of the multitudes, and prayed for the wicked."[28]

While Christians have seen here an allusion to Christ's suffering, it seems unlikely that Jews at the time would have understood that the servant in question is the Messiah, or if so, that the Messiah was Jesus. Why unlikely? Because the "servant," as elsewhere in Isaiah, is none other than the people Israel. Isaiah in fact has four separate poetic passages that describe a suffering servant. Of these, chapter 53 is the fourth and last. In chapter 49, the servant himself makes the equation: "[God] said to me: You are my servant, Israel, in whom I take glory."[29] God says explicitly in chapter 44, "Remember these things, Jacob and Israel, for you are My servant." Also: "But hear now, Jacob, My servant, and Israel, whom I have chosen."[30] Yet again: "Fear not, My servant Jacob and Jeshurun, whom I have chosen."[31] Jacob and Jeshurun are scriptural designations for Israel.[32]

Mark and Luke direct our attention to Isaiah 53:12 with its description of the servant being numbered for execution among the "transgressors" or the "wicked." The same verse has the servant "pour[ing] out his soul for death"—which has been taken as a proof that in the course of his work, the Messiah will be killed. So too the verse that reads, "He was persecuted and afflicted, but he did not open his mouth; like a sheep being led to the slaughter or a ewe that is silent before her shearers, he did not open his mouth."[33] Again, for any biblically knowledgeable Jew, the latter phrase would have carried definite associations with Israel and no suggestion of extinction, but rather of the servant's merely being *willing* to die. In Psalm 44, the Jewish people speak in anguishingly beautiful language of the trials they have undergone for their faith, including unto death itself: "Because for Your sake we are killed all the time, we are considered as sheep for slaughter." But, the psalm declares, "you have saved us from our oppressors, and You have shamed those who hate us."[34] The meaning is that while Israel went willingly to the slaughter, and while many individual Jews were killed, the people itself was *saved* from its enemies and did *not* die. The meaning of the other phrase, to "pour out his soul for death," would then bear the same connotation: to go willingly to death, without necessarily suffering total extinction. Indeed, Isaiah 53 positively indicates that the servant will *not* lose his life, for he will "see offspring and live long days."[35] While later Christian and Jewish interpreters have put their own fascinating spins on this text, to those contemporaries of Jesus who saw him die and knew he neither had offspring nor "live[d] long days," applying it to the man from Nazareth would have seemed unsupportable.

Of the other prophecies supposed by the Gospels to have been fulfilled at the Crucifixion, a number are drawn from Psalm 22, which however it has been interpreted by later Jews and Christians gives no indication in the text itself that the author, King David, meant to proclaim a vision of the future. Anyone picking up the text and reading it, without a background in the Christian scriptures, would simply find David's heartrending memories of personal suffering, which of course he recorded as a prayer to be said by the many future readers of his poem who would find themselves cast into the maw of their own pains and trials. Matthew and Mark give us to understand that Jesus applied it to himself at the ninth hour of his death, crying out, "My God, my God, why hast thou forsaken me?"—which is the psalm's second verse. But if he really said it, this proved only that he possessed a biblical consciousness and put the psalm to the use its author intended.

All four Gospels deploy another verse from Psalm 22, "They divide my garments among themselves, and cast lots for my clothing," which the Roman soldiers are reported to have done with Jesus's clothing after they crucified him.[36] But here, too, even if it happened just this way, nothing about anyone's candidacy for the role of Messiah would be indicated. Whether the event occurred as the Gospels say, in all its supposedly prophecy-fulfilling details, is of course an open question; but we can be sure that first-century Jews were confronted by Christians pressing these biblical texts on them as proof for their claims on behalf of the dead Messiah. The Jews can only have been baffled as to why this psalm would be relevant at all.

ONE LAST PROPHECY relating to the Crucifixion, which leads us to a question with a surprising answer: Was there in Jewish tradition any room for a dead Messiah? Didn't Jesus's death tend to cast doubt on his ability to accomplish all the world-transforming things the Messiah was supposed to do?

John's Gospel cites a verse from Zechariah, "They will look on him whom they have pierced," which the evangelist understands as a reference to the grief Jews will feel one day when they look back on their crime of having "pierced" the hands and feet of Christ when he was nailed to the cross.[37] Strictly speaking, the Gospels depict not the Jews but Roman soldiers as those who did the actual piercing, so from that perspective John's assurance that "these things took place that the scripture might be fulfilled" seems dubious.[38] With a little context added, what Zechariah says, quoting God, is this: "I will pour out upon the house of David and upon the inhabitants of Jerusalem a spirit of grace and supplications. They will look toward Me because of whom they have stabbed; they will mourn over him as one mourns over an only [child], and be embittered over a [deceased] firstborn."[39] When you consider that the verse can just as well be translated, "They will look *upon* [rather than *toward*] me [or Me] whom they have stabbed," it's easy to see why Christians have understood this as referring to Christ, whom they identify with God and who was pierced or stabbed at his crucifixion. This is a fine example of how cryptic the prophets can be, providing many a foothold either for Jewish tradition or Christian interpretation.

You may find this startling, but there is an ancient Jewish tradition that this refers to a messiah who, in the course of his work, dies at the hand of enemies. I say *a* messiah since in an orally reported teaching recorded in the Talmud's tractate *Sukkah*, there is a reference to *two* messiahs. One is the *Mashiach ben Yosef* ("Messiah son of Joseph"); the other is the *Mashiach ben David* ("Messiah son of David"). The latter, descended from King David, is the familiar Messiah who conquers and rules the nations and liberates the Jews. The former—a descendant not of David but of an earlier biblical figure, Joseph, a son of the patriarch Jacob—is a sort of forerunner to the Davidic Messiah with a specific mission preparatory to his. Intriguingly, as a proof text alluding to the *Mashiach ben Yosef*, the Talmud cites the very verse from Zechariah that John quotes.[40] The same Talmudic text says the forerunner messiah will die, while the Messiah son of David will live.

No one knows how far back this teaching goes. The fact that the Talmud cites it in the name of Rabbi Dosa, who probably lived in the second century, doesn't mean it dates from the second century. On the contrary, the rabbi refers to this idea of a messianic forerunner in such a way, without explanation or elaboration, as to suggest that the idea was so well-known that there was no need to explain or elaborate.

Of course, the *Mashiach ben Yosef* is not *the* Messiah, the Messiah who is to be a scion of King David. Yet even regarding the latter personality, the rabbis did not find it unthinkable that before being revealed, he would first have experienced death. Consider Rav, a foremost disciple of Rabbi Judah the Prince, born about 150 CE. His teaching on this point is recorded in the Talmud's tractate *Sanhedrin* and likely was not originated by him: It was that the Messiah could come either from the living or from the dead. "Rav said: If [the Messiah] is from among the living, he is [someone] like our holy Rabbi [meaning Rabbi Judah the Prince, editor of the Mishnah]. If he is from among the dead, he is [someone] like Daniel the Greatly Beloved [meaning the prophet Daniel, who had died centuries earlier]."[41]

Were these ideas known to Jesus's contemporaries? If so, perhaps they also knew of a related teaching that the specific role of the *Mashiach ben Yosef* was to defeat the power of "Esau," brother of the biblical patriarch Jacob, who stands in Jewish tradition as a figure for Rome. This was based on a rabbinic reading of a verse from yet another prophet, Obadiah, who states that "the house of Jacob will be fire, the house of Joseph a flame, and the house of Esau for straw; and they will ignite them and devour them. There will be no survivor to the house of Esau, for the Lord has spoken."[42]

Maybe the notion of a messiah who dies *was* known in Jesus's day. Then the fact of his death would not, in itself, disqualify him. However, the Gospels' assertion that Jesus came from the tribe of Judah (David's ancestor), rather than from that of Joseph, would rule him out as a potential *Mashiach ben Yosef*, as would the not negligible fact that he didn't even attempt to upset the power of Rome, aka Esau. If the idea was *not* familiar to first-century Jews, then they must have understood the verse from Zechariah in some other way, in which case since nothing about the passage points explicitly to a messianic connection, a murdered messiah would have seemed a contradiction in terms.

TO WHAT I'VE SAID HERE about prophecy fulfillment and the Messiah, it might be objected that while the Gospels' interpretations of these verses may be highly imaginative—or, to put it another way, highly strained—rabbinic exegesis is no less so. Finding a reference to *Mashiach ben Yosef* in Zechariah's cryptic verse is a good example of how such traditional Jewish interpretations may seem completely untethered to what the scriptural text actually says. So why would first-century believers in rabbinic Judaism reject Matthew's or John's understanding of the prophecies in question, subjecting them to a higher level of scrutiny than was applied to the teachings of the rabbis? Doesn't that suggest precisely the sort of willfulness, the refusal to believe in Christ despite all the evidence, that the Gospels themselves attribute to the Jews?

A Jew of this period would have offered a twofold answer. First, "tradition" is not the same as "interpretation." As we saw in chapter 1, the rabbis held that their traditions were really orally transmitted data that originated at Mount Sinai, from the mind of God Himself. It didn't matter if the tradition seemed untethered. The text was merely shorthand, code, a mnemonic. It was not at all to be assumed that if you just stared at the scriptural words long enough—"interpreting" them, guided by your intellect and a general background in biblical studies—their esoteric meaning could be intuited.

Second, our first-century Jew would reply that the centrality of the Christian doctrines at stake here is such that, to be plausible, they really need a firmer support in Hebrew scriptures than the imaginative interpretations of prophecy that the Gospels in fact offer. By contrast, the foundations of Jewish practice and doctrine are almost without exception stated plainly in the Hebrew scriptures.

To this generation of Jews, the importance of the issue of prophetic fulfillment cannot be exaggerated. Not surprisingly, then, early Christians must have felt the need for a firmer basis on which to establish their readings of the prophetic passages.

The Gospel of Luke tries to give them one. After Jesus died, it was said that his tomb had been found empty, that he had been resurrected and appeared to his followers. Luke reports about the risen Jesus: "Then he said to them, 'These are my words which I spoke to you, while I was still with you, that everything written about me in the law of Moses and the prophets and the psalms must be fulfilled.' Then he opened their minds to understand the Scriptures, and said to them, 'Thus it is written, that the Christ should suffer and on the third day rise from the dead . . .' "[43]

He *opened their minds*—meaning he gave them to understand scripture in a way that neither the plain text nor rabbinic tradition could support. The idea of a resurrection "on the third day" is a nice illustration of how, according to Luke, this worked. The citation offered by Jesus, "Thus it is written, that the Christ should suffer and on the third day rise from the dead," apparently refers to Hosea's prophecy. There, the speaker is the people Israel, who have suffered divine chastisements and now wish to repent: "Come, let us return to the Lord, for He has mangled [us] and He will heal us; He has smitten and He will bandage us. He will heal us after two days; on the third day He will raise us up and we will live before Him."[44] It goes without saying that applying this to Jesus—whom the early Christians regarded as morally perfect, thus in no need of "returning" to the Lord in repentance for healing— was to violate the obvious meaning of the text.

As an answer to the authority that the rabbis were credited with possessing to say what scripture meant, Jesus's act of opening his followers' minds makes sense *only* if what he meant to do was found a new religion. Up until now we have been operating on the assumption that, as a Jew speaking to other Jews, he meant to do no such thing. Of course, we can only guess at what the historical Jesus actually taught, but the Jesus of Luke's narrative is clearly moving in a fresh direction. Not an entirely new one, admittedly. Jesus rejected the oral law and seemed to set himself up as an alternative authority with no less power than the rabbis had to "interpret" scripture. Now, however, he was passing on that authority to his followers. This is one definition of a religion: a group of authoritative teachers empowered to interpret sacred scripture and to transfer their authority to others.

Which is to say, the resurrection works as a proof that Jesus was "the Christ" only if you have already accepted his authority to render interpretations of scripture contrary to the obvious meaning of the words. That is, it works only if you are already a Christian. If you are not a Christian, then Hosea's prophecy means merely what it seems to mean. It refers only to whom it seems to refer: Israel. There is nothing incoherent or unserious about accepting Jesus's authority to change the meaning of scripture. Jews accept the authority of the oral tradition, conveyed by the rabbis, to render some pretty mind-bending readings of biblical verses. But citing the resurrection as a proof to a non-Christian, even if it happened, is circular reasoning. It assumes from the beginning what it sets out to prove.

Yet we know that when Christians give the resurrection as the ultimate evidence that Jesus and his mission were vindicated by God, they don't necessarily have in mind only the question of whether that first Easter—the finding of the empty tomb, followed by the appearance of a risen Jesus to multiple witnesses—did or did not fulfill this or that prophecy. From a more expansive perspective, it was the resurrection by itself, on its own merits entirely independent of prophecy, that deserves to elevate Jesus from the rank of mere prophet and wonderworker to that of Son of God. Could the Jews of his time possibly be expected to see things this way?

No, they could not. I say this for three reasons. First, I have emphasized prophecy fulfillment here because that happens to be the way Jews' minds worked at the time. The words of the prophets, and of scripture generally, were their critical test, their standard criteria, for accepting or rejecting religious claims. That is why the Gospels themselves emphasize prophecy as they do. They are making their best pitch. If no verse in the prophets unambiguously presented resurrection as a criterion for recognizing the Messiah—and none does—then such a hypothetical wonder would prove nothing.

Second, the fact that the resurrected Jesus had appeared, if he did so at all, to so few people was curious. In the context of witnesses to miracles, the Jews were accustomed to far higher standards of reliability. When God spoke to the people Israel at Mount Sinai, commissioning them in their mission to uphold the Torah covenant, there were, according to the Pentateuch, about two million witnesses—the entire Jewish nation. In subsequent generations, no one ever objected to the Torah's account, "Wait, my ancestors are supposed to have been there, but *my* family has no tradition of a revelation at Sinai!" Jesus, on the other hand, appeared to his eleven disciples. If he also showed himself to many more people—thousands? tens of thousands?—why don't the Gospels mention that? If it was God's habit to seek mass witness to His greatest deeds, as the Sinai event suggests, then why not here with Jesus's resurrection?

Third, even if prophecy is relegated to a lesser status than it actually possessed in Jesus's time, and even if the historical truth of the resurrection is taken as a given, as something that we can all agree happened, it's still unclear what the event would prove. Later generations of Jews—from the coming of the apostle Paul onward, as we'll see in the next chapter—were asked by Christians to give up the whole structure of their faith, the Sinai covenant, centered on the commandments that God had given them to believe would be eternal. Jesus himself did not stand for the idea of the total nullification of the Sinai covenant. In his few sayings, recorded in the Gospels, during the forty days between the resurrection and his being taken up into heaven, he never says anything indicating such a thing to be the true meaning of his previous statements when still alive. So how could his resurrection demonstrate that God had canceled Sinai? How did *Jesus's* resurrection vindicate *Paul?* It did so only if you had already accepted Paul's reading of the events of Jesus's life and death—which again catches us in the trap of circular reasoning.

Or of a totally new religion. Up until this point, Jews could have argued with Jesus within the framework of Jewish tradition itself—on the basis of its doctrines and practices. Now, the faith centered upon him was moving out of the shadow of Judaism, getting ready for what would come next: the birth of the religion of Christianity, something new under the sun.

The Jewish rejection of the Jewish Jesus was one thing, with its own reasons. The Jewish rejection of the *Christian* Jesus, the Jesus of the church once it had been established under gentile auspices, is quite another. Of course, the new religion did not emerge as a fully separate entity right away—that would happen later, when a final break was made with the Jewish mother faith. But the seeds of it were planted, one might speculate, as soon as the presumed Messiah died on the cross. This required a radical reinterpretation of everything the first Jewish followers of Jesus thought they knew about the Messiah. If Jesus was the Messiah, the son of David, and if he had now died, and if the rabbis taught that the *Mashiach ben David* would not die before completing his mission, then it stood to reason that the rabbis must be wrong—indeed, deniers of Christ.

The extreme hostility of the Gospels toward the Pharisaic teachers thus falls into place. So, as we'll see, does that of Paul toward Judaism as a whole. We shall now bring into focus the Jesus whose face the Jews would next be confronted with to accept or reject—a new Jesus, an entirely non-Jewish one, the Jesus of the apostle Paul.

CHAPTER FOUR

A NEW RELIGION
THE CURSE OF THE TORAH

The Jews who knew of Jesus were not unanimous in rejecting him—neither in his lifetime nor immediately after his death.

I might in fact have more accurately, if less succinctly, titled this book *Why the Jews Who Rejected Jesus Did So*. The community of believers he left behind became the earliest church, headquartered in Jerusalem under the leadership of his brother James. Following John's Gospel in the order of the books of the New Testament, the book of the Acts of the Apostles tells the story of the infancy of the early Christian church. The time frame includes the martyrdom of the preacher Stephen at the hands of the Sanhedrin and the subsequent rise of a "great persecution . . . against the church in Jerusalem."[1] About this harried fellowship there are many misconceptions.

If we try to imagine them as modern-style Evangelical Christians transported backward in time, outfitted with appropriate period dress and a working knowledge of conversational Aramaic—James Dobson riding a donkey—we will be seriously misled. Unlike my politically conservative Christian friends nowadays, they were, for instance, fire-breathing communists, requiring that community members donate *all* their belongings to the common good. Once the apostle Peter, another church leader, got wind that a certain married couple in the church had held back some of their own money from the communal purse. According to Acts, Peter upbraided them harshly and thereby killed both on the spot.² Another misconception about the early Christians is that they were Christians.

At least, they were not so in most of the ways that in our time would make somebody recognizably Christian. True, they awaited the imminent return of the Christ, their Messiah, not unlike the way other Jews awaited the Messiah's first and only coming; but apart from this they were practicing Jews, worshipping in the Jewish Temple, eating only kosher food, circumcising their newborn boys, living the lives of Jews quite separately from anyone of gentile birth. Their "bishop," James, appears in ancient Christian accounts as a most pious and observant Jew. Though he occupied an episcopal throne—the chair was still preserved almost three centuries later, as the fourth-century church historian Eusebius records—he could not be confused with any bishop nowadays. One Jewish-Christian writer who lived in Palestine in the second century, Hegesippus, records a tradition that James was a Nazirite, a kind of Jewish ascetic described in the book of Numbers who would abstain from wine and not cut his hair for a certain period of time, possibly as a penitential practice. James went beyond what the Torah requires of such a person: "He drank no wine or intoxicating liquor and ate no animal food; no razor came near his head; he did not smear himself with oil, and took no baths." James was a frequent worshipper at the Temple: "He used to enter the Sanctuary alone, and was often found on his knees beseeching forgiveness for the people, so that his knees grew hard like a camel's."³ Though this last detail is not altogether plausible, since the Sanctuary was the domain of the Jewish hereditary priests, the whole picture is of a Jew who observed his ancestral religion in full. With hindsight, we may wonder how Jesus's message—if later believing Christians are right about what that message was, in having left Jewish religious observance behind in its entirety—came to be so thoroughly misunderstood immediately upon his death among the people who knew him best in his lifetime.

Was there some contradiction between being a Jew like James and his followers and awaiting Jesus's return to earth as Messiah? In itself, no. James's posture really was not so different from that of those followers of the Lubavitcher rebbe (1902–1994) who have continued to hope for his return. The fact that the proposed Messiah had died would not alone make Jesus, in the eyes of these believing Jews, an unequivocally failed candidate for that exalted office. As we saw in chapter 3, there was nothing ironclad in Jewish tradition at this time either to require or to preclude a messiah who will die and be resurrected.

We can get a fuller picture of what the original church community was like from considering the path taken by Jewish followers of Jesus whose tradition survived, as if in amber, after Christianity split decisively from Judaism. After the Jewish church had disappeared entirely from the holy city, with the destruction of Jerusalem in 70, Jewish followers of Jesus were still scattered about, at odds with the rest of the Christian world on basic questions of religious belief and practice. These Jewish "Christians" came in several varieties. Hence the catchall name applied to them later by the rabbis: *minim*, which means "varieties" or "types." There were other groups that also received this sobriquet, but typically when the Talmud and other rabbinic texts speak of a *min,* it refers to a Jewish Christian.[4] In the holy land, there predominated those who held fast to the way of James, whose successors on the bishop's throne of the Jerusalem church for a hundred years after the Crucifixion were all circumcised Jews. Among these Jewish followers of Jesus, one found the Ebionites. Some were Pharisaic in their Torah observance: What distinguished most of them from other Jews was their belief that Jesus had been a prophet and the Messiah, but not a divine person. Other Ebionites, however, did see Jesus in a divine role, while still holding fast to Jewish religious practices.

Yet I should add that while other Jews would have recognized their Temple worship and their circumcision, or James's Nazirite vow, as authentically Jewish, and while the hope of Jesus's return in itself was not blatantly heterodox, this does not mean the Jews who didn't follow Jesus would entirely embrace those who did. Acts speaks of Jewish persecutions of the early church, and Hegesippus portrays James as a martyr about the year 62, pushed from atop the Temple parapet by his fellow Jews and then stoned. The present text of Josephus's *Antiquities* alludes to James's condemnation to be stoned, but this reads like a later Christian insert. There may have been something objectionable about the earliest proto-Jewish-Christian movement led by James, though it's hard to say what that was. Could it be that James advocated the same overruling of the ancient *oral* Torah, as distinct from the written Torah, that Jesus himself did? Just as the pearl in the oyster develops not from nothing, but from the tiniest irritation caused by a grain of sand, there was undoubtedly some grain of what Jews would have regarded as error in Jesus's teachings, and James's, that allowed the Jesus movement to develop into a new religion, turning its back on the essence of Judaism, the commandments. But in the Jewish church, the grain of sand was still only that. It was not yet the fully developed pearl.

That is one end of the Jewish-Christian spectrum, the Jewish end. This "Jewish Christianity" soon withered into a mere heresy in the wider gentile church and within several centuries would be totally extinct. At the other end of the spectrum, we find those followers of Jesus shaped by the writing of the apostle Paul, whom we'll meet in this chapter. They really begin to deserve the epithet "Christian." One such category of *mimim*, called Nazarenes, observed the commandments, worshipped Jesus as the Son of God, and also accepted Paul as an authoritative teacher, which the Ebionites did not.[5] There was also a more purely Pauline variety that had given up Torah observance. They seem to have been located mostly in the Diaspora.

Acceptance of Paul, not Jesus, in other words, marks the breaking point between those who still practiced a version of Judaism and those who had abandoned their mother faith. Paul's teaching spelled the end of any Jesus-based religion that could still claim to be "Jewish."

WHO WAS PAUL? One of the church's most ardent persecutors was a Jew from Tarsus by the name of Saul. As the story is told in Acts, this Saul, supposedly an agent of the high priest, is dispatched to torment the members of the church at Damascus. But on the way he suffers a blinding revelation of Jesus Christ. After this he joins forces with the Jerusalem church, under a new name, Paul, which means "small." The rest of the book recounts his journeying and preaching, to Jews at first but, when rebuffed, increasingly to non-Jews. The tenor of the reception that Jews gave Paul is notable. We have accounts of his outreach efforts in synagogues in Asia Minor, mostly what is today Turkey, and across the Aegean to Greece. He preached to Jews at Antioch of Pisidia, Iconium, Thessalonica, Beroea, Athens, Corinth, Ephesus, and Achaia. Almost everywhere he went, whenever he presented the case for Jesus Christ to fellow Jews, he set off storms of hostility and derision.

The Jews "contradicted what was spoken by Paul, and reviled him."[6] They "opposed and reviled him."[7] They "stoned Paul and dragged him out of the city, supposing that he was dead."[8] He himself recounts in a letter, "Five times I have had at the hands of the Jews the forty lashes minus one. Three times I have been beaten with rods; once I was stoned."[9]

He was to become the apostle to the gentiles, forsaking the Jews, whom he regarded as incorrigibly, willfully blind to spiritual reality.[10] It was precisely because the Jews vigorously opposed him that he turned his attention to the gentiles. He said, "Since you [Jews] thrust it [the Gospel of Jesus Christ] from you, and judge yourselves unworthy of eternal life, behold, we turn to the Gentiles."[11] Another time, "Your blood be upon your heads! I am innocent. From now on I will go to Gentiles."[12]

The book of Acts also alludes to a conflict with Paul's fellow leaders of the early church over issues touching upon the place of gentiles, their responsibilities and existential condition, in the new religious community. At a council meeting in Jerusalem, the leader of the church, James, strikes a compromise, after which Paul departs for more journeying and preaching.

His final visit to Jerusalem ends badly. Certain Jewish believers in Jesus, apparently taking a different view of Judaism from Paul's, seize him in the Temple. They almost murder him, but Paul is saved by a cohort of Roman soldiers from the nearby Antonia fortress. The military tribune of the cohort puts him under arrest, and so he remains, appearing before a very hostile Sanhedrin and finally being sent under military guard to Caesaria on the coast and then on to Rome for trial. The book concludes with Paul living for two years under house arrest in the

Roman capital—where, according to Christian tradition, he would finally be executed as a martyr.

In all this, as in the letters he wrote to the various congregations of believers in Jesus that he knew of or founded, Paul is depicted as a Jew of the most solid family lineage, religious principles, and educational background that one could imagine. Who would dare suspect such a person of trying to undermine his inherited faith?

He tells the Jewish mob gathered against him on the steps of the Antonia, "I am a Jew, born at Tarsus in Cilicia, but brought up in this city at the feet of Gamaliel, educated according to the strict manner of the law of our fathers, being zealous for God as you all are this day."[13] As the author of Acts mentions twice, finding the fact to be highly significant, the Jews are momentarily impressed and silenced when Paul is able to address them in the holy tongue, Hebrew, in contrast with the normal spoken language of the day, Aramaic.

He declared, "I am a Pharisee, a son of Pharisees," a believer in "everything laid down by the law or written in the prophets."[14] In his letters, he boasted of his grasp of the higher levels of Jewish learning: "I advanced in Judaism beyond many of my own age among my people, so extremely zealous was I for the traditions of my fathers."[15] To the believers in Jesus at Philippi in Macedonia, he described himself this way: "circumcised on the eighth day, of the people of Israel, of the tribe of Benjamin, a Hebrew born of Hebrews; as to the law a Pharisee, as to zeal a persecutor of the church, as to righteousness under the law blameless."[16]

The insistence on his own Jewish authenticity is so, well, insistent that you start to wonder. What does this Pharisee of Pharisees, this Hebrew of Hebrews, feel he needs to prove, and why?

Jews, that critical people, to this day are quick to notice subtle suggestions of inauthenticity—hints that individuals who claim to be Jewish or to represent Jewish values are nothing and do nothing of the sort. There is a certain quivering sensitivity in the Jewish soul, almost a sixth sense. With Paul, the hints that he was not what he claimed to be were right on the surface. A perusal of his letters immediately raises troubling questions about the veracity of his self-description.

Take his claim to be the son of Pharisees. As scholars point out, it is hard enough to believe that there were significant numbers of Pharisees in Jesus's Galilee, as opposed to farther south in Judea, the vicinity of Jerusalem. The presence of such Jews in Tarsus, far to the north in what is today Turkey, seems even less probable. That there were Jews in that city is not hard to believe—the vast majority of Jews at this time lived in the Greek-speaking Diaspora outside Palestine. But the spirituality of these Hellenistic Jews was mostly of a different character from that of the rabbis and their followers in the holy land. It would be as if a Jew today told you he descends from a long line of Orthodox Jews from, say, Arkansas or Alaska. Not impossible, but not likely.

Or consider the boast that his family came from the tribe of Benjamin. This is hard to believe simply because sometime after the return from the Babylonian exile in 536 BCE, such tribal distinctions were lost. That a family from the Jewish hinterlands of Tarsus in the first century CE could trace its lineage to Benjamin seems dubious. The Talmud states explicitly that "we do not know whether we are descended from Rachel or Leah"—those two matriarchs being the mothers (along with their two handmaidens) of all the eponymous tribal founders of Israel, the twelve sons of the patriarch Jacob.[17] Religiously literate Jews would have known this, though Paul's gentile converts likely would not.[18]

Then there is the assertion that he knew Hebrew. Most Jews of his time, including those living in Palestine, were unlearned in the ancient holy language. That is why important Aramaic translations (*targumim*) of scripture were composed. One of these, attributed to the first-century convert Onkelos, is still traditionally printed alongside the Hebrew text of the Torah. It seems clear that Paul in fact was among those who could not read Hebrew. Whenever he cites from the Bible, it is evident that he was consulting the Greek translation, the Septuagint, which does not always adhere to an accurate rendering of the original meaning. This could result in substantial misunderstandings of what the Torah was actually getting at, including misunderstandings of crucial passages that passed from Paul into the body of Christianity as a whole.[19]

If Paul was not sufficiently fluent to read the Bible in Hebrew, as modern historians tend to agree, then the notion that he was ever a student of the great Gamaliel is called into question. Gamaliel, who lived in the first half of the first century and served as president (*nasi*) of the Sanhedrin, was not a children's Sunday school teacher but rather the leading sage of his day. Anyone who had the privilege of studying "at his feet" would by definition also be among the foremost Jewish scholars. That such a person would be able to understand the Bible in its original language should go without saying. It's interesting to note, then, the admission in the book of Acts itself that the Jews regarded Paul as "uneducated."[20]

These are just a few suggestions as to why so many Jews, when they met the apostle, distrusted him. To the more discerning, he must have appeared a charlatan. But that doesn't yet explain the level of outrage his message provoked.

UNDERSTANDING THIS IS important because the rejection of Paul, or rather of Paul's conception of Jesus Christ, was the very turning point of Western history. It seems that he set out on the first of three missionary journeys with the intention of taking his testimony to other Jews. His itinerary of synagogues, as given in Acts, testifies to this. Probably like Jesus before him, Paul thought that he was living in the final stage of history, foreseen by the prophets. As he wrote around the year 50 in his earliest surviving correspondence, soon "the Lord himself will descend from heaven with a cry of command, with the archangel's call, and with the sound of the trumpet of God. And the dead in Christ will rise first; then we who are alive, who are left, shall be caught up together with them in the clouds to meet the Lord in the air; and so we shall always be with the Lord."[21] Paul wanted to warn his fellow Jews that the end was nearing and if they wanted to be among the saved, they must accept Christ in their heart.

Meanwhile, the early church at Jerusalem faced a dilemma. Jesus had left no directions to his followers on the question of how to deal with gentiles. There were some believers who held that to be saved— that is, to be among those who were going to be caught up to the clouds to meet the Lord—non-Jews must undergo formal conversion to Judaism. This would include being circumcised as well as agreeing to keep all the other commandments, down to such details as what food can and cannot be eaten. Paul calls this faction "the circumcision party" and associates them with the leadership of Jesus's brother James.[22]

The church stood at a crossroads. Under James and the circumcisers, it might have remained, in its attitude to Judaism, what the Jesus movement had been during the latter's own lifetime: opposed to the authority of the rabbis and of the oral tradition, but otherwise loyal to the practice of the commandments found in the written Torah. Any gentile wishing to join the followers of Jesus (and James) would have to accept the whole program of action and faith described in the first five books of the Bible. According to Acts, this faction included Pharisees who said, "It is necessary to circumcise them, and to charge them to keep the law of Moses."[23]

Another faction in the church was developing under the influence of Paul. Rejected by the Jews, he took his preaching to the gentiles. In his hands, the message was suitably reshaped, the requirements of Torah jettisoned. At the critical moment in Jerusalem, about the year 49, when the leadership of the church chose between these approaches, the decision was made *not* to subject non-Jews to the practice of the commandments in all their details. As the account of the Jerusalem council in Acts makes clear, the decision took shape under the heavy influence of Paul, who "related what signs and wonders God had done through [him] among the Gentiles."[24] We can assume that the Jewish rejection of Jesus and his own teachings, told in the preceding chapters, played a key role in guiding the outcome of the meeting.

The apostles and elders approved a letter setting out three minimal requirements that would from now on be asked of converts to the church. New Christians must abstain from eating food sacrificed to idols, from certain nonkosher meats, and from immoral sexual practices. Notably lacking was the requirement to be circumcised.

In this letter, composed at James's direction, we have what is effectively the founding document of Western civilization. Had the "circumcision party" won the day, Christianity would have remained a Jewish sect whose members obeyed the dictates of Jewish law, at least of the written Torah. This sect would have been intrinsically bound to the Jewish people, and bound to remain small, as the people Israel have always been small in numbers. The fact is that the practice of the commandments is a discipline unsuited to the requirements of a mass religion. Even with the oral Torah jettisoned, Judaism requires expertise. It's not for everyone.

With the demands of the faith whittled down to three—and two of these, the ones having to do with food, would themselves be lifted—the new church was all set to accomplish what it did: over the course of some centuries, convert all of Europe. Had the "circumcision party" prevailed, the continent as a whole would have remained pagan, with all that implies. None of the achievements in culture, law, morality, or science associated with the rise of the church would have taken place, at least not in the forms in which we know them.

Different people react differently to the rejection of their beliefs by the audience they most urgently wish to convince. Some give up the fight. Some never relinquish hope and never change even the smallest detail of their message, but keep on preaching it until their last day, when they are carried off by a broken heart. Others, in bitterness and disgust, choose to reject their audience and seek other listeners with a message changed to suit the new audience. This last was Paul's way. "Since you thrust it from you, and judge yourselves unworthy of eternal life, behold, we turn to the Gentiles."

Paul spoke those words to the Jews at Antioch of Pisidia during his first journey, at the conclusion of which he went up to Jerusalem to meet with James and the elders. From that meeting came the decision to dissolve the requirement that converts obey the dictates of the Torah. Because the Jews rejected Paul, there is such a thing as Christian civilization.

WHY THE JEWS FELT so strongly about Paul isn't immediately obvious. After all, even as the two religions were beginning to diverge, on basic points of belief there was substantial overlap. In the area of ethics, it has been plausibly, but incorrectly, argued that Paul was only teaching non-Jews the Noachide laws that the rabbis said all non-Jews were obliged to observe—seven laws, or really categories of laws, that

Jewish tradition considered the essentials for a civilized culture whatever its national origin. In fact, his message was more radical than that, especially where it pertained not to gentiles but to Jews—but we'll come to that shortly. In the area of metaphysics, Pauline Christianity largely took over Jewish assumptions on matters like reward and punishment after death, eternal life, and salvation. This may sound strange, because our own modern culture is so pervaded with misconceptions about Judaism, thanks in large part to misinformed Jews. I once received a startling inquiry from an opinion page editor at a major U.S. daily newspaper. She was editing an article I had written that mentioned that Jews and Christians both believe in an eternal life— "Heaven." The editor told me she had received queries from the Jews on her staff who had read the article. They all said this was a factual error: Jews don't believe in eternal life! Or do they? Yes, I said, of course they do and have done so for thousands of years. The Talmud is replete with discussions of the afterlife, which will follow the resurrection of the dead, and the Hebrew Bible also alludes to it, if in a veiled fashion.

As for how one gets to heaven, again Paul borrowed the basic assumption of Judaism that salvation is God's gift, not something you buy with deeds. In his belief system, God gave the gift in the form of Jesus's saving death. Those who rejected the gift naturally would not receive it. Christian theologians have taken this notion of God's unmerited "grace" to be a unique and superior feature of their religion, as if the Jews could only understand buying their salvation as one buys a roast chicken at the market, except that in Judaism you bought it not with dollars or shekels, but with brownie points earned by performing commandments. This is absolutely wrong. King Solomon in the book of Ecclesiastes had written, "Go, eat your bread with joy and drink your wine with a glad heart, for God has already approved your deeds." At the same time, Solomon crystallized what he took to be the heart of biblical religion: "Be in awe of God and keep His commandments, for that is man's whole duty."[25] How were the two ideas reconcilable? In the Jewish understanding, salvation came to the Jews in the form of the Sinai covenant, God's gift. The commandments a Jew performed in his life did not "earn" him salvation. They were merely the response that God asked for to the fact that he was *already saved*—"God has already approved your deeds." As the Mishnah puts it, "All of Israel has a share in the World to Come."[26] Jews who rejected the gift naturally would not receive it. Those who purposefully exclude themselves from the covenant will be denied their share, will have no place in "heaven." Those who merely, out of weakness or self-indulgence, violate its laws and who fail to repent will, of course, pay some price after death. But the price is of limited duration, less than a year in what we may call "hell"; and with the price having been paid, they then receive their eternal reward.[27] Nor did the Jews who stood at Sinai somehow earn the covenant. The Talmud relates that while God indeed chose them for His covenant, they were His last choice, all the other nations of the world having turned down the offer. We shall return to this issue in chapter 7.

If we want to know why many Jews reviled Paul, we need to sort out some of the unsatisfactory explanations given in Acts and other New Testament books, from the real reason. Because we have no contemporaneous literature written by Jews about the apostle, I must necessarily offer an educated guess, based on what is known about him and about the Jews and Judaism of his time. Let's begin with the three inadequate explanations:

JESUS AS CHRIST? From a reading of Acts, we might come away thinking that what drove the Jews berserk was Paul's contention that Jesus was "the Christ," which is to say the Messiah. No sooner than the "scales [had fallen] from his eyes" at Damascus, following his miraculous conversion, then Paul—who was still called "Saul" at the time—entered the synagogues of the city and began proclaiming of Jesus, "He is the Son of God." The narrator tells us, "Saul increased all the more in strength, and confounded the Jews who lived in Damascus by proving that Jesus was the Christ."[28] Later, on his third missionary circuit, at Achaea, he "powerfully confuted the Jews in public, showing by the scriptures that the Christ [Messiah] was Jesus."[29]

It might seem reasonable to assume that it was precisely the fact that Jesus had died that, in Jewish eyes, ruled him out as a candidate for the role of Messiah. At Thessalonica, Paul spent three weeks at a certain synagogue "explaining and proving that it was necessary for the Christ [Messiah] to suffer and to rise from the dead, and saying 'This Jesus, whom I proclaim to you, is the Christ.' " Hearing this, the Jews "gathered a crowd, set the city in an uproar, and attacked the house of [Paul's host] Jason . . ."[30]

This whole issue of a dead messiah is, as we have already observed, a bit of a red herring. The Jews would likely have been puzzled by Paul's insistence that it could be proved from the Bible that the Messiah must die and rise again. In making his case, perhaps he deployed the prophecy from Hosea also alluded to in Luke's Gospel: "Come, let us return to the Lord, for He has mangled [us] and He will heal us; He has smitten and He will bandage us. He will heal us after two days; on the third day He will raise us up and we will live before Him." As we noted in the last chapter, that verse requires exegetical acrobatics if it is to be applied to Jesus.

Or perhaps he argued from the fifty-third chapter of Isaiah, which in the Christian arsenal of proof texts would become the chief item of prophetic evidence that Messiah must die for the sins of the people. Around the time of Paul's conversion, the apostle Philip used Isaiah 53 to convert an Ethiopian eunuch, a gentile pilgrim to the holy land. The eunuch was sitting in his chariot, puzzling over Isaiah's text, and Philip hopped aboard and explained how the person referred to there, "as a sheep led to the slaughter," was Jesus—not the Jewish people, as the context suggested.[31] This might well have convinced an Ethiopian visitor, probably a newcomer to biblical religion. It was less likely to sway a Jewish audience, which evaluated any claim for Jesus from the perspective of what was already known from the Hebrew Bible.

If in the idea of a resurrected messiah the rabbis themselves saw nothing blatantly contradictory of biblical tradition, then it appears unlikely that Paul's nomination of a deceased person for the messianic office would by itself have driven the Jews to apoplexy. Still, however, they would have dismissed the apostle's ideas as hasty and presumptuous. For Jesus had left undone all the principal acts the Messiah was expected to accomplish. He had not gathered the exiles, overthrown the Roman oppressors, or established a just kingdom on earth. That alone didn't prove he could not at a future date be revealed as the Messiah. At that point, hypothetically, he could indeed perform all the requisite mighty deeds. It simply meant that about him, as about many other dead Jews from the near or distant past, the most you could say was that the jury was still out.

The book of Acts could be right when it asserts that no less a figure than the sage Gamaliel himself defended the followers of the purported Messiah, urging that they be tolerated, calling for an attitude of suspended judgment, of wait-and-see. On the other hand, if Gamaliel knew of Jesus's dismissive attitude to the oral tradition, this alone would have curdled any regard he felt for the man. Gamaliel was credited in the Mishnah with the admonishment that every Jew must "seek for yourself a [Torah] master, and remove yourself from doubt"—meaning, rely on the tradition of your teacher rather than on your own doubtful interpretations.[32] If Jesus set himself up as an authority independent of Jewish tradition, this—rather than the fact that he died—would have definitely ruled him out as a claimant to the exalted messianic role.

JESUS AS GOD? Merely calling Jesus the *Christos*, or Messiah, would open Paul to nothing worse than ridicule. What about calling him by such titles as "the likeness of God" and "the image of the invisible God, the first-born of all creation," as Paul did in letters to his followers at Corinth in Greece and at Colossae in Asia Minor? As used in Jesus's lifetime, it is not clear what the phrase *Son of God*, which Paul also applied to Jesus, actually meant. Seemingly in itself it did not attribute divine personhood to Jesus.

While Jesus likely did not think of himself as divine, Paul edged closer to this. Is that what so enraged his Jewish listeners? At Achaea, according to Acts, a group of Jews charged Paul, making "a united attack" on him, before the proconsul of Roman Asia, Gallio. The Jews alleged, "This man is persuading men to worship God contrary to the law." But Gallio dismissed their accusation, saying he could not be bothered with charges having to do with "words and names and your own law; I refuse to be a judge of these things."[33]

Could it have been Paul's "words" about Jesus, the divine-sounding "names"—such as "Lord," "Son of God," "likeness" or "image" of God—

he applied to him that set off the Jewish attack? I don't think so, at least not these "words" and "names" by themselves. True, Paul seems to place Jesus somehow on a level with God: "For us there is one God, the Father, from whom are all things and for whom we exist, and one Lord, Jesus Christ, through whom are all things and through whom we exist."[34]

We have already considered the phrase *Son of God*, with its ambiguities. That same quality of slipperiness is to be found in Paul's other expression about Jesus. In Greek as in Hebrew, there was a secular as well as, alternatively, a divine meaning to the word *lord*. It might mean simply a person of exalted importance, or it might mean God. So too with calling somebody the "image" or "likeness" of God. Had not the first chapter of Genesis, in describing the creation of the first man, portrayed God as saying to Himself, "Let us make man in Our image, after Our likeness"?[35] Jewish tradition understood the Hebrew *ki'demutenu* in that verse, "after Our likeness," to refer particularly to man's capacity for understanding and intellect, which we share with God.[36] On the face of it, saying that Jesus possessed this quality didn't invest him with divinity, any more than Genesis itself had meant to attribute divinity to all mankind.

What Paul in his heart meant by these "words" and "names" is another question, probably an unanswerable one. His letters are not logical, syllogistic, or even coherent much of the time. They are ecstatic and poetic. If we could go back in time and interview him, really press him on what he intended to communicate about the relationship of God and Jesus, I doubt we would get a clear, straight answer. In the history of Christianity, a need for definitions and unambiguous creeds would come later. For us it is sufficient to see that Paul's language preserved enough ambiguity on this subject that an educated, committed Jew in his audience, knowing nothing about the future of the religion the apostle was in the process of founding, probably would have felt uneasy at hearing Jesus called "Lord" and all the rest of it. However, this by itself would not have driven our Jew into a fit of indignation.

THE GENTILE PROBLEM. From the book of Acts, it appears that a main point of controversy between the apostle and his fellow Jews had to do with gentiles and their religious status. The Jews are said to be "jealous" of the non-Jews who have been flocking to hear Paul preach. That is, they were "jealous" of others who might wish to share God with them. The Jews wanted Him all for themselves. Once, on a Sabbath in Antioch of Pisidia, "almost the whole city gathered together to hear the word of God. But when the Jews saw the multitudes, they were filled with jealousy, and contradicted what was spoken by Paul, and reviled him." Subsequently, "the Jews incited the devout women of high standing and the leading men of the city, and stirred up persecution against Paul . . ."[37]

Maybe Paul would have said it was this same jealousy that drove his opponents among the Jewish Christians: the "circumcision party." The latter taught that "unless you are circumcised according to the custom of Moses, you cannot be saved."[38] In other words, they held that admission to the community of the church was open only to practicing Jews or former gentiles who had undergone formal conversion, including circumcision (as the Bible prescribed) along with ritual immersion and a special animal sacrifice at the Temple (if the "circumcision party" recognized Jewish oral tradition on this point). It was Paul's dispute with the circumcisers that led to the council of Jerusalem, which in turn led to the fateful decision to exempt non-Jews from the obligations on every Jew entailed by the Torah.

Paul did not require non-Jews, if they wished to enjoy a blessed hereafter, to observe the Torah's commandments. This sparked disagreement in the early community of Jesus's followers. But is it plausible that his view would inspire persecutory zeal among non-Christian Jews?

In the Talmud one finds evidence of a lively discussion among the rabbis on the very question that divided Paul from the "circumcision party." While there was agreement that all Jews had a share in the hereafter, the World to Come, Rabbi Joshua ben Hananiah and Rabbi Eliezer ben Hyrcanus argued over a verse from Psalms, "The wicked will return to the grave, all peoples who are forgetful of God."[39] Rabbi Eliezer understood this to mean that all the peoples, the non-Jews, have shown themselves to be unworthy of reward in the afterlife.

Rabbi Joshua disagreed, arguing that the verse applied only to those non-Jews who were "forgetful of God," while others, who remembered God, would enjoy an eternal reward just as the Jews would.

Presumably some Jews held the disturbing and unappealing view articulated by Eliezer. Among these were the members of the "circumcision party." But the normative view was Joshua's, and it passed down as such into the stream of Jewish tradition.[40] In line with Joshua's understanding, the Talmud elsewhere lays out a system of ethics for the "children of Noah"—that is, for all the world's peoples, descended as they are from the sole survivors of the great flood recounted in the book of Genesis: Noah and his family, who repopulated the desolate earth. These moral prescriptions constitute something like a natural law, known to all peoples. Non-Jews who live moral lives, as per the Noachide code, were assured of a happy destiny in the next world.[41] The subject of Noachide law is complex, but one point only needs to be absorbed: For non-Jews, there was no requirement of circumcision.

In short, when Paul argued with Jewish Christians who said that "unless you are circumcised according to the custom of Moses, you cannot be saved," he was arguing with Jews who, in the context of first- and second-century Judaism, held a distinctly minority view. As for any non-Christian Jews who objected to teaching non-Jews about God, they all the more so would have to be dismissed as a marginal case. The Noachide code did include a prohibition of idolatry. So from a Jewish perspective, teaching to gentiles about God could only be applauded. It simply is not plausible that Jews who knew anything about Judaism could have been stirred up to persecute the apostle by the mere fact that he taught "the word of God" to non-Jews.

WHAT REALLY OUTRAGED so many of the Jews who heard Paul can be expressed simply: He presented himself as an exponent of, and an expert in, their faith, but what he really sought to do was undermine it from within. While maintaining, in broad outline, some of the major assumptions of Judaism, he otherwise wished to hollow out the accepted meaning of the Hebrew scriptures, replacing it with a new religion, albeit fitted out in biblical trappings. This was internal subversion, much more troubling than if Paul had been an acknowledged outsider. If a pagan gentile critiqued Judaism and sought to turn Jews from their ancestral religion, that would be resented, too, and resisted, but human beings by instinct find the traitor far more disturbing a figure than the foreign enemy. For one thing, the traitor is more dangerous, since as a native son, he knows the ways of his nation, its vulnerabilities, which he can exploit easily in a way the alien interloper cannot. What if Paul succeeded? The urgency of the Jews' distress, their anger at him, can be explained by reflecting on the Jewish belief that when Jews turn away from God's commandments, the whole community will suffer.

Some hint of this is given in Acts. The commandment of circumcision is used as a kind of shorthand for the whole structure of Jewish religious practice. Among Jewish Christians who still observed the Lord's commands, worrisome rumors circulated about Paul that "you teach all the Jews who are among the Gentiles to forsake Moses, telling them not to circumcise their children or observe the customs." The worry emerged not from mere nitpicking punctiliousness. There was one language God had given the Jews in which to express their relationship with Him: the commandments. It wasn't the Jewish people who established the Sinai covenant as the basis for this relationship. That was God's choice, and He had promised it would not be changed forever—as the Bible often poetically expressed this, "for a thousand generations."[42] Take the commandments away, and the Jews were rendered mute, unable to conduct their love affair with God in the idiom He chose for them, unable any longer to respond to His gift of the covenant. Rejecting this gift meant rejecting God. Any Jew who knowingly did this would lose his share in the World to Come. The Asian Jews who seized Paul in the Temple were acting on the belief that he sought to nullify the covenant.[43]

The rumors were perfectly true. The apostle's letters make this clear. On the question of circumcision itself, he stressed that the patriarch Abraham had been accounted righteous even before he became the first Hebrew to be circumcised. Hence God cared nothing about circumcision as a literal matter: "Real circumcision is a matter of the heart, spiritual and not literal."[44]

This distinctive surgery was specially charged with symbolic meaning. To begin with, it was a rather high hurdle for any gentile male who contemplated accepting the yoke of the commandments. It was also, unlike the Torah precepts that Jesus critiqued, not a matter of oral tradition but was clearly stated in the written Torah, given not only to Abraham, but again to Moses at Mount Sinai.[45] Like Jesus, Paul dismissed the oral law as "human precepts and doctrines."[46] Where he departed from Jesus's thought was in broadening the exception to include all of Torah law.

In general, he argued, what concerned God was not "works," fulfilling the commandments, but "faith." He wrote, "Do we then overthrow the law by this faith? By no means! On the contrary, we uphold the law."[47] But this was merely playing games with words. He "upheld" the commandments only in the sense that he believed they had played a useful if negative purpose. "If it had not been for the law, I should not have known sin," he wrote.[48] Since he held that it was impossible to fulfill the Torah's commands, for as a rule "the evil I do not want is what I do," the law merely served to make obvious man's inherent sinfulness.[49] Thus he pointed to the need for an alternative mode of achieving salvation. That was the belief in Christ.

Again and again, addressing Christians of Jewish and non-Jewish background, he granted full liberty from the law. "Now we are discharged from the law, dead to that which held us captive."[50] Christ was "the end of the law."[51] Regarding the Jewish dietary regulations, these could be dismissed unless one found them personally meaningful: "Nothing is unclean in itself; but it is unclean for any one who thinks it unclean."[52]

If he personally sometimes obeyed the laws, this was only for appearances' sake. It made observant Jews who had not as yet accepted Christ feel comfortable. He admits this plainly: "To the Jews I became as a Jew, in order to win Jews; to those under the law I became as one under the law—though not being myself under the law—that I might win those under the law . . . I have become all things to all men, that I might by all means save some."[53] Since all that I have previously quoted from his letters to the scattered Christian communities was meant for circulation among believers, it's obvious that after a Jew had accepted Paul as his teacher, the full implications of the novel doctrine would be revealed to him. Henceforth this new Jewish believer would be "discharged" from the commandments.

Why did Jews find this not only mistaken but outrageous? As Paul's reasoning about Abraham shows, he presented his ideas as if they flowed naturally from a sensitive reading of the Hebrew scriptures—as if his doctrine were *necessitated* by the internal logic of the Pentateuch and the prophets. This was a gross distortion, but it was more than that.

Paul taught the dissolution of the terms of every Jew's relationship with God: the commandments. However, in the Hebrew Bible, there is no escape clause, no honorable "discharge." As we saw in chapter 1, everywhere the assumption is that the commandments are well within man's reach to follow and that God "commanded His covenant for eternity."[54] Paul taught that at the center of his system was "faith," as opposed to "works," and in this point above all others he thought that his understanding of what God wants differed from that of the Jews. He was wrong about this, too. The rabbis considered faith in God, the cultivation of a relationship with Him based on trust, to be the very heart of their religion. To prove it from the Bible, they even cited the same verse that Paul did, from the prophet Habakkuk: "But the righteous person shall live through his faith."[55] There was, however, a grammar to this relationship, which was the commandments.

If Paul knew anything about Judaism, how did he reach the conclusions about the Bible that he did? As scholars have observed, the fact is that Paul *began* with the assumption that salvation can be found only through faith in Christ and reasoned *from there*.

We arrive here at the very heart of the difference between Judaism and the religion that Paul originated. The difference is still observable in the faith of Christians, as compared with that of Jews, down to our own time. Followers of Paul read and understand the Hebrew Bible through a certain philosophical lens—they bring to it the premise that

Jesus is the savior, that salvation is from him. They read the Old Testament from the perspective of the New. They prioritize the New over the Old.

Jews who believe as Jews do just the reverse. They prioritize the Old over the New. They begin with the premise that God speaks through the Hebrew Bible. With this in mind, they may proceed to evaluate the claims of Christianity. Because they approach and interpret scripture in chronological order—as seems reasonable, after all—they find that the New Testament does not arise naturally or logically from the foundation document, the Old Testament.

Of course, Paul had only the Jewish scriptures, but like Christians today, he approached and interpreted them from the perspective of those premises that would later be enshrined in the New Testament. The Christian scholar George F. Moore sought to identify what those premises were. He said there were two of them, which he frankly acknowledged to be "equally alien to Jewish thought and repugnant to its spirit."[56]

The first alien premise was that from a Jew who seeks God through the medium of the commandments, "under the law," God requires nothing less than perfection. What was needed in order to be "saved" was absolute, total conformity with the law. Paul taught, "For all who rely on works of the law are under a curse; for it is written [in Deuteronomy 27:26], 'Cursed be every one who does not abide by all things written in the book of the law, and do them.' "[57] The second repugnant premise was that under the economy of the law, God can't, or won't, freely forgive the penitent sinner. From these postulates there logically followed the need for some sort of intervention from heaven, the circumventing of the law. This was accomplished through the death of Christ, which offered a new route to salvation. As Moore argues, this was Paul's "predetermined conclusion," but the apostle "can hardly have expected the argument to have effect with Jews, who would deny both premises."

For one thing, Paul had misunderstood the verse just quoted from Deuteronomy: "Cursed be every one who does not *abide* by all things written in the book of the law, and do them." The Hebrew word that he took to mean "abide by" really means "uphold." In other words, the Jew was expected to *uphold* all the Torah's commandments, affirming that they were God's will. But there was no expectation of perfect conformity in his actions. The rabbis made this clear.[58]

As for God's attitude of strictness toward those "under the law," that idea was explicitly contradicted by the Hebrew scriptures themselves. The Psalms speak of this with special eloquence: "[God] has not treated us according to our sin, nor repaid us according to our iniquities."[59] "And do not enter into strict judgment with Your servant, for no living creature would be vindicated before You."[60] Obviously the Psalmist, traditionally held to be King David, would not have prayed this way if God's standard operating procedure was indeed to hold humans to "strict judgment." Elsewhere David cried out, "Let me fall into the Lord's hand, for His mercies are abundant; but let me not fall into the hand of man."[61]

What a contrast to the anonymous Letter to the Hebrews, which some early church authorities attributed to Paul. An extended polemic against Judaism, it asserted that "without the shedding of blood there is no forgiveness of sins."[62] God needed blood, as in blood sacrifice, foremost the blood of the crucified Jesus, His sacrificed Son. The point was greatly sharpened with the destruction of the Temple with its sacrificial system, but whether before or after that year the idea that penitence was not enough would have come as a surprise to the large majority of first-century Jews, who lived in the Diaspora and therefore had no regular access to the Temple rites. In not availing themselves of these rites at all times, they were relying on scripture, which taught that forgiveness could be secured without sacrifice. King Solomon had said that when the Jews were in exile from their land, without a Temple, they "should repent . . . saying, 'We have sinned; we have been iniquitous; we have been wicked,' and they [will] return to You with all their heart and with all their soul . . . May You hear their prayer and their supplication from Heaven . . . and forgive Your people who sinned against You."[63]

In the Jewish understanding, which arose from the Hebrew Bible, repentance was always available to those who wished to "get right" with God. The Temple cult, prescribed in the Pentateuch, was an aid to this, not a precondition. Since that was the case, any new mechanism for winning God's forgiveness that someone should propose, such as the atoning death of Jesus Christ, would be superfluous. This was surely proved by the exile of the Jews to Babylon after the fall of Jerusalem in 586 BCE. The First Temple then lay in ruins for seventy years, a lifetime. If God saw no need then for a sacrificed Son, why would there ever be such a need?

George F. Moore's argument, that Paul began from premises alien to believers in the Hebrew Bible, has been streamlined by E. P. Sanders, also a Christian: "It appears that the conclusion that all the world—both Jew and Greek—equally stands in need of a savior [namely, Christ] *springs from* the prior conclusion that God had provided such a savior. If he did so, it follows that such a savior *must* have been needed, and then only consequently that all other possible ways of salvation are wrong. The point is made explicitly in Galatians 2:21: if righteousness could come through the law, Christ died in vain."[64]

Something like one of these approaches, Moore's or Sanders's, is the only way to explain how a Jew like Paul could have become the first person to imagine the essence of what would become Christian theology. The Bible he read and obviously cared for did not in any sense lead to the conclusion he said he drew from it. So the conclusion must have come first and in turn redirected and transformed his understanding of the Hebrew Bible as a whole. After formulating his belief about Jesus, when he reread scripture he in effect was reading a different book from the one other Jews read.

THAT IS, ASSUMING THAT Paul was a Jew. Was he really? This biographical detail is based on his own strenuous insistence, an insistence that, as we've seen, itself raises disturbing questions about his truthfulness. I would like to suggest that many Jews found him to be an outrageous character not only because he led Jews away from the commandments, and not only because he did this based on a reading of scripture distorted by his own "predetermined conclusion." They also sensed him to be a deceiver. Any observant Jews who heard him must have found it hard to believe he had ever been a Pharisee. He claimed to speak about Judaism as an expert, who had experienced the spiritual world of Torah from inside. Yet his words belie this.

He spoke of the Torah in the most negative terms. It was a curse: "Christ redeemed us from the curse of the law."[65] It held the Jews "captive." He described the anguish of trying to keep the commandments: "For I do not do the good I want, but the evil I do not want is what I do."[66] Besides contradicting what scripture itself said about the accessibility of the Torah—"it is not hidden from you and it is not distant. It is not in heaven . . . nor is it across the sea"—this would have struck committed Jews as an alien distortion of the experience of observing the commandments. It could come only from the mouth or pen of a person who had never really experienced the life of Torah.

How would a Jew know that? In part because the biblical books speak so ecstatically about Torah, known to Paul as "the Law," about its observance and contemplation.[67] It is interesting to consider the apostle's depiction of being held "captive" by the "curse" of "the Law" in light of, for instance, Psalm 119: "I occupy myself with your statutes . . . Teach me, O Lord, the way of Your statutes, and I will cherish it to the utmost. Grant me understanding so that I may cherish Your Torah, and keep it with [my] whole heart. Lead me on the path of your commandments, for that is my desire . . . I will be preoccupied with Your commandments that I love, and I will lift my hands to Your commandments, which I love, and I will discuss Your statutes . . . Had your Torah not been my preoccupation, then I would have perished in my affliction . . . O how I love Your Torah! All day long it is my conversation . . . Therefore I have loved your commandments more than gold, even more than fine gold . . . There is abundant peace to the lovers of your Torah, and there is no stumbling block for them."[68]

In Paul's day and in our own, Torah observance looks radically different to those who have only read about it in books than it does to those who have experienced it firsthand. The Pentateuch itself gives a lovely illustration of this. In Torah's symbolic nomenclature, Torah itself is in many places represented by water, while man is "a tree of the field."[69] Immediately after the Israelites had escaped from bondage in Egypt, they were crossing the Wilderness of Shur. Parched from thirst, they came to a place called Marah where there was a spring. But the water there was bitter and undrinkable. Moses then "cried out to the Lord, and the Lord showed him a tree; he threw it into the water and the water became sweet."[70]

The tree is man, the water is Torah. When the tree stands outside the water, it tastes bitter. When the tree plunges into the water, it turns sweet. Before a Jew "takes the plunge" and immerses himself in the life of Torah, all the rules and laws seem bitter—a "curse," a "captor." But once he has jumped in and experienced it for himself, it becomes sweet.[71]

How a person talks about the commandments is a reliable indicator of what he has experienced personally. Simply using certain words tells your listener or reader a lot about you. As evidence of this, I can cite to you the innumerable conversations about Judaism I have had with people of various religious perspectives. Consider the word *ritual*. Hardly anyone who has tried living a Torah life, really gotten *into* it, *ever* speaks of Jewish "rituals." The word means scripted actions of religious significance, but it connotes pure outwardness: actions that possess no inherent power to link God with man. Once you have made these "rituals" your way of life, you find they aren't rituals after all, so you stop using that word.

Paul presented himself as a Pharisee of Pharisees by training and experience, a sage who had plumbed the depths of Judaism. But anyone who has been that tree soaking in the sweet spring of Marah knows that the apostle's depiction of Judaism is one that likely came from someone who had at most put a toe in the water.

Once, in composing his letter to the community at Galatia, the apostle made an intriguing slip in his choice of pronouns, writing as if he himself were a non-Jew: ". . . that in Christ the blessing of Abraham might come upon the Gentiles, that we might receive the promise of the Spirit through faith."[72] There were, in fact, Jews in late antiquity who said they possessed a tradition that he was not even a Jew: the Ebionites, those last holdouts of the Jewish followers of Jesus who persisted in adhering to Jewish religious practices. In the fourth century, the Christian writer Epiphanius, who cataloged heresies, sought to document their beliefs. He wrote, "They declare that [Paul] was a Greek . . . He went up to Jerusalem, they say, and when he had spent some time there, he was seized with passion to marry the daughter of [a Jewish] priest. For this reason he became a proselyte and was circumcised. Then, when he failed to get the girl, he flew into a rage and wrote against circumcision and against the Sabbath and the Law."[73]

Whatever the historical value of this tradition, it does indicate that Jews who observed the commandments, even if they also believed in Jesus, found something suspect about Paul's Jewishness. In all the ancient Jewish polemics against Jesus himself, which we'll consider in the next chapter, there is no hint anywhere that *he* was not a Jew by birth. Only Paul aroused this suspicion.

With all this going against him, one can well see why certain members of the Jewish communities he visited would take umbrage at him, maybe even motivating some hotheads to action, whipping, beating, and stoning him.

This observation brings us into a confrontation with today's dominant academic opinion. That opinion sees Jesus in many ways as a typical Orthodox Jew of his day, with typical religious beliefs. Similarly, it is argued that Paul never meant to break with Judaism. His own claim to be a lifelong believing "Pharisee," a Jew of traditional inclinations, a student of the great rabbi Gamaliel, is taken at face value. True, his fellow Jews expressed violent outrage at his teachings. But we are asked to believe that the problem was merely one of Paul's brusque, undiplomatic manners.

The contemporary scholars who say this are wrong. The Jews that Paul encountered in his journeys around the Mediterranean world, besides coming close to killing him, rejected his message—to put it mildly—because they perceived him as misrepresenting and thereby overturning their religion. They regarded him as a faker who didn't understand the faith he so passionately critiqued. And *they* were right.

From the start, the religion he founded had woven into it his own misunderstandings. The rabbis would soon anathematize the incipient movement of Jewish Christians for representing a completely unacceptable innovation. Standing for faith in the Bible and in tradition, the rabbis could hardly do otherwise.

THE OFFENSE THAT JEWS took at Paul's doctrines increased with the decades that followed. The book of Acts depicts Paul's alleged teacher, Gamaliel, as urging tolerance of the followers of Jesus. About half a century later, the tide of Jewish opinion took a decisive turn against those Jews, the *minim* and Nazarenes.

By the end of the first century, they were found so repugnant by the rabbis that a special malediction upon them was inserted in the central Jewish prayer, the *Shemoneh Esrei*.[74] One version read: "May the apostates have no hope, unless they return to Your Torah, and may the Nazarenes and the Minim disappear in a moment. May they be erased from the book of life, and not be inscribed with the righteous." Down to today, traditional Jews say a variation of this three times daily, no longer mentioning Nazarenes and *minim* by name. Ideologically, the writing of this malediction into the *Shemoneh Esrei* was the event that ensured there could never be any philosophical mixing of the two faiths. It was no longer acceptable to be a Jewish Christian. What prepared the ground for this decisive moment in Jewish religious history was the destruction of the Temple.

In early Christian times, the *minim* were viewed as beyond the pale not only by Jews, but also by gentile Christians. About the year 107, Ignatius, bishop of Antioch, commented that "it is monstrous to talk of Jesus Christ and to practice Judaism."[75] St. Jerome wrote in a letter to St. Augustine, "As long as they wish to be Jews and Christians, they are neither Jews nor Christians." The rabbis considered Jewish Christians worse than idolaters. In the Talmud, Rabbi Tarphon, who lived in the second century, says that if he were being chased by an enemy and his life were in danger, he would flee for safety into a pagan temple but would give up his life before entering a house of *minim*, a Jewish-Christian church.[76]

The Talmud gives a clue about the essence of what made, and still makes, Jewish Christians so problematic in Jewish eyes. Rabbi Ishmael, another second-century figure, said they "arouse jealousy, enmity, and dissension between Israel and [our] Father in Heaven."

The time period in which the anathema upon the *minim* was sealed in Jewish liturgy is crucial to understanding its motivation. If it was composed about 80 CE, as historians indicate, that was only ten years after the burning and ruin of the Second Temple by Titus and his Roman legions. Only two gates were left standing when the Romans were done. For this disaster, some Jews blamed the rise of Christianity, seeing the spiritual desertion of the Christian Jews as a cause of "enmity" between the people Israel and their God.

The Talmud states that from forty years before the Temple's destruction and onward, there were supernatural omens of the disaster to come—that is, starting from the very inception of the Christian religion following the death of Jesus. The eternal fire on the Temple altar would not stay lit. The monumental bronze Temple gates opened by themselves.[77] Josephus confirms the Talmud's account of the inner Sanctuary's east gate and its mysterious openings. He adds other portents from these years: a bright light shining around the altar and Sanctuary at three in the morning, a cow brought for sacrifice giving birth to a lamb, apparitions of chariots and armies flying through the sky above the whole land of Israel. Was God not warning the people of the disastrous course some had set out upon?[78]

An ancient midrashic teaching attributes the dispersion that followed to the fact that some in Israel renounced monotheism, circumcision, the Ten Commandments, and the Torah as a whole—as did those Jews who followed Paul.[79] The Torah itself had said this would happen if Jews abrogated the covenant. While some Jewish Christians still practiced some commandments, the rabbis did not find it worthwhile to make fine distinctions among subcategories of *minim*. The fact that Jesus had planted the seeds of a religion whose overall message abrogated Torah observance was enough to condemn all Jews who counted themselves as his followers.

While the Jewish-Christian problem was spiritual, it was also practical. Eusebius wrote that the Jewish Christians in Jerusalem abandoned the defense of the holy city before it fell. They fled across the Jordan River to a place called Pella—a desertion their fellow Jews never forgot.

From then onward in Jewish hearts there would linger an inherited suspicion of such syncretists as betrayers whose actions led to catastrophe. Jewish Christians were now, in theological terms, persona non grata. Theologically, the Jewish break with Christianity was complete.

But our story is far from over. Historians continue to refine their views about when the separation of the Jewish from the Christian communities occurred, in the holy land and in the Diaspora. There is evidence of communal mixing of Orthodox Jews with Christian Jews and with gentile Christians for centuries after the Crucifixion. Scholars now gravitate to the view that (socially, at least, as opposed to theologically) there may never have been an identifiable "parting of the ways."

Such contact generated friction, taking the form of sharp words aimed like arrows. Until now we have had to speculate, based on reasonable assumptions, about what Jews who were alive at the time would have said about Jesus and Paul. Contemporary opinions somehow were not written down, probably because the Christian phenomenon initially seemed too small to worry about. That would soon change. As we'll see in the next two chapters, by the second century a tradition of polemic had developed among advocates of the two faiths, continuing through late antiquity and documented in rabbinic sources like the Talmud, of which the medieval disputations between Christians and Jews were a development and continuation. The reasons for the Jewish rejection of Christ were only now starting to take vivid focus.

CHAPTER FIVE

AFTER CHRIST, BEFORE CONSTANTINE

CONVERSATIONS WITH *MINIM*

W hen the Jews had their own state with its capital at
Jerusalem, even if subjugated to Rome, they were in some
sense still masters of their own destiny. They could deal
with challenges to their faith, such as Pauline Christianity, as they
wished. With the destruction of Jerusalem and her Temple, Jewish history entered a dangerous new phase, when Judaism was no longer the
state religion anywhere and Jews were thus increasingly vulnerable to
the attraction of other religions and cultures. In this context, the encounter with Christianity unfolded. The last chapter took us up to
about the year 80, when Judaism officially made its break with the followers of Jesus. During the next few centuries, which are the subject of
this chapter, Jews and Christians competed more or less on a level playing field. Toward the end of the period, Christians would gain an enor-
mous and permanent upper hand with the conversion of the emperor
Constantine and later the adoption of Christianity by most of the empire's citizenry.

Through it all, there persisted the Christian preoccupation with
showing Jews their error. Even after Paul said he was taking leave of his
fellow Israelites, giving up on them in favor of evangelizing the gentiles, Christians could never entirely abandon the project of winning

over the Jews. After all, if the Jews did not accept Jesus—his very own people!—as messianic savior, this constituted a serious stain on the honor of Christianity and on its own sense of internal coherence. The Jews had given to the world the very books of the Bible that Christians said proved Jesus's case. They knew those books as well as, or better than, anyone—yet those who remained identifiably Jewish rejected him! Some part of the Christian soul would always be troubled by this, disturbed by the apprehension, however suppressed, that the Jews were right. To Christian challenges, the Jews felt obliged to respond. The Jews also mounted their own intellectual attacks.

It was in this period that the penchant for arguing from scripture took shape. We have the extensive literary record of an ordinary Jew debating a learned Christian on the question of Jesus as God and Messiah. Rabbis sparred with Jewish Christians, too, but it wasn't until Christianity had emerged as the state religion that the Jews composed their most serious and monumental responses to the believers in Jesus, implicitly defending their continuing refusal to accept the offer of Christian faith. Future Jewish-Christian disputations, into and beyond the time when Christianity became a crusading faith with its own armies, kings, and body of theological doctrine, all may be traced to these first centuries after the fall of Jerusalem.

Of course, we should also not forget that the world was disturbed by more than just intellectual warfare. The rebellion of the Jews against the Roman imperial enemy that resulted in the destruction of the Temple did not conclude with that disaster. There was a hiatus of six decades, and then the Jewish war resumed, to be brutally and finally terminated under the reign of the emperor Aelius Hadrianus in 135.

The second Jewish war was led by Simeon Bar Kochbah, a man hailed by the greatest sage of the day, Rabbi Akiba, as Messiah. This failed Messiah was killed in the Roman siege of the Jewish city of Beitar, but not before he secured an independent Jewish Jerusalem for two and a half years and even started construction of a Third Temple, clearing the Temple Mount and beginning with a foundation along the lines of Ezekiel's prophecy of what the messianic Temple would look like. Akiba and other rabbis were prepared to follow him for one of the very same reasons that they could not accept the Christian claim for Jesus: Bar Kochbah got things done, he led a genuine uprising, he was on his way to rebuilding the Temple. These things defined a plausible messianic bid. That is, of course, until the presumptive Messiah's death, which seemed to prove that Akiba had been overhasty.

When Bar Kochbah died, so did hope of any immediate resumption of cultic Temple worship or of Jewish sovereignty in the holy land. The emperor restored Jerusalem as "Aelia," a pagan city with a temple of Jupiter where the holy Temple had stood. Jews were barred from entering. Even Christian Jews were banned, so that there ensued the end of the line for the "bishops of the Circumcision," as Eusebius called the leaders of the Jerusalem church.[1] Gentile Christianity was now on the ascendant.

As the religion centered upon Jesus grew, continuing to draw some Jews to its banner, the Jewish response would change, taking the religion with more seriousness than had been the case in the first century.

TO SET THE STAGE for these theological and philosophical engagements between the two faiths, we might wish to clarify our understanding of the period by asking what kind of threat to Jewish ranks the new religion posed. In the opening centuries of the Christian era, how many Jews became Christians? The number appears to have been small—and that should surprise us.

Between about 40 and 120 CE, literary references to Christians, by pagans and Jews alike, suggest that the church as a whole expanded slowly. Though the Alexandrian Jewish philosopher Philo wrote an account of Pontius Pilate's career, he neglected to mention the Crucifixion of Jesus, either because he didn't know of it or because he didn't consider it a significant event. Among gentile writers, Tacitus, Pliny the Younger, and Suetonius knew of the existence of the Christian movement but regarded it as a novelty in need of explaining: They assumed their readers would be unfamiliar with the religion.[2]

As for Christianity's success among the Jews, we have one ancient attempt to come up with a total number of converts. Origen (185–254

CE), the celebrated Christian Bible scholar and theologian, thought that from Christ's time to his own, the figure was fewer than 144,000. Recall that in the first century there were about a million Jews in the holy land alone and five times that number in the Diaspora, where the appeal of Christianity was probably higher. In short, Jews were not becoming Christians in droves.

Yet according to a modern historian and sociologist, Rodney Stark, this is not what we should expect. Stark offers a provocative comparison between the situation of so-called Hellenized Jews, imbued with Greek culture, living in the Diaspora in these early Christian centuries, and that of secularized German Jews in the nineteenth and twentieth centuries. Wealthy and in other ways quite comfortable in a non-Jewish society, the latter still identified as Jews; but in terms of Jewish religious practice, they had become marginal. They were caught between their loyalties to their adopted homeland, on the one hand, and to their religious heritage on the other. Often their level of religious education was low. Similarly, Hellenism was a cultural orientation dominated by Greek values and embraced by large numbers of well-to-do Greek-speaking Jews who had ceased to feel compelled by the traditional faith of their people. Many Hellenized Jews knew no Hebrew, or much else about Judaism. Their cultural hero was Philo, a Jew who sought to meld Greek philosophy with biblical faith.

The problem for both groups of Jews, separated by a vast distance of centuries, was that no one likes to be marginal. As humans, we seek to feel that we belong wholly to a culture rather than straddle two cultures at once. German Jews thus invented a new Judaism, under the banner of the Reform movement, which shed many of the particularistic aspects of the old religion: Protestant-style worship was adopted, complete with choirs and organs and German-language liturgy, and the whole system of commandments was largely discarded along with the ancient longing to return to the land of Israel.

Stark (who is a Christian) points out that the Christian movement offered many of the same benefits to Hellenized Jews that Reform did to secularized German Jews. It was a way to integrate yourself more fully with the surrounding gentile culture, also including the opportunity to jettison the obligation to observe the commandments—but without giving up your Jewishness altogether. Men and women being what they are, we should have expected many Hellenized Jews to accept the bargain and become Christians, just as German Jews filled the pews of Reform temples. By the end of the second century, the record of Alexandrian Jewish literature comes to an end: Hellenistic Jewish culture had been swallowed up either by rabbinic Jewish faith or by Christianity, or by both.

Have historians underestimated the number of Jews who turned Christian? One intriguing piece of evidence is the fact that the church so vigorously rejected the heresy of Marcion, who from the 140s on mounted a serious challenge to Christian orthodoxy. Headquartered in Rome, Marcion taught that the New Testament had radically superseded the Old, that in fact the God of the Hebrew Bible was a different being from the God of Jesus and Paul. The Jewish God was an inferior creator deity whose worship Christians needed to reject. Marcion tossed out the entire Old Testament along with the Gospels of Matthew, Mark, and John (the three Jewish Gospel authors), accepting only the Gospel of Luke (a gentile) along with Paul's letters.

Stark asks why orthodox Christians were so adamant in assailing Marcion's teaching. He argues that it may well have been because, as of the second century, Christian communities included so many born-Jews, who bridled at Marcion's anti-Jewish stance. After all, the "heretic" was right, in a sense. In the second century, when the Christian canon was still in formation, sensitive readers of scripture must have noted the radical disjunction between the Hebrew Bible and the Christian Gospels and epistles: "Even today, after nearly two millennia of rationalization, the fit between the Old and the New Testaments often seems awkward." Yet another modern Christian historian, Paul Johnson, admits that when we juxtapose the Hebrew with the Greek scriptures, the Jewish deity indeed appears to be "a quite different God."[3]

Arguing that Jews likely converted in larger numbers than we realize is one way to construe these facts. Another is to suggest that it was precisely the "awkward" fit between the Old and the New that warned even superficially educated Hellenized Jews away from the new religion. Origen's figure of fewer than 144,000 Jewish converts in two centuries would then make sense. Those who scrutinized the offer of the new faith from the perspective of what they already knew of the Hebrew Bible would have a devilishly hard time justifying the leap across the scriptural divide. This was not the case with Reform, where at least there was the comforting thought that you were staying in the same religion, albeit with all the disturbing, seemingly anachronistic parts pruned away.

We should recall, incidentally, that potential gentile converts would not have had to overcome the same hurdle their Jewish counterparts did. For they approached the whole matter from a different perspective. With no Old Testament "baggage," they could much more naturally interpret the Hebrew Bible *in the light of* the Christian scriptures — instead of the other way around, as a Jew, raised on the Hebrew Bible, would most naturally do. This tended to eliminate the problem of the awkward fit. A gentile could be given the Christian Gospels and epistles *first*, which then colored his subsequent reading of the Hebrew scriptural books. As treated by Christian interpreters from the New Testament on, everything in the Old that clashes with the New was "spiritualized" or otherwise given a new meaning. We'll now see how the newly formed theology did this and how Jews responded — the Hellenized and the fully committed, each after their fashion.

THOSE JEWS WITH A less certain grounding in their tradition were more vulnerable to Christian arguments. This emerges clearly, if unintentionally, from a fascinating and important document: Justin Martyr's *Dialogue with Trypho the Jew*. The author (c. 100–165 CE) was born to pagan parents in the city that is today called Nablus, on Israel's West Bank. He was a philosopher and remained one after converting, becoming the greatest of those early Christian apologists who sought to defend their faith on rational grounds. Their interest was in attracting sophisticated gentiles. Justin had a school in Rome and met his death as a martyr, scourged and beheaded for refusing to sacrifice to the pagan gods.

About the year 135 he was living in Ephesus, a large city on the Aegean (today the coast of Turkey) where Paul had lived and preached for three years. As he tells the story in his *Dialogue*, one morning he was walking in the city, dressed in his philosopher's robe. (Since this was a professional role at the time, by custom the practitioner wore a special woolen blanketlike garment, just as today a medical doctor wears a white coat.) A Jew called Trypho approached in company with some boorish friends, also Jews. He introduced himself to Justin and initiated a Platonic-style dialogue, with Justin playing the Socratic lead part of pedagogical inquisitor. The subject was God's new covenant with the Christians, as compared with the old one with the Jews.

There is no way of telling if the encounter actually happened as described, but Justin certainly presents it as if it did. Historians wonder about the identity of Trypho. Eusebius, our most vivid Christian witness to this period, described him as an "eminent Hebrew."[4] Some scholars have said he might be the very same Rabbi Tarphon we met in the last chapter—the fellow who said he would rather die than enter a Jewish-Christian house of worship. Not likely! Trypho displays far more tolerance than Tarphon. Also, Trypho's schooling clearly was not rabbinic: He speaks of having been "taught in Argos by Corinthus of the school of Socrates."[5] It becomes apparent that, like Paul, both Trypho and Justin are unable to understand the Bible in its original Hebrew and must rely on the problematic Greek translation, the Septuagint. In short, Trypho gives every indication of being a rather typical Hellenized Jew, out of his depth when talk turns to the interpretation of biblical texts. I am inclined to credit the truth of Justin's account, if only because he so nicely depicts how easy it was for a Christian scholar to outmaneuver a Greek Jew who, however philosophically sophisticated and however emotionally loyal to Judaism, hadn't received a thorough Jewish education.

For his part, Justin is a philosophic bullyboy, hectoring Trypho, demanding that he assent to questionable propositions. He then uses these to build the rest of his argument as if they were proven facts. Trypho's companions laugh and shout rudely at the Christian sage, evidently unable to offer cogent responses of their own. Trypho himself remains respectful—though he does object at one point that "I would have you know that you are out of your mind when you say all this."[6] This is just bluster, as Trypho quickly shows what a pushover he is.

For example, Justin wishes to demonstrate that the church has taken the place of the Jewish people in God's plan for the salvation of mankind. Thus, whenever the Old Testament refers to "Israel" in a favorable way, it is a reference to Christians; wherever in an unfavorable way, it's a reference to the Jews. In the Bible itself, one finds no internal clues that God or the prophets are to be understood as speaking of two Israels—one good and one bad. Rather, Israel is a complicated spiritual entity, sometimes good and sometimes bad. But Justin's interpretation requires two Israels, so this is taken as fact. Trypho never points out the obvious circularity.

Again and again, the Jew has little to reply to Justin's speeches. But in fact there's always plenty to reply. So Justin lays stress on God's alleged eternal rejection of Temple sacrifice. He quotes the prophet Amos: "I hate and loathe your festive offerings, and I will not be appeased by your assemblies."[7] But as Trypho fails to point out, two verses later it becomes clear that God hates only those festive offerings offered without righteous intentions, for He also says: "Remove from before Me the multitude of your songs, and the music of your lutes I will not hear."[8] Does this mean that God eternally rejects music and songs? Presumably not.

Justin adduces two of the strongest prophetic passages in the Christian arsenal. One is Jeremiah 31:30–31, which speaks of a "new covenant": "Behold, days are coming—the word of the Lord—when I will seal a new covenant with the House of Israel and with the House of Judah: not like the covenant that I sealed with their forefathers . . ." In Justin's treatment, this new covenant is identical with Jesus Christ. Trypho had nothing to say in response; but as we saw in chapter 1, it seems much more likely that the new covenant is simply the ancient system of commandments, changed only by the fact that the Jewish people bring to it a renewed commitment: "If these laws could be removed from before me . . . so could the seed of Israel cease from being a people before me forever" (31:35).

Justin also confronts Trypho with Ezekiel's prophecy, in which God says He "gave them [that is, the Jews] decrees that were not good and laws by which they could not live."[9] By this the Christian sage means to denigrate the observance of the commandments.

Is it really the Sabbath and circumcision and all the rest that Ezekiel speaks of here as "laws by which they could not live"? Trypho doesn't inquire, but he would have done so had he looked more closely at the preceding verses. God laments: "But the children rebelled against Me. They did not follow my decrees and did not observe My laws, to fulfill them, through which, if a man fulfills them, he will live through them; and they desecrated my Sabbaths; so I spoke [to Myself] to pour out My wrath upon them . . ."[10]

Evidently two sets of legislation are referred to here. First, God gave laws that were life-giving. Then, when the Jews rebelled, they were subjected to "decrees that were not good." To identify the *second* set of laws with the traditional commandments like the Sabbath and circumcision, as Justin does, makes little sense. Because, as the Bible narrates Jewish history, they were the first laws to be given to the Jews, they must be the first, good decrees referred to in Ezekiel's prophecy. Here again, the context defeats Justin's interpretation. More plausibly, Jewish sages have long understood the second, bad laws to be those imposed by harsh foreign rulers, like the Greeks and Romans, who subjugated the Jews when the latter shrugged off their true and eternal Ruler.

Justin wants his Jewish listeners to understand that their traditional laws are rendered moot by the coming of Christ. As has surely started to become clear in our survey of the Jewish-Christian debate about Jesus, this is one of the chief Jewish objections to the proposition that the itinerant preacher from Nazareth was the Jewish Messiah. Probably it is the most decisive of all. In Deuteronomy, Moses had forewarned the Jews that God would test their love for Him, raising up in their midst prophets and dreamers who would lure them from the true path of monotheism and observance of the commandments. Could the true Messiah be someone who founded a religion that told the Jews that these very same commandments were "not good"? Poor

Trypho is so flooded and overwhelmed by his interlocutor with out-of-context prophetic citations, he fails to see this basic problem with Justin's presentation.

Also in Deuteronomy, Moses warns that the false prophet or dreamer will produce signs and wonders and say, "Let us follow gods of others that you did not know and we shall worship them!"[11] A Jew steeped in scripture would have thought of this as he listened to Justin explain how the Bible itself shows the existence of multiple divine personalities. Thus, God will sometimes speak in a royal plural, as if He comprised more than one personality. And sometimes an angel will speak in His voice, as if the angel were a deity. Justin tries to show that when this happens, we are listening to the voice of Christ, who entered the world as an incarnate being on various occasions before being born to Mary and growing up to be Jesus the Messiah.

Trypho is typically unprepared to answer. "It is plain that Scripture compels us to acknowledge this," he says at one point.[12]

At the end of the *Dialogue*, Trypho and Justin part as the best of friends, with the Jew pronouncing himself to have been "extraordinarily charmed with our intercourse . . . For we [Trypho and his companions] have found more than we expected, or than it was even possible for us to expect."[13] He isn't ready yet to become a Christian, but we are left to wonder if perhaps it is only a matter of time.

AS TRYPHO THE HELLENIZED JEW stood in the streets of Ephesus and found himself rendered defenseless as a debater, the rabbis in the holy land were likewise encountering Christians who wanted to spar with them on the same issues, adducing much the same evidence from scripture. Except that here the Jews were in command of their sources.

Such conversations between sages and *minim* amount to a pattern of interactions, mostly casual but sometimes formal. Christian sages wrote of debates with Jews. Because the Jews had not yet experienced Christian anti-Jewish persecution and so felt free to speak their minds, often they themselves initiated the encounters. Jerome, translator of the Hebrew Bible into Latin, described his aggressive Jewish interlocutors with even greater dislike than he felt toward Jewish Christians: "with loose lips and twisted tongue, and with spittle spluttering from their shaven, grinning jaws." Other Christians who sparred with Jewish opponents include Tertullian (160–225 CE), a native of Carthage in North Africa, and Origen, the third-century theologian who hailed from Alexandria.

From the formulation of the anathema against the *minim* about the year 80, the history of Jewish counter-Christian polemic begins. In rabbinic sources such as the Babylonian and Jerusalem Talmuds and the midrashic collections, where we find records of this polemic tradition, the names of certain sages active in the Jewish-Christian debate keep coming up. In the second century, we have Rabbis Eliezer ben Hyrcanus, Joshua ben Hananiah, Eleazar of Modein, Tarphon, Bar Kappara, and Joshua ben Levi; in the third century, we have Rabbis Simlai, Samuel bar Nachman, and Abahu.[14]

These sages operated in various localities around the land of Israel. In the Galilee, there were Sepphoris, on a lovely hilltop, and Tiberias by the shore of the Sea of Galilee. Another was Lydda, now familiar as Lud, the location of Ben-Gurion Airport. A fourth, the most prominent venue for Jewish-Christian sparring, was Caesarea on the Mediterranean coast. We may want to try to imagine the atmosphere there, so different from the places where Jews would later debate Christians in the medieval European disputations. No clammy cathedrals or chilly palaces at Caesarea, but rather the hot blue skies and blowing sands of a great Mediterranean harbor. Rome had its provincial capital here, backed by a major garrison of troops. Some splendid ruins may be visited today. They include the impressive amphitheater where the Jewish king Agrippa I was struck by a mortal illness in 44 CE under supernatural circumstances, an angel appearing in the sky above him, after the spectators acclaimed him a god.[15]

The danger of confusing men with gods formed one of the themes of Abahu, among the foremost sages who taught at Caesarea. He would lecture on a verse from Numbers: "God is not a man that He should be deceitful, nor a son of man that He should repent."[16] Clearly he had in mind Jesus, whose followers hailed him as God and also as the "son of man," for the sage said, "If a man tells you, 'I am God,' he is a liar; if [he says, 'I am] the son of man,' in the end people will laugh at him."[17]

Another of his favorite verses was from Isaiah. There the Lord said, "I am the first and I am the last, and aside from Me there is no God." To Abahu, the relevance to Christianity with its "Son of God" was apparent. He taught that God was unlike a human king, who might have a sibling or a child. Rather, God meant us to understand through Isaiah's words: " 'I am the first,' for I have no father; 'and I am the last,' for I have no son; 'and beside Me there is no God,' for I have no brother."[18]

The rabbi knew of an intriguing institution called the Be Abidan, of which there was probably one in Caesarea itself. The references in the Talmud are vague, but it seems to have been a forum for disputations among advocates of competing religions and philosophies. (The name may derive from the Greek *Odeon*, a theatrical venue where philosophical discourses could also be heard.) Books of scripture, Jewish and otherwise, were kept handy there for reference. While some Jewish sages declined on principle to participate in such debates with Christians, others were willing to attend.[19] Probably Abahu was among the latter.

For remarkably he not only critiqued Christian doctrine, but also served as a teacher of *minim* who wished to learn from Jewish scholarship. The Talmud relates a story about a group of these to whom he recommended a colleague, Rabbi Saphra, as a paid teacher. But when the *minim* were dissatisfied with Saphra's ability to clarify a difficult scriptural passage, they asked Abahu to take over the instruction, which he did.[20]

There was also a darker side to the interaction with Christians. Some generations before Abahu, Rabbi Eliezer ran into serious trouble, probably also at Caesarea. About 109 CE during an anti-Christian persecution across the holy land by Roman authorities, Eliezer was somehow caught in the imperial dragnet. Arrested and put on trial as a suspected *min*, he appeared before the governor, who asked, "How does it come to be that an old man like you busies himself with such foolish matters?" Knowing it was in vain to argue, Eliezer simply replied, "Faithful is the Judge concerning me." The governor thought this was in reference to himself and, flattered, chose to dismiss the case and release Eliezer.

Afterward, the rabbi was troubled at the evil fortune that had overtaken him. He thought it must reflect some misdeed he had committed. His student Rabbi Akiba asked, "Rabbi, perhaps there came some bit of heresy [*minut*] into your hand and it pleased you, and because of that you were arrested for *minut*." The sage replied that he did indeed remember such an occurrence. Once he had been walking in Sepphoris when a follower of Jesus approached him with a question about a verse in Deuteronomy. Eliezer didn't answer, so the *min*, whose name was Jacob, reported the explanation that Jesus gave to the verse, which is obscure and need not detain us. Eliezer admitted to Akiba that the Christian interpretation had pleased him, and to this lapse he attributed his rough handling by the Romans.[21]

God was evidently teaching the elderly sage a lesson about listening to Christians. If Eliezer did so, he stood in danger of being mistaken for one. The moral is that when it comes to sin, as soon as you have got yourself into a situation where you have granted an audience to someone who wishes to lead you astray—whether that someone is another person or whether it is yourself, when the voice of temptation speaks in your own heart—you have already set off down the road to sin, even if you have taken no outwardly observable immoral action. The first woman, Eve, learned this lesson after she simply agreed to listen to the serpent in the Garden of Eden. From that moment, before she had taken a bite of the apple, her downfall was all but accomplished.[22]

WE CAN SEE WHY SOME rabbis chose not to engage directly with Christians in controversies. Yet they had no reservations about speaking to their own students on why they found Christian doctrine unacceptable. These teachings were not laid out in the manner of comprehensive, point-by-point refutations, like those we find in the medieval period. As represented in the Talmud and midrashic sources, they give an impression of being offhand, almost casual. This may be because in the period we are describing—before the emergence of a Christian state—the new faith was not regarded with great seriousness as a rival or danger. We must keep in mind, however, that, as everywhere in Jewish tradition, the brief, clipped remarks of the sages are often intended to be cryptic. They conceal depths of meaning in a few coded words.

Whether casual or not, we may distinguish motifs in the rabbis' treatment of Christianity. The top four are the seeming reversion from monotheism to the worship of multiple deities; the problem of Christianity's abrogation of the law of the Torah; the true Messiah; and the person of Jesus himself. There is some overlap with what I suggested were the reasons the Jews in the first century so violently rebuffed the apostle Paul, but now for the first time, starting in the second century, we begin to hear the Jews' reasoning in their own words.

TWO GODS OR ONE? In Talmudic and other early rabbinic literature, the most often heard polemical theme directed against Christians has to do with the charge that the latter worshipped two gods. Not three, as in the later Christian formulations—Father, Son, and Holy Spirit—but two. In the first centuries of our era, not all Christians had yet become formal Trinitarians, for the Holy Spirit had not yet joined the pantheon. This is not to say the rabbis went out of their way to appreciate subtle theological distinctions that Christians might advance.

Thus, in his *Dialogue* Justin cited a verse from Genesis describing the destruction of Sodom and Gomorrah, the sinful cities: "And the Lord rained down upon Sodom and Gomorrah sulfur and fire from the Lord."[23] The Christian apologist asked, didn't this suggest there were at least two personalities comprehended by the phrase *the Lord*—namely, the Father and the Son? Otherwise, it would have made more sense simply to say that the Lord rained down sulfur and fire "from Him."

On an occasion within a few decades of Justin's discussion with Trypho, a Jewish Christian put the same query to Rabbi Ishmael, the son of Rabbi Yose. Probably the scene was Sepphoris, not far from where Jesus had his ministry. As the Talmud recounts, Rabbi Ishmael was about to answer when someone in the audience, a Jew who was not even a scholar but only a simple launderer of clothing, jumped up and cried: "Leave him [to me]. I will answer him." Ishmael deferred to the launderer, who pointed out another verse in Genesis that uses a similar grammatical construction, but in reference to a mortal. An early descendant of the first humans, Adam and Eve, called Lemech, had said to his two wives, "Adah and Tzilah, hear my voice; wives of Lemech, give heed to my speech."[24] As in the statement about Sodom and Gomorrah, Lemech referred to himself twice. Did this mean there were two Lemechs? No, it was simply an example of scriptural idiomatic usage.

Justin also cited an earlier verse from Genesis, describing the Creation of the world. God said, "Let us make man in our image."[25] The Christian sage reasoned, why would the verse be in the plural if not to indicate that God had a partner in the Creation—namely, the cosmic Christ?

A century later, a Jewish Christian asked this question of Rabbi Yochanan (c. 200–279 CE), who taught and lived in Tiberias, by the Sea of Galilee. Yochanan told his students, "Wherever the *minim* use a [scriptural verse] to support their heresy, the reply [to their argument can be found] in the immediate context [of the verse]." Which is to say, Jewish Christians were apt to take verses out of their proper context and thus distort their meaning. In the case at hand, Rabbi Yochanan pointed out that the very next verse shows that only the One God was involved: "God created man in His image," with both the verb and pronoun appearing in the singular.[26] The sage went on to cite a lovely tradition that the Torah phrased the earlier verse in the plural because God sought to model proper, humble conduct: "The Holy One, Blessed be He, does not do anything unless He [first] consults the Heavenly Court"—that is, His retinue of angels.[27] Just so, humans should act in a deferential manner to subordinates by asking their opinion before acting.

Yet the rabbis understood that the verse about God making man "in our image" was charged with danger. Moses himself had foreseen this. A third-century Palestinian sage, Rabbi Jonathan, reported a tradition about a conversation between God and His lawgiver. At the

Lord's direction, Moses was composing the Torah. When he came to these words, he burst out in dismay, "What a pretext [for heresy] You have given to the *minim*! I am amazed!" To this God replied, "Write! And he who wishes to err, let him err!"[28] Meaning that the intention of the verse was clear, given the context. Although heretics would claim to find proof of God's multiplicity, they were led by their own willfulness, not by a sober reading of the text.

THE ETERNAL LAW. Did God intend the Torah's commandments, 613 in all according to Talmudic tradition, to be observed forever? To show that the law was only temporary and had been rendered obsolete by the coming of Jesus, Christians pointed to Abraham, whom God regarded as righteous even before, at age ninety-nine, he had received the command to circumcise himself. If Abraham's righteousness didn't depend on this most onerous of religious obligations, surely any Jew could be considered righteous without resting on the Sabbath or giving tithes, without observing the dietary laws or the rules governing marital relations (no sex during the period of menstruation and for a week after), and all the rest.

Over in Caesarea, the fourth-century Christian historian Eusebius (260–339?) was merely restating a long-standing Christian belief going back to Paul's teaching when he wrote, "Christians alone can be seen throughout the world practicing religion in the very form in which Abraham practiced it." As part of the same atmosphere of growing Jewish-Christian controversy that the rabbis participated in, Eusebius was busy writing his voluminous works, which included a series of "special pamphlets" entitled *Selections from the Prophets*, just as Christians today put together pamphlets with prophetic selections showing to their satisfaction how Isaiah, Jeremiah, and the rest foretold the career of Jesus Christ. He argued that Abraham and his predecessors, Adam and Noah and their families, were in fact—Christians! "They cared nothing for bodily circumcision—nor do we; nor for the keeping of Sabbath—nor do we; nor for abstentions from certain foods or distinctions between others (all that Moses was the first man ever to hand down, for later generations to carry out, in symbols)—nor do these things matter to Christians now."[29]

In line with this notion that the commandments were meant as symbols only, some Christian thinking sought to define their individual symbolic meanings. Thus, one of the earliest examples of Christian anti-Jewish polemic, the epistle of Barnabas (c. 135 CE but anachronistically attributed to Paul's traveling companion Barnabas), explains the moral lessons alluded to through the Bible's rendering of the rules of kosher food. For example, in symbolic terms, eating rabbit is forbidden not literally, but only to warn against sexually molesting children: "You shall not be a corrupter of children; nor liken yourself to such persons. For the rabbit every year acquires an extra anus; and as many years as it lives, so many it has."[30] One sees why such an analysis would provoke skepticism from Jews and indeed from gentiles. A disinterested reading of the text can't help but lead to the conclusion that these commandments, whatever symbolic meanings they also possess, were first and foremost meant to be carried out as concrete actions.

The more serious point was that having to do with Abraham. The rabbis replied with received traditions to the effect that the patriarch had in fact kept *all* the commandments, not just circumcision, including those conveyed not in the plain text of the Torah itself, but only through oral transmission from the revelation at Mount Sinai as well as those that the rabbis would later enact, down to the most precise details. They noted a verse in Genesis: "Because Abraham obeyed My voice, and observed My safeguards, My commandments, My decrees, and My Torahs." The last word, *v'torotai* ("and My Torahs"), indicated not only the written but also the oral Torah.[31]

There were other hints of this in scripture. For instance, Abraham's nephew Lot, educated in Abraham's household, had served unleavened bread (matzo), of the kind Jews would later be commanded to eat at Passover, to the angels who came to save him from Sodom, where he lived, just prior to the city's destruction: "He made a feast for them and baked unleavened cakes [matzoth], and they ate."[32] The rabbis explained that it was Passover, and Lot had learned to eat matzo then from his uncle.[33]

As for the question raised by Christian teachers of why, if circumcision is so important, God waited until Abraham was ninety-nine to give the instruction, the rabbis had an answer. It was so as not to "shut the door in the face of converts" to Abraham's primordial religion of monotheism, whom the patriarch sought to proselytize. As Paul could have confirmed, they might balk at being circumcised as adults. Initially, God decided it was important that this not stand in Abraham's way.[34]

This addressed the covenant's eternality extending back into the past. What of the future? Perhaps it was built into the structure of the commandments that there would come a time when they would no longer have the force of obligation. Paul used the image of a child's tutor, who instructs the youth until the latter has grown up enough not to require tutoring.

Apart from the obvious point that the Torah itself never indicated that its role was only as a temporary tutorial, fascinatingly, some rabbis made what may at first sound like an admission. The mainstream rabbinic view was that there would be no radical difference between our world and the world ruled over by the coming Messiah except that freedom and virtue would reign: The domination of the wicked governments, especially Rome, would be forever ended. But another view held that the difference between present and future would be far more profound. The Talmud cites the view of Rabbi Simeon ben Eleazar (c. 150 CE) that in the messianic era "there [will be] neither merit nor guilt."[35] In other words, anyone wanting to acquire merit through the commandments had better do it now, rather than wait for the denouement of history, when it would be too late.

Did this mean that with the Messiah's coming, Jews would no longer keep kosher or circumcise their baby boys? Judging only from his lone statement, Simeon ben Eleazar is too cryptically terse for us to say for certain. But other rabbinic teachings, reflecting the same general viewpoint, resolve the question. Rabbi Joseph (who died about 333 CE) taught that the "commandments will be abolished in the Hereafter"! But as Rabbi Yochanan had told his students, context is everything. The context for Rabbi Joseph's statement is a discussion in the

Talmud of whether a corpse may be buried wearing a shroud woven from a mixture of wool and flax, which the Bible forbids. The rabbis said such a garment for the dead was acceptable, which Joseph saw as confirming that when we are resurrected in the messianic age, it will be too late to attain merit through the commandments—for example, by obeying the commandment not to mix wool and flax. After rising from the grave, you will next be judged for what you did during your life. Yochanan himself clarified the matter: "As soon as a man dies he is free from the commandments."[36]

With this in mind we can understand some later, quite startling rabbinic statements. The *midrash* on Psalms explicates a phrase in the biblical book of Psalms (146:7): ". . . the Lord releases the bound." What are the bonds from which He'll free us? This midrash records an opinion that all kinds of animal flesh will be permitted for consumption and that a man will be allowed to engage in intimacy with his wife even when she is menstruating. But the *midrash* goes on to indicate that the "bonds" that will most dramatically be loosened are those of death. In other words, all this applies only to the time when death has been abolished—that is, after the resurrection of the dead.

The reason the rabbis singled out the commandments having to do with eating nonkosher meat and engaging in intimacy during menstruation is that both arise from God's will that Jews separate themselves from morbid reminders of death. Meat that has been improperly slaughtered, or the forbidden mixing of milk (symbolizing life) with meat (symbolizing death), conveys the spiritual infection of a crushing awareness of death, an awareness that Jewish law calls *tumah*. So, too, when a woman menstruates, a potential life—the egg she bears—has been lost. At such a time, husband and wife separate so as not to taint the act of sex (the creation of a life) with the reminder of death.

But with the advent of the true Messiah, there will no longer be a reason to worry about mixing life with death, because there will be no death! So according to this particular midrashic opinion, the two commandments having to do with meat and sex will be rendered inoperative.[37]

To summarize: The Jewish answer to Christian teachings about the abolition of Torah law was twofold. The eternality of the Torah extended back to Abraham, who merely discovered certain preexisting, timeless principles, much as a scientist would discover principles of physics that had always operated, but unrecognized. And the eternality of the commandments extended into the endless future, or at least until such time as death is no more.

THE TRUE MESSIAH. Christianity said the Jews could dispense with the commandments prescribed in the written and oral Torahs, the very grammar of a Jew's relationship with God. No true Messiah would found a religion that presumed to abolish the commandments. Still, it remains evident that some rabbis thought the messianic age would bring about a new situation, following the resurrection, in which at least some commandments would be transformed. Noting this, a Christian might argue, But the messianic era has begun! Was it not possible that the promised age commenced with the first coming of Christ, his death and resurrection, to be followed at some later date by his return and the calling of the dead back to life? In that case, the question of whether the commandments have really been abrogated would turn upon the related question of whether the Messiah has come.

A Jew who believed in his own religious tradition could only respond that the world as he knew it was nothing like the coming world that the Messiah would herald. When they taught about this subject, the rabbis saw themselves as interpreting scripture in three ways. At the simplest level, they read it like any sensitive reader. In chapter 1, we saw what the Bible itself indicates about the wondrous future age, presided over by a scion of King David. The prophets agreed that there was a sequence of events related to the unfolding of the age.

We found that Ezekiel, in his thirty-sixth and thirty-seventh chapters, may be the clearest and most detailed prophetic voice in laying out this sequence: 1) gathering of exiles; 2) reign of the Messianic king; 3) a new covenant characterized by scrupulous observance of the commandments; 4) eternal peace; 5) a new Temple; 6) the nations recognize God. There was no suggestion of a pause between a first and second coming of the messianic king. On the contrary, the prophets' frequent use of the phrase *on that day* suggested a single sweeping redemptive process. The fact that the Jews of the exile had manifestly not been gathered argued strongly that the sequence had yet to begin. A renewed commitment to the commandments, eternal peace, a new Temple, and universal worship of the God of Israel were also conspicuously lacking.

But Christians disagreed about the interpretation of scripture. Rabbinic Judaism thus brought forward two additional perspectives. First, exegesis was not a free-for-all. Because understanding the Bible as the Lord meant it to be understood was crucial, and because the text was so manifestly cryptic, at Mount Sinai He had given not only the Torah, but also certain fixed rules for interpreting it.[38] These rules had been passed down from teacher to student orally. Second, there were traditions, also emanating from the Sinai revelation and transmitted orally, that could not be derived by exegesis. Indeed, everything that was a matter of oral tradition had first been revealed, in some essential or embryonic form, at Sinai.[39]

So in responding to Christian arguments, any believing Jew would naturally turn to the oral traditions. The rabbis who instructed and ministered in the period immediately after the editing of the Mishnah, the *amoraim*, picked up the thread of messianic teachings that started with the Bible. In the Talmud, especially the eleventh chapter of its tractate *Sanhedrin*, we find their voluminous rendering of the traditions about events that will accompany the appearance of the Messiah.

One of these teachings portrayed world history as being divided into three epochs of two thousand years each, starting with the creation of Adam and Eve. First came two thousand years of human alienation from God. At the beginning of the second epoch, about 1758 BCE by modern calculations, Abraham began to teach Torah to the world. Two thousand years after that, or 242 CE, was supposed to begin "the Days of the Messiah." But "because of our sins, which are numerous," the redeemer has been delayed.[40]

However, he cannot be delayed beyond the end of the framework of six thousand years. For those keeping count, that means he must appear by the year 2242. After this, the world would hibernate in a condition of desolation for thousands of years, before the breaking forth of the World to Come, a supernatural existence to be enjoyed by the virtuous dead who were resurrected.

That was in the future. In the meantime, there were certain things that rabbis said they knew. For one, they knew that no one could predict the exact time of the Messiah's appearing. There were figures in biblical history who had known the date, namely the patriarch Jacob and the prophet Daniel, but God had forbidden them to reveal it. His coming would be a surprise: "Three things turn up when [they are] not expected. They are: the Messiah, a found object [that had been lost], and a scorpion."[41] Yet there were signs of his imminent approach: increased insolence and disrespect for sages and elders, falsehood, wars.

But the Messiah's coming would not be a product of happenstance. The preeminent condition that would cause him to appear was repentance. The book of Deuteronomy said just this. There, Moses had spoken prophetically of a time when the people Israel were dispersed everywhere in the world but then repented, reembraced God's commandments, and subsequently were gathered together again. "It will be that when all these things come upon you—the blessing and the curse that I have presented before you—then you will take it to your heart among all the nations where the Lord, your God, has dispersed you; and you will return unto the Lord, your God, and listen to His voice, according to everything that I command you today . . . If your dispersed will be at the ends of heaven, from there the Lord, your God, will gather you in . . . You shall return and listen to the voice of the Lord, and perform all His commandments that I command you today . . . The Lord will return to rejoice over you for good . . . when you listen to the voice of the Lord, your God, to observe His commandments and His decrees, that are written in this Book of the Torah . . ."[42]

God's rejoicing and the return of the exiles were tied explicitly with the "commandments and . . . decrees, that are written in this Book of the Torah." The very commandments whose observance Christians said their Messiah had dispensed with were the very preconditions for the promised redemption.

Citing from Isaiah, the Talmudic rabbis made this clear. Rabbi Simeon ben Yohai, who lived through the Hadrianic war, taught that the Messiah would come if all Israel observed two Sabbaths according to the laws.[43] Rabbi Yochanan, whom we've already met, said the messianic age would dawn only upon a generation that was entirely righteous or upon one that was entirely wicked. However, the Talmud, where his statement is recorded, immediately jumps in to explain that in the latter case, God will bring sufferings on the people that will cause them to repent and become righteous so as to prepare the way for the Messiah's footsteps.[44] Thus, either way, the Messiah will come only to a generation that has repented.

One thing that Jews could agree on with Christians was that the generation of Jesus had not been outstandingly righteous. They had witnessed the destruction of the Temple, after all, a sorry reflection on their moral condition. To a Jew, it would have been clear that the Messiah had not come in the first century.

THE PERSON OF JESUS. A check of the editions of the Talmud printed in recent centuries will reveal no mention of Jesus. This is thanks to a thorough censorship of rabbinic literature. Starting from 1578 to 1580, in the version of the Talmud edited in Basle, Switzerland, every explicit reference to Jesus was excised to evade Christian wrath. In earlier manuscripts, we in fact find clear references and allusions to "Yeshu ha'Notzri," Jesus of Nazareth, who emerges a rather different figure from the Jesus of the Gospels or of modern scholarly books. Today, these censored passages appear only at the very back of some Talmud editions, separated from the text itself and cryptically headed, in very small type like addenda.

This material, forming a relatively coherent tradition about Jesus, has been traced to its likely originator, Rabbi Eliezer, whose own teacher, Yochanan ben Zakkai, died at a ripe age before 80 CE and could have encountered Jesus in the flesh. Sometimes Jesus is called by other names or appears in historical contexts at variance with the time frame set in the Gospels, but there is little room for doubt that the rabbis had in mind the Jesus of Nazareth who healed, taught, performed wonders, and inspired the Christian religion.[45] This was certainly the opinion of the foremost sage of the past thousand years, Moses Maimonides, as he made clear both in his *Mishneh Torah* and in his "Epistle to Yemen."[46] Other modern rabbis have argued that the Jesus of the Talmud is a different Jesus of Nazareth. Their view seems to be inspired mainly by a wish to avoid giving ammunition to Jew haters. However commendable this intention, it comes too late. As a quick Internet search will reveal, these sources are already well-known to anti-Semitic fringe groups and to others.

Whatever we make of the value of the stories and polemics about "Yeshu" as a source of historical truth, they reveal the predominant attitude among the most influential Jewish teachers. Jesus is revealed as a former student of Torah who went seriously off the rails and became a spiritual danger to the people Israel.

His mother was Miriam ("Mary"), a "women's hairdresser," who was married but conceived the baby Yeshu by another man, Pandira—hence one of Jesus's alternative designations in the Talmud, "Ben Pandira," the "Son of Pandira."[47] About Miriam, it is said that she was of a royal bloodline but "played the harlot with carpenters," suggesting that it was the paramour, Pandira, who was the carpenter—not Jesus's adoptive father, Joseph, as in the Gospel story.[48] Yeshu grew up to be a disciple of a great rabbi, Joshua ben Perachya. Inconveniently, the latter is known to have lived a century before the Jesus known to us from history. Yet as we said, rabbinic tradition (as conveyed by Maimonides) equates this Yeshu with the familiar Jesus. So either the displacement in time was meant, by the Talmud's editor, to disguise the story, giving a cover to those who later would try to argue that it referred to a different Jesus of Nazareth—or the narrative simply became confused over time as the rabbis, who after all didn't spend that much time thinking about Jesus in the first place, forgot exactly when it was he had lived.

In any event, on a certain occasion Yeshu and Joshua ben Perachya were staying at an inn.[49] The teacher made an offhand comment about what a beautiful place it was to spend the night. Tragically, there was a misunderstanding. When the older sage spoke of the inn as an *acsania*—which can also mean a female innkeeper—Yeshu thought his teacher was making a leering comment about their hostess, and he replied in kind: "But Rabbi, her eyes are so narrow!"

We can only infer that Yeshu had a bad habit of making inappropriate remarks about women, because the teacher immediately took furious offense and cast him out of Rabbi Joshua's circle.

Some time went by and Yeshu repeatedly asked his master to accept him back into the society of sages, but Joshua refused. Finally, Rabbi Joshua decided that next time Yeshu came, he would accept him as a penitent. The occasion came, but when Yeshu arrived Joshua happened to be in the middle of his prayers and could not be disturbed. However, he gestured to Yeshu in what he thought was a friendly, beckoning way. Another misunderstanding transpired! Yeshu thought he was being dismissed yet again. He went away; and during this period, he conceived and began instructing others in his heretical ideas. Thus the personal becomes political or, rather, theological. The hurt that Yeshu suffered motivated him to stray in his beliefs and his teachings.

At last the teacher sought out the former student and begged him to return to the fold, but Yeshu refused. He explained, "I have learned this from you: everyone who sins and causes other people to sin will not receive the opportunity to repent."

The future of Yeshu, and the course of his new religion, were thus sealed. Intriguingly, the Talmud partly blames his teacher for this, rendering the moral that one should "always let the left hand push away, while the right hand invites." In other words, don't be overly harsh, like Joshua ben Perachya, but rather, when dealing with a wayward fellow man, balance chastisement with gestures of love and reconciliation.

At the end of this narrative, the Talmud gives the outcome of the sad chain of events: "Yeshu ha'Notzri practiced magic and led astray and deceived Israel." As we saw in chapter 3, the same indictment is given in a Talmudic account of his trial and death.[50]

There is a pathetic quality to the rabbis' portrait of Jesus. He went astray because of a character flaw of his own, indicated by the tension that evidently had been building between him and his teacher even before they arrived at the inn, the *acsania*. Yet however flawed the personality, his downfall was occasioned by the insensitive treatment he received from a mentor. For that he cannot be blamed. In the full classical sense of the word, the story of Jesus can be called tragic.

This degree of sympathy, however modest, that the rabbis felt for their fallen student is reflected in a grotesque allegory about Yeshu's fate after death—in hell. Of all allusions and references in the Talmud to Jesus, this is the one that I, as a Jew, most hesitate to reveal to those readers who aren't already familiar with it. However, an account of the Jewish-Christian debate through the ages would be incomplete and therefore dishonest without it.

The story is told of Onkelos, a gentile who wished to convert to Judaism. This ambition was complicated by the fact that he was a nephew of Titus, the Roman general who conquered Israel and burned the Temple in the year 70. Onkelos used magic to raise his uncle's spirit from hell, where his punishment was to be burned every day, only to have his ashes gathered and his body revived and rejoined with the soul, so that he could be burned again the next day.

Onkelos asked what nation, in the afterworld, is most highly esteemed. Titus replied, "Israel." When the nephew said he was considering conversion, Titus said that, on the contrary, he should become an oppressor of the Jews because this was a sure way to worldly advancement. It helped Titus himself rise to the emperor's throne, which he inherited from his father, Vespasian, in 79.

When Onkelos then raised the spirit of another individual who gave trouble to Israel, namely Jesus, the latter agreed with Titus that Israel was honored in the eternal world. But his practical advice was markedly different: "Seek their good. Do not seek their harm. Everyone who hurts them is like one who has hurt the apple of his [own] eye." When Onkelos proceeded to ask Jesus what punishment he suffered, he answered that it was to be boiled in excrement. The narrative concludes, "Everyone who mocks the words of the wise is punished by boiling excrement."[51]

However objectionable this image may be to us with our modern sensitivities, it would have appeared less remarkable to an earthy

Christian like Martin Luther, whose language, not least when discussing Jews, was laced with the crudest vulgarity. It's simply a fact that earlier generations were more comfortable with scatology than we are: They lived with it in a way that we, with our sanitized restrooms and regular garbage collection, do not. Keep in mind, too, that one point of the story is to give credit to Jesus, as compared with enemies like Titus who sought Israel's outright destruction. Anyway, the rabbis viewed boiling in excrement as a symbolically appropriate punishment. If we take a moment to consider it from their perspective, we can see why. One needs to keep in mind the centrality, in Judaism, of the authority of those who convey the tradition. From the event at Mount Sinai, when God revealed the Torah with its oral explanation to the Jewish people and thus to the world, everything we know about God comes through the chain of tradition. As we found in the Gospels, Jesus was dismissive of Torah's oral transmission, which he regarded as a human invention. He felt empowered to read and interpret the Torah for himself, casting aside the wisdom of his elders. To the extent his teaching caught on, it would mean the end of any reliable way of gaining access to the heritage of the oral Torah, and hence to God. In Jewish mysticism, the backside from which excrement is released stands in symbolic terms for the "backside" of ultimate reality. Believers in false religious ideas see this reality in a distorted form—as if from the back—hence the form of Jesus's punishment.

The rabbis understandably felt some hostility to him, for his teaching did catch on. In Paul's hands the entire Torah, not only the oral but the written, was dismissed as a "captor" and a "curse." This development was inevitable, since one Torah without the other is like a wife sundered from her husband. When the couple has separated, there is no longer a marriage—no husband and no wife.

THE UNFOLDING OF CHRISTIAN HISTORY did not become a very grave concern, however, until the religion was embraced by the Roman state. Before 312 CE, debates and polemics between Jews and Christians were sporadic, episodic, altogether casual. In that year, the emperor Constantine became a Christian. By 429, most of the population of the empire was Christian. This called for a new Jewish response, a far more serious and sustained answer to the claim that the Christ had come. This took the form of a whole library of new holy books, collecting older teachings from the rabbis, of which we've already sampled many.

One of the most fascinating and important figures of this period was Julian the Apostate (331–363 CE). He was a nephew of Constantine, and he became emperor himself. Raised a Christian, Julian reverted passionately and publicly back to the old pagan religion. In his day many conservative pagans, not yet Christianized, had come to see Judaism as an ally against the radical new religion that threatened to undermine Roman civilization. Emperor Julian took this view.

As Christian sources report, in 362 he called together Jewish representatives from Syria and Asia Minor to tell them he intended to strike against the Christian faith by rebuilding the Temple. Jews blew *shofars* in celebration and flocked to the ruined holy city. But then an earthquake destroyed the construction work that had already been undertaken on the Temple Mount, causing gases trapped under the platform to explode in flame. Meanwhile, Julian himself was killed in battle against Persia. That was the end of Jewish hopes that the Temple would stand again thanks to Roman patronage, and a terrible mourning ensued.

In all this, while ordinary Jews let themselves be carried away with enthusiasm, the rabbis held back, aloof. There is no record of their meeting with Julian, or any other tribute to him, in the Talmud. They were respectful in dealing with the emperors, but cool, corresponding with them as a "servant" addressing his "lord." Perhaps they had in mind the Talmudic teaching that in the End of Days, the biblical patriarch Jacob's brother, Esau, standing in rabbinic thought for Rome, would "put on his *tallith* [prayer shawl] and sit down with the righteous in Paradise; and the Holy One, blessed be He, will drag him and cast him forth from thence."[52] Esau would come to be understood as the animating spirit of Christianity. Just as Esau persecuted Jacob in the Bible, the Christianized empire began to persecute its Jews. By 425, Judaism had been formally subjugated to Christianity.

Not coincidentally, it was at this time that the rabbis produced the first Talmud, in Palestine, called the Jerusalem Talmud (though it was not edited in Jerusalem). Its more famous successor, the Babylonian Talmud, was shaped and edited by Rabbi Ashi, who died in Babylon in 430. The Talmuds are oral Torah. So is the midrashic collection *Genesis Rabbah*, expounding upon the book of Genesis, which was also drawn together sometime after 400. Why, now, was it felt to be necessary to write down all this material? Scholars today recognize the extent to which the formulation of these encyclopedia-length works was meant—implicitly, not explicitly—to address the spiritual challenge of a permanently Christian state, coupled with the radical disappointment of the people at Julian's failure to rebuild the Temple.[53] The existence of a Christian Rome posed at least four different challenges to the Jewish rejection of Jesus. To each, the Jews with their newly published holy books responded massively.

First, from very early on, maybe starting with Jesus himself, it had been a staple of Christian teaching to question the authenticity of the oral tradition, which taught merely "as [divine] doctrines the precepts of men."[54] In other words, the rabbis made it all up. The increased stature of the now state-sponsored religion heightened the challenge.

The Talmuds were the answer. They differ from the Mishnah in one very obvious way. While the Mishnah almost never cites the scriptural sources for its laws, the Talmuds make an obsessive habit of it. The Torah was regarded as shorthand or code, to which only Jewish tradition possessed the key. Much of the sprawling Talmudic verbiage is concerned with tracking down the words in scripture that allude, in however veiled or indirect a fashion, to a given religious practice or belief not otherwise expressly stated. The editor of the Mishnah, Rabbi Judah the Prince, in about the year 200, hadn't felt it necessary to supply these sources. But now Christianity compelled the sages to reveal their hand.

Second, the advent of Christianity succeeded in changing the whole matrix in which the two religions expressed their rivalry. As the scholar Jacob Neusner has neatly put it, the Mishnah offered a system of sanctification rather than salvation. For the rabbis who survived the destruction of the Temple were left with a dilemma: how to provide to the Jews the quality of holiness in daily life that the Temple had once supplied. In painstaking detail, the Mishnah gives the solution. Jewish practice henceforth must provide avenues for approaching God at every moment of the day. There is always some commandment to fulfill, from the very mundane, like eating your kosher lunch or saying a blessing on exiting the bathroom, to the more exalted realms of prayer and meditating on Torah. In this way, for a Jew, there really is no "secular" life.

Torah indeed also offered salvation. The Jews had firm beliefs about what happened after death, about the hope of a messiah and of claiming one's place in paradise. But the Mishnah largely ignores these themes because they were less pertinent to the emergency that presented itself after 70 CE—namely, filling the spiritual hole that the lost Temple had left.

With the coming of state-endorsed Christianity, there was a different emergency. The new religion claimed to be the exclusive path to salvation in the afterlife. Again, the rabbis offered their response. In lush detail, the Talmuds lay out the Jewish system of salvation: the covenant with Israel and the parallel one with the "children of Noah," the gentiles, both offering the reward of experiencing God's love eternally.

Third, there was to contend with the very specific implications of a Christian state. Christians were starting to write their own history, the history of the church, to whose establishment the whole narrative of human experience had been leading. In their understanding, the dawn of a Christian empire was the climax of a long process of human spiritual evolution—proof that God claimed the church as His very own enterprise.

The Jews responded by telling the story of history their own way. It was also a process that would build to a climax, but that climax had not come yet. Theirs was a history told as genealogy. The biblical patriarch Abraham started it all. His son Isaac had two sons, Jacob and Esau. As *Genesis Rabbah* recorded the midrashic tradition, Jacob was the ancestor of all Israel, while Esau's children founded the city, later the empire, of Rome. History would take mankind through a series of world empires, Babylon, Persia, Greece, Rome. The Roman domination would not last indefinitely. Finally, Rome would fall, to be replaced by the enlightened kingdom of the Messiah of Israel. In the end, Jacob would triumph over Esau.[55]

Fourth, there was the disturbing fact that the Temple, more than three centuries after its destruction, still lay in ruins. Revered Christian preachers like John Chrysostom pointed to this as proof that the Christ had come and that he was Jesus. After all, the savior had "predicted the Temple would be destroyed, that Jerusalem would be captured, and that the city would no longer be the city of the Jews as it had been in the past." Chrysostom triumphantly informed the Jews that after all this time had gone by, there was not "a shadow of the change for which you are waiting."[56]

Once more, the rabbis of the Talmud had their reply. We have seen it already in this chapter. Redemption awaited repentance. It was absurd to look for the Messiah when the world still rolled along as always, mired in corruption and sin. Thus, the Mishnah's system of sanctification was not separate from the Talmud's system of salvation: The two were yoked together. Righteous behavior, as the Mishnah codified it, would bring the ultimate salvation of mankind that the Talmud portrayed. The Messiah would come, Esau would be defeated and Rome would fall, salvation would be won, and Jewish tradition would be vindicated.

CHAPTER SIX

MEDIEVAL MINDS
THE GREAT DEBATE

In Jesus's own lifetime, the Jews took little notice of him. In Paul's day, they disgustedly refused a hearing to the chief apostle of Christ. Over the centuries in which the Mishnah and the two Talmuds were compiled, the explicit comments of the sages about Jesus and the new religion he inspired were neither systematic nor abundant. The rabbis seem to have been aware of the Christian religion only peripherally, out of the corner of an eye. In medieval Spain, Germany, and France, all this changed. If we want to know why the Jews rejected Christ, the time and place we should seek is the High Middle Ages in Western Europe. Here the question of Jesus—who was he, Son of God or insidious deceiver?—was debated between Jews and Christians in more detail, with more vigor and urgency, than anywhere else at any time in history.

The decision on the part of the Jews to fully state their objections to Christianity was taken at first under conditions of terror, as Jews were forced to engage in public "disputations," elaborate formal debates, with learned Christians, intended to humiliate the Jewish debaters and lead their communities to accept baptism. However, some Jews seemed to relish the opportunity to point out to Christians where their faith fell short. A minority even sought out such opportunities and composed handbooks for Jewish debaters, giving the best arguments in their arsenal. This is quite contrary to the accepted sentimental view of Jews huddling pitiably in Christian Europe, always avoiding offense and seeking only to be left alone. The Middle Ages lasted a long time and had many phases. Not all Jews were cowed. The more aggressive had no objection either to debating with Christians, or to converting them.

we left off in the previous chapter with the editing of the Babylonian Talmud by Rabbi Ashi, completed about the same time that Rome fell to the Visigoths. The latter occurred in 410, thus commencing the period of European history called the Middle Ages. In this chapter, then, we will deal with the centuries during which the Jews contemplated their oral traditions in the written format of the Talmud as well as the midrash, finding there, among much else of equal or greater interest, new ways to formulate the reasons behind their rejection of Jesus. This period would end with the rise of the Protestant Reformation in the sixteenth century, with all the occasions for doubting tradition itself that were stirred up then among Jews and Christians alike, forming the subject matter for our next and final chapter.

The Jewish voices recorded in the Talmuds originated in the Roman and Persian East, now Israel and Iraq. These were the centers of Jewish religious life. Meanwhile, Jewish settlements around the rim of the Mediterranean were in the process of shifting to the north and west. In Roman imperial antiquity, Jews already had settled in areas that are today France, Germany, and Spain. From here they spread to the Baltic region, Poland, and Ukraine. Major centers of Talmudic learning flourished in the Rhineland and in southern France, in Provence.

To appreciate the setting, we would do well to keep in mind a brief outline of the major events of the Jewish Middle Ages. One focal point of the life of the Jewish people then was in Babylon (today's Iraq), where the great Talmudic academies were at Sura, Nehardea, and Pumbedita. The Jews enjoyed a degree of self-rule under their own *resh galuta* (meaning "leader of the exiled community"), also called the exilarch, the holders of which office claimed descent from King David.

There was still an exilarch in Baghdad as late as 1401. But since the Babylonian Jews were in only limited contact with Christianity, we need not deal with them further here.

Under the Christian Byzantine—that is, eastern—Roman Empire, the Jews were treated harshly. What tranquillity they enjoyed was thanks in part to the theology of Saint Augustine (354–430), which was deeply influential in the Christian world. He found a stable place for the Jews in his religious outlook. In the unfolding to the world of salvation through Christ, it was their role to play the witness. They were Christ's people. They possessed the scriptural books that demonstrated that the promise of his coming had been given by God to the Hebrew prophets. In Augustine's view, the continued existence of the Jews was to be accepted gracefully, in that it proved the Christian account of history to be true. The Jewish people were a useful relic.

This relatively benign perspective was upset by the teaching of Pope Gregory the Great, who served in that office from 590 to 604. He saw the Jews not as simply ignorant of the salvation offered by Christ, but willfully, wickedly hostile to it. They knew Christ was the divine Messiah. They had always known this—which, rather than the charge of deicide, was their most heinous crime. It was only out of some black, demonic depths in their souls that they refused to worship God's Son. What proof could there be for this? Well, did not their very own Hebrew Bible show how perverse the Jewish nation was? Again and again prophets from their midst railed against their rebellious spirit. The rejection of Jesus was just another in a long succession of Jewish acts of spite against God.

For five hundred years, this hateful teaching worked under the surface of European culture. In Visigothic Spain of the seventh century, anti-Jewish persecution was particularly enthusiastic, in both the economic and the religious realms, extending to the suppression of Jewish observances (Sabbaths and holy days, circumcision) and forced conversions to Christianity. Spain was thus first introduced to the figure of the *Marrano*, the insincere Jewish convert to Christianity who waited secretly for the opportunity to return to his own traditions. The position of the Jews was ameliorated with the coming of the Berber Muslims in

711. Under Abd al-Rahman, who arrived as a refugee from Damascus in 755, the Umayyad dynasty was established in Spain, creating a haven for Jews on the Iberian peninsula. The house of Umayyad was remarkable for its tolerant worldliness, if not for its devotion to Islam. A comparatively peaceful and fruitful time for the Jews was beginning.

In accounts of the golden period of Spanish Jewry, between the eighth and eleventh centuries, the adjectives most often applied by historians—"luminous," "dazzling," "sparkling"—make this era sound rather like a very long cocktail party. Umayyad rule came to a rude close in 1013 when more fanatically purist Muslims invaded, capturing the capital, Cordoba, to the distress of the large and wealthy Jewish community there as well as in other Jewish strongholds, like Granada and Tarragona, the Upper West Side (of New York) and Beverly Hills of their day. A new fundamentalist Islamic dynasty, the Almoravids, was set up, followed in the twelfth century by the Almohads—which for the Jews meant massacres, forcible conversions, the outlawing of Jewish religious study and worship. Rabbi Moses ben Maimon, known as Maimonides (1135–1204), was a refugee from the Almohads, fleeing Cordoba to Fez, Morocco. After a period spent in hiding, he settled in Cairo, where he directed some extremely frank Jewish evaluations not only of Islam, but of Christianity. In short, Jewish life was not always so good under Muslim rule. Many Jews must initially have welcomed the Christian reconquest of Spain, finally completed in 1492.

Meanwhile, elsewhere in Europe, resentment of the Christ-denying Jews mounted slowly like the tension in a fault line, which finally shook the heart of the continent in a violent earthquake of anti-Jewish hatred accompanying the call to the First Crusade, in 1095. On their way to liberate the holy land from its Muslim occupiers, Crusaders devastated the ancient Jewish communities of the Rhineland, bringing the choice of conversion or the sword. The Jews in Spain, however, remained isolated from the worst anti-Semitic agitation of the era of the Crusades—that is, until 1391, when the wave at last broke upon the Spanish peninsula. A century later, in 1492, Spanish Jews were offered the alternatives of conversion or expulsion. It is a shaming memory in the otherwise proud history of Sephardic (Spanish) Jewry that the Sephardim were on the whole less willing to suffer for their faith than were the German Jews, the Ashkenazim. The latter accepted martyrdom in far larger numbers, often feigning a willingness to become Christian only for the chance to spit on the cross or curse the name of Jesus on the way up to the baptismal font.

Keeping in mind the critical years 1095 and 1391, we can appreciate the timing of the three most famous, or notorious, disputations pitting Jews against Christians over the question of Jesus. In Paris in 1240, Rabbi Yechiel ben Yosef, the head of the Paris yeshiva (Talmudic academy), was called upon by King Louis IX to defend the Talmud against charges that it falsified scripture and defamed Christ.

The French king was of the opinion that the best answer to a Jewish opponent of the church was a sword through the abdomen. (He was later canonized as Saint Louis.) It was not surprising, then, that the Paris disputation was not an especially enlightening affair. The event was memorable primarily for Rabbi Yechiel's valiant if hopeless attempts to show that the "Yeshu ha'Notzri" depicted in such troubling, offensive passages in the Talmud was actually a *different* Jesus of Nazareth from the Jesus who founded Christianity. As the terrified rabbi cried out before the priests, "May I live and return to my house, the Talmud was not referring to the Christian Jesus when it spoke of one who is punished in hell in boiling excrement!"¹

The disputation at Barcelona, in 1263, presided over by the liberal-minded King James I of Aragon, is of far more substantive interest, not least because the Jewish disputant was the greatest Talmudist and mystic of his day, Rabbi Moses ben Nachman, known as Nachmanides. Born in 1194 in Gerona and a physician by trade, Ramban (his acronym) left Spain for Palestine four years after the disputation. In the ruined holy city, he established an academy but soon relocated to the Crusader capital of Acre, on the coast, becoming chief rabbi there and dying in the same city in 1270. The approach of his Christian opponent in the disputation, the baptized Jew Pablo Christiani, was the exact opposite of the other converted Jew, Nicholas Donin, who "debated" with Rabbi Yechiel in Paris. Rather than attacking the Talmud, Christiani tried to show that it preserved traditions from the ancient rabbis that actually proved Jesus was the Messiah. After his conversion, Christiani had joined the proselytizing Dominican order, teaching Hebrew to his fellow Christian missionaries so as to maximize their effectiveness. He would later advise the king of France, Louis IX, to impose on unconverted Jews the stigma of wearing a special "Jew badge." From Nachmanides's own account of the debate, it's obvious that in tearing apart his opponent, the rabbi enjoyed himself. He even relaxed enough to indulge a taste for sarcastic wit, as when the king asked, If Jesus wasn't the Messiah, where was he, then? Nachmanides replied that they might find the true Messiah even now, if James would send a runner to seek him, sitting before the gates of Toledo.

Still another Jew turned Christian, an intellectual bully called Geronimo de Santa Fe (the former Joshua Lorki, died c. 1419), ran the disputation held at Tortosa, Spain, which extended over a period of twenty-one months in 1413–1414. Here as at Paris, the intention was not to debate substance, as James I had conducted the Barcelona disputation, but rather to cow and humiliate the Jewish debaters and provoke Jewish conversions. The historical situation was propitious for the Christian side, since the event followed by a mere two decades the 1391 outbreak of anti-Semitic violence in Spain. Whether out of fear or sincere spiritual conviction, groups of Jews stepped up during the proceedings to be baptized—ten families on one day, eleven the next, and so on.

Whereas Nachmanides relished tripping up his less sophisticated opponent, there was no such pleasure to be taken by the Jewish disputants at Tortosa. An account of the dreary affair written by a Jew who witnessed it, Solomon Ibn Verga, is lightened only by the chronicler's humorously dyspeptic comments about his coreligionists. Thus the Jewish team agreed beforehand "that their procedure would not be in the style of the Jews taught in their academies, to interrupt each other and to abuse each other in disagreements, so that they would not be humiliated before the Pope," Benedict XIII, who presided. Elsewhere, Ibn Verga recalls, "And some of us were happy at the words of the Pope," who ordered that the Jews be given proper lodgings along with kosher food, "and some of us were unhappy, as is the character of the Jew."[2] Otherwise, it is apparent that the Jews were in great distress, censuring those among their company who were too bold in addressing the Christian side. When Rabbi Astruk Halevi made a sharp reply to the pope, who had questioned the Jewish belief that the Messiah has indeed been born and waits in the Garden of Eden—"Our lord Pope! While you believe in so many far-fetched things about your Messiah, allow us to believe one about our Messiah"—the rabbi's colleagues immediately went ashen. Later, all the Jews repaired to their rooms, "and we all cried out against Rabbi Astruk, saying, 'Fie on you, and on your words, for you have put a sword in the hand of our enemies.' "[3]

From such contemporary accounts we get a sampling of the arguments deployed by Jews in explaining their rejection of Jesus. So, too, from the literature of Jewish anti-Christian polemic that appears from the twelfth century on, replying to the far greater volume of Christian literature that was being written, aimed at debunking Judaism.

A taste of the delightful fighting spirit of these Jewish polemical works, the willingness to give offense to Christian opponents if necessary (and even if not necessary), can be had from this passage found in the *Nitzachon Vetus* (or "Old Polemic"), by an anonymous thirteenth-century German Jew:

"When you speak to them, do not allow your antagonist to change the subject, for it is the usual method of the assertive and impatient Gentile to skip from one subject to another . . . For when he realizes his inability to verify statements, he begins to discuss other matters. One who argues with them should be strong-willed by asking questions or giving responses that deal with the specific issue at hand and not permitting his antagonist to extricate himself . . . Then, you will find the Gentile thoroughly embarrassed; indeed he will be found to have denied their central dogmas . . ."[4]

Many of the Jewish polemics were in effect handbooks for debaters, not unlike the fat briefing notebooks prepared for U.S. presidential candidates before debating one another on television. The *Nitzachon Vetus* advises the Jew on how, referring to his Christian opponent, "you can trip him up and refute him."[5] Other interesting or unusual examples include Jacob ben Reuben's *Sefer Milchamot ha-Shem* ("Book of the Wars of the Lord"), an early example of the genre, written in 1170; *Nusach ha-Ketav* ("Written Tradition"), by the previously mentioned Joshua Lorki before he turned Christian; *Bittul Iqqare ha-Notzrim* ("Refutation of Christian Principles"), by the Jewish philosopher Hasdai Crescas (1340–1410), whose only son was among those massacred by Christians in the 1391 Spanish anti-Semitic outbreak; and a late example of the genre, *Hizzuk Emunah* ("Strengthening Faith"), by Isaac ben Abraham of Troki (c. 1533–1594), a Lithuanian Jew professing the Karaite heresy that denied the oral tradition and yet whose attacks on Christian doctrine were much prized by Orthodox Jews.

Perhaps the most colorful of the polemicists, Isaac Profiat Duran, wrote *Al Tehi ka' Avotecha* ("Do Not Be Like Your Fathers") in a fit of disgust at his close friend David Bonet Bonjorn. They were Spanish Jews who had been forced to the baptismal font in the riots of 1391 but who resolved to flee Spain for Palestine in search of the freedom to practice Judaism. At the last minute, when Duran's friend was supposed to meet him in preparation for an imminent departure, Bonjorn failed to show up. Duran later learned he had decided to embrace Christianity after all. From a port in southern France in 1396, Duran wrote him a furiously mocking letter sarcastically praising Bonjorn for the decision to become an apostate. The letter began, parodying the opening verse of Psalm 34: "To David, when he changed his mind, before the Ruler of the world and sang of the death of the son who suffered for him and carried the burden for him. He said to his father: 'I do not know thee,' and does not ask after the forefathers anymore. I called him once my brother. Maestro Bonet Bonjorn, the new Christian, is his name. In Israel he was called once David Bonet ben Goron." Duran went on to bitterly berate the "new Christian": "Where penalties threaten, believe that it is always better to permit. Eat of pork, of all animals in the water, on the earth and in the air, which have been forbidden to you once.

"To be sure have not the disciples of the [Christian] Messiah themselves forbidden this to the faithful people, in the book of their teaching called 'The Acts of the Apostles'? [chapter 15] . . . Did not those men as the descendants of Abraham keep rigidly the Law? Even after the death of their leader? Even after their baptism? But why should I mention them, seeing that the Messiah himself confirmed the permanence of the Law! [Matt. 5:17]."[6] It was a very early polemical deployment of what later historians would call the "Jesus of history," the Jesus who apparently himself upheld the major outline of Jewish religious observances, as against the "Jesus of faith," whom Christian theology presents as the first believer in Christianity. When Duran's letter was made public, church authorities, not getting the joke, earnestly applauded him, regarding the text as suitable for the edification of not-yet-converted Jews.

Apart from formal debates and written critiques of the competing faith, Jews engaged in other arguments and encounters as needs and opportunities arose. Some shrank from giving offense, while others, despite the obvious danger to which they were exposing themselves, didn't hesitate to insult the Christian faith in the face of its most ardent believers. One rabbi claimed to have told the king of Germany, "If one were to load a donkey with vomit and filth and lead him through the church, he would remain unharmed."[7]

Among the most vituperative of the Jewish disputants were those who had converted from Christianity. They were also some of the most active proselytizers for Judaism. It is a modern myth that Jews have always disdained seeking to convert others, an activity for which Christian authorities in this period were often driven to reprimand and persecute Jewish missionaries. One historian, Jeremy Cohen, estimates that in the early Middle Ages, before the worst persecutions, converts to Judaism from among the gentiles may have outnumbered converts to Christianity from among the Jews. These included ex-priests, such as Wecelin, who ministered to the household of a certain Duke Conrad in the early eleventh century. He converted to Judaism and sparked a bitter controversy by writing an anti-Christian pamphlet. A young priest in Oppido, Italy, named John (he was of Norman descent) wrote of his own conversation to Judaism, telling also the story of Archbishop Andreas of Bari, in southern Italy, who in about 1078 took shelter in Egypt in order to become a Jew. Fleeing to Muslim-held areas was a course often taken by new Jews. In one famous instance, a deacon named Bodo in the court of Emperor Louis the Pious (778–840) crossed the Pyrenees Mountains to Muslim Spain, where he lived as a Jew, got married, and changed his name to Eleazar. Possibly the oldest text in the Jewish polemical genre, *Sefer Nestor ha-Komer* ("Polemic of Nestor the Priest"), was composed no later than the eighth century by a priest turned Jew living in the Muslim east.

Thus, we are in possession of a record of the reasons medieval Jews themselves gave for disbelieving the Christian assertion that Jesus was their long-awaited Messiah. Those reasons fall into three major categories: arguments based on biblical prophecy, by far the largest area of dispute; those based on the Talmud and other rabbinic literature; and those based on philosophical considerations. We shall have occasion to reflect, however, on whether or not any of these stated objections was the truest cause—the ultimate and most profound one—for the Jewish rejection of Jesus.

OBJECTIONS FROM BIBLICAL PROPHECY. There are certain events in life of which, when they occur, no one can be in doubt. It's a question not of weighing the evidence, but simply of opening your eyes and looking around. For example, consider the growth of a baby in the womb. When a woman's pregnancy has advanced to the late stages, no acquaintance who bumps into her on the street will have to ask, "So, did you have the baby yet?" The coming of the Jewish Messiah had always been expected to be such an event. He would prove himself in the historical arena. Neither in the Bible nor in the later Jewish sources was there any notion that a person would have to wonder whether or not the Messiah had appeared. Maimonides, the Spanish Jewish philosopher par excellence, wrote, "Anyone who does not believe in [the Messiah] or does not await his coming [thereby implicitly] denies not only the other prophets but also the Torah [itself] and Moses our teacher"— Moses being the preeminent prophet.[8] But the point was that the criteria for identifying the Messiah were so clearly spelled out in Jewish tradition, and the fulfillment of these criteria would be so obvious, that only a denier (*kofer*) of the whole tradition could fail to recognize him when he comes. Such a person would in fact have to be a denier not only of the Bible, but of the very reality in front of him.

This perspective was a refrain among the Jewish polemicists, as dictated by the words of the prophets. In the Hebrew Bible, the kind of salvation that received the most attention, and thus presumably mattered most to God, was not of the individual soul, but of the people altogether. So Isaiah had said, "Your people will all be righteous; they will inherit the land forever."[9] Hence the ultimate messianic redemption must take place on a world historical stage, visible to everyone. Yet while Christians asserted that the Messiah had come, the world had not changed its cruel, violent nature. To put it another way, in the Barcelona disputation, Nachmanides reasonably could have rested his case with the statement "Look around you. Open your eyes." What he did declare before James of Aragon was, "The prophet [Jeremiah] says that in the time of the Messiah, 'They shall teach no more every man his neighbor, and every man his brother, saying, Know the Lord: for they shall all know me' [31:34]; also 'The earth shall be full of the knowledge of the Lord, as the waters cover the sea' [Isa. 11:9]; also, 'They shall beat their swords into ploughshares . . . nation shall not lift up sword against nation, neither shall they learn war anymore' [Isa. 2:4]. Yet from the days of Jesus until now, the whole world has been full of violence and plundering, and the Christians are greater spillers of blood than all the rest of the peoples, and they are also practicers of adultery and incest. And how hard it would be for you, my lord King, and for your knights, if they were not to learn war anymore!"[10]

He pointed out the rule that a sound proposition needn't be provable but should be falsifiable. That is, there must be some way of testing it, showing it to be false. But with the Christian assertion about Jesus, this was not so. Take, for example, what the book of Genesis indicates about the curse that befell mankind through the sin of Adam and Eve: From then on, men have been compelled to earn their living through "the sweat of your brow," while women give birth only in great pain. If humanity has been redeemed, this curse should have been lifted in a way that would be obvious to all: Men would not slave away at their jobs to earn bread, women would not scream in labor. Christians, however, held that the redemption had been effected in ways that cannot "be observed and sensed"—which was suspiciously convenient, "because this is a matter in which nobody can refute you."[11]

Joseph Kimchi, a twelfth-century Provençal sage and author of *Sefer ha'Brit* ("Book of the Covenant"), composed his polemic in the form of an imaginary dialogue with a Christian. He wrote: "You claim that Jesus saved the world from the day he came, but he accomplished nothing which can actually be seen."[12]

Kimchi's son David (called by the acronym Radak, c. 1160–1235), a still more distinguished commentator on the Bible than his father, stressed the plain, simple meaning of the scriptural text and rarely lost a chance to take a swing at Christian prophetic interpretations. In Isaiah's prophecies, a cycle of poems about a mysterious "servant" of God was taken by Christians and some Jews as referring to the Messiah. (We'll return to one of these poems, the famous Isaiah 52:13–53:12.) On verse 52:13, which reads, "Behold, My servant will succeed; he will be exalted and become high and exceedingly lofty," David Kimchi wrote scornfully that the only place that Jesus "was lifted up and exalted was the tree on which they hung him!"

Another passage, Micah 5:1, was also agreed upon by Jews and Christians to have a messianic significance, including the biographical fact that he would come from Bethlehem: "Bethlehem—Ephratah—you are too small to be among the thousands of Judah, but from you someone will emerge for Me to be a ruler over Israel . . ." But was Jesus a ruler over Israel? On the contrary, the younger Kimchi pointed out, "He did not govern Israel but they governed him"—an apparent reference to the belief also agreed upon by Jews and Christians that Jesus in his last hours was ruled over quite harshly by the Jewish authorities, who either killed him themselves (the Talmud's version) or connived with the Romans to do so (the Gospels' version).[13] As Maimonides wrote, "Finally he was overpowered and put a stop to by us when he fell into our hands, and his fate is well known."[14]

The author of the *Nitzachon Vetus* asked, "Were the prophecies . . . fulfilled during the time of Jesus, as it is written, 'The wolf also shall dwell with the lamb, and the leopard shall lie down with the kid' [Isa. 11:6]? If [your Christian debating opponent] will then assert that this is to be understood allegorically, i.e., that at that time evil and righteous men will live together, such a situation would be nothing new. Has this not been the case from time immemorial? It is also written, 'They shall not do evil nor destroy in all my holy mountain' [Isa. 11:9]; now, was there no evil done in Jerusalem from then on, and was the land not destroyed? Why, several wars were waged there after that time both while Israel dwelt there . . . and afterwards."[15]

It was a general rule that where biblical prophecy taken literally would refute the belief in Jesus as Messiah, Christians would opt for a symbolic or "spiritualized" interpretation; but where the converse was true and the prophecy taken literally appeared to support their belief, they embraced the literal interpretation. So in regard to the prophecies that described the general state of the messianic world, Jews thought they must be fulfilled both in a plainly visible sense and also, where appropriate, in a spiritual one—Christians only in the spiritual dimension. But when it came to other prophecies, Christians could be sticklers for a literal reading—that is, a literal reading of verses that seemed to point to Jesus. To this latter category belong a handful of biblical passages—in Genesis, Isaiah, Jeremiah, Psalms—that became the principal foci of the Jewish-Christian debate. However, other verses *in the very same* passages that ruled Jesus out as the referent could in the Christian reading be ignored or, again, interpreted allegorically. Jews objected to the highly circular "Heads I win, tails you lose" approach to scriptural exegesis. We'll consider some illustrations.

Proceeding from the first book of the Hebrew Bible, Genesis 49:10 is a deeply cryptic verse that received obsessive attention from medieval disputants. It appears in the context of the patriarch Jacob's blessing of his twelve sons. Each son became the founder of one of the tribes of Israel, which became the Jewish people. Judah was the royal tribe, from whom the Jewish king was to be selected: King David was a descendant of Judah and so would be the Messiah.

Here is what Genesis 49:10 says: "The scepter shall not depart from Judah nor a scholar from among his descendants until Shiloh comes and his will be an assemblage of nations." In the Bible, Shiloh is the name of a locality in Israel. Curiously, since Christians rejected the oral Torah, on this point they embraced an arcane rabbinic tradition that "Shiloh" was also a designation of the Messiah. The earliest source for this identification is an ancient Aramaic translation, which the rabbis held to have been revealed at Sinai but later lost and then rediscovered (about 90 CE) by the famous convert to Judaism named Onkelos.

As Christians understood the verse, it meant that a descendant of Judah would rule as king of the Jewish people until the Messiah comes. Thus, when the "scepter" of rule departed from the tribe of Judah with the destruction of the Jewish commonwealth by Rome in 70 CE, it meant the Messiah had arrived. In the Barcelona disputation, Nachmanides's opponent, Pablo Christiani, opened his presentation with this argument: "Scripture says, 'The scepter shall not depart from Judah . . . until Shiloh comes.' Shiloh is the Messiah, and the prophet says that Judah will always have power until the coming of the Messiah who goes forth from him. And if so, today when you [Jews] have not a single scepter or a single ruler, the Messiah who is of the seed of Judah and has the right of rulership must have come."[16]

Nachmanides's reply was simple. The verse could not mean what Christiani said because centuries before Jesus the kingship had lapsed altogether. That was in 586 BCE, during the exile of the Jews to Babylon for seventy years. Later, about 164 BCE, a dynasty had been set up from the tribe of Levi, the Hasmonaeans, whose revolution against the Greek oppressors is celebrated on the Jewish holiday of Hanukkah. The Hasmonaeans in turn were displaced by the dynasty of Herod, who was not even a Jew, much less from the tribe of Judah. Herod was supposed to have been on the throne when Jesus was born.

Thus, following Christiani's logic, the Messiah must have come not in Jesus's time, but more than five centuries earlier, with the Babylonian exile, or certainly by the time of the Hasmonaeans. In which case the Messiah must have been not Jesus, but some other person unknown to Jews or Christians.

As Nachmanides explained, "The prophet [Jacob] does not mean that the kingdom of Judah would continue without any interruption, but that it would never pass away from him [Judah] and cease forever. And he means that whenever Israel does have a royal ruler, he has to be a member of the tribe of Judah; and if their kingdom should lapse for a while because of sin, when it returns it must return to Judah."

The author of *Nitzachon Vetus* characteristically drops the courtly formality adopted by Nachmanides. Some Christians seeking to win Jewish converts claimed that the verse was actually an acrostic. Look at the words *Until Shiloh comes and to him* in Hebrew, and you find that the first letters of the last three words spell *Yeshu*, or Jesus. Our polemicist replied by pointing out that when one takes into account the words preceding that phrase in the same verse, a fuller acrostic is to be found, spelling out "There is no blemish as evil as Jesus."

He asked other pointed questions. On what basis was Jesus to be identified with the final and greatest king from the line of Judah—that is, the Messiah? In the Gospel account, the man's claim to descent from Judah was through his mother's husband, Joseph. If he wasn't Joseph's son, he cannot be the Messiah. If he was Joseph's son, he cannot be the son of God: "Understand, then, that they are refuted by their own words," by "the book of their error"—namely, the New Testament.[17]

Moving on from the Pentateuch to the prophets, we come to the chapter in the Bible that has probably been adduced more often and with greater conviction in support of Jesus's claim than any other passage, Isaiah 53.

In the King James Version, its stately verses are familiar, etched on the consciousness even of secular folk today: "He is despised and rejected of men; a man of sorrows, and acquainted with grief: and we hid as it were our faces from him; he was despised, and we esteemed him not. Surely he hath borne our griefs, and carried our sorrows; yet we did esteem him stricken, smitten by God, and afflicted. But he was wounded for our transgressions, he was bruised for our iniquities; the chastisements of our peace was upon him; and with his stripes we are healed."[18]

Christians identified this suffering "servant" of God with Jesus, whose death brought atonement to the world: "he was wounded for our transgressions." No idea could be more central to the Christian message, and according to the Christian reading, in Isaiah 53 it receives its most poignant statement in all the Hebrew Bible.

The Jewish reaction to this understanding illustrates the massive divide between the Jewish and Christian ways of reading the Bible—in the Middle Ages, as today, it is as if the two faiths occupy alternative universes. In one the Christological import of this chapter from Isaiah is perfectly clear, just like the Christological interpretation of so many other verses. In the other, these readings appear so ill founded that one hardly knows where to begin. As Nachmanides boldly said in addressing the king of Aragon, one could believe such things only if he was brought up on them from earliest youth, fed them almost with his mother's milk. Or as Joseph Kimchi incredulously declared to his imagined Christian debating opponent, "How can you!?"

Here, of course, the name of Jesus himself nowhere appears in our passage; neither does the title "Messiah" or "king" or "son of David" or any other expression that would point to a messianic interpretation. The "man of sorrow" is God's nameless "servant," that is all. Furthermore, who is the speaker in the chapter, the "we" whose transgressions are forgiven through the servant's chastisements? To find evidence that the servant is Jesus, that the "we" is humankind, one has to come to the passage looking for confirmation of something one already believes or wants to believe.

The greatest of medieval exegetes, Rabbi Solomon bar Isaac (called Rashi, 1040–1105), answered that it was clear from context that the "servant" was none other than the Jewish people. Living in Troyes, France, he is thought to have been familiar with church traditions, possibly through his grandson Rabbi Samuel ben Meir (called Rashbam), who polemicized directly against the Latin Bible.[19] Rashi preferred to respond to Christian interpretations implicitly. He explained that it was "the way of this prophet [Isaiah] to speak of all Israel as if they were one man," as God's "servant."[20] In other passages, Rashi notes, Isaiah has God speaking to "Israel, My servant" (41:8), "Fear not, My servant Jacob" (44:2), "And now hearken, Jacob, My servant" (44:1). "Jacob" was another name for "Israel," for the patriarch Jacob received from God the personal name "Israel." His sons, eponymous founders of the twelve tribes, established the national entity called "Israel" after their father.

The speaker in Isaiah 53 was not humanity in general, but the gentile nations in particular that oppressed Israel. At the End of Days, they will express their dread and amazement at how they have "despised" and "rejected" the "man of sorrows," whom God has now revealed to them as His own "servant." As Rashi summarized, "So will the nations say, each to his neighbor, 'If we had heard from the mouth of another [besides God] that which we have seen [namely, the exaltation of Israel], we would not have believed it.' "[21]

What's amazing is that the Jewish exegetes did not reject the conception, shared with Christians, that the servant's pains vicariously atoned for the sins of others. Rashi again paraphrases the collective statement of the gentiles at the end of history: "Now we see that not because of [Israel's] lowliness did this [suffering] come upon him but rather he was chastised with pains so that the peoples should be forgiven through the sufferings of Israel. The illness that rightly should have come upon us, he bore [on himself]."[22]

A slightly later rabbinic Bible commentator, Abraham Ibn Ezra, was more direct in objecting to the Christian view. He was born in Toledo about 1093, traveled as far as England, Palestine, and India, and died in Rome in 1168. A grammarian of exacting standards, impatient with fanciful interpretations of scripture, the worldly Ibn Ezra noted that Christians were flat-out "wrong" when they pointed triumphantly to verses in this and other prophecies that, read literally, seemed to allude to Jesus. For they dropped their hyperliteralism when a commonsense understanding of a given verse failed to match the particulars of Jesus's life or death. In the case at hand, Isaiah spoke of the servant's reward—the latter would "see his seed," that is, have children; "prolong his days," that is, live a long life; and "divide the spoil with the strong," a reference to divvying up the booty of war (53:10, 12). Jesus did none of these things.

But the "ultimate proof," said Ibn Ezra, that the servant could not be Jesus was the context. Isaiah 53 is not a freestanding literary work. It appears in the prophet's book immediately preceded and followed by other passages clearly meant to give consolation to Israel. Immediately preceding, we find the Lord comforting "His people; He will have redeemed Jerusalem. The Lord has bared His holy arm before the eyes of all nations; all ends of the earth will see the salvation of our God."[23] Immediately following, God speaks encouragingly to the distressed people of Jerusalem: "Sing out, O barren one who has not given birth; break into glad song and be jubilant, you who have not been in birth travail. For the children of the desolate [Jerusalem] will outnumber the children of the inhabited one, said the Lord."[24] Try reading Isaiah's work as a whole, proceeding from chapter 51 through to 54 and keeping in mind that the original text had no separate or numbered chapters at all—they were a later, Christian innovation. A sudden diversion from the prophet's words about Israel, to a discourse on Jesus's saving death, and back to further consolations for Israel would be a most peculiar way for a writer to compose his work.

We may deal briefly with other frequently disputed prophetic verses.

On Isaiah 7:14, "Behold, a virgin shall conceive, and bear a son, and shall call his name Immanuel" (King James Version), Christians commented that this predicted the birth of Jesus to the Virgin Mary. Beyond the elementary point that Jews had been making for a thousand years, that the word translated "virgin" actually meant "maiden" and carried no intimation of sexual purity, Joseph Kimchi made some commonsense observations.

First, in context, this prophecy was given by Isaiah to King Ahaz of Judah as a sign, as assurance, that his kingdom would not be conquered in an impending attack by two aggressor nations from the north. If the sign came about only centuries after Ahaz died, how was it supposed to reassure him? "Let it be known to you," wrote Kimchi, stating the obvious, "that nothing which comes after the event is ever called a sign."[25] Also, from a grammatical perspective, the *Nitzachon Vetus* noted that what the verse actually says is that the maiden "*has* conceived and *will* bear a son." In other words, the lady was already pregnant at the time of prophecy, long before Mary was born.

On Jeremiah 31:31, "I will seal a new covenant with the House of Israel and with the House of Judah," Christians called this an unambiguous reference to the new covenant or testament of Jesus, replacing the Torah of the Jews. If so, the author of *Nitzachon Vetus* replied, the prophet had a fine opportunity to make this clear, but he declined to do so. Jeremiah writes (31:32–33) that this new covenant will "not [be] like the covenant that I sealed with their forefathers on the day that I took hold of their hand to take them out of the land of Egypt . . . For this is the covenant that I shall seal with the house of Israel . . ." Right here, says our polemicist, "is where he should have publicly written [of] that new Torah of Jesus. All he does say, however, is, 'I will place My Torah within them'; it is therefore clear that this was said about the Torah that he had already given which they had forgotten and that he was promising that He would write it on their hearts so that it would no longer be forgotten."[26] Also, if this was really the new "Torah of Jesus" being referred to, why does the prophet not mention the other nations who supposedly will also have Jesus's law of love inscribed within them?

On Psalm 22:16, "they pierced my hands and my feet" (King James Version), Christians here found a famous example of an explicit prefiguration of Jesus's sufferings. In the Gospel story, the Romans pierce his hands and feet with nails in preparation for his being hung upon the cross. *Nitzachon Vetus* answered that the word given in the Latin translation as "they pierced" is written in the Hebrew original not as *karu* ("they pierced"), but as *ka'ari* ("like a lion"). The entire verse is properly translated, "For dogs have surrounded me; a pack of evildoers has enclosed me, like a lion [at] my hands and my feet." In biblical poetry, such as in the book of Psalms, the second half of a verse typically echoes the first. With this in mind, we should expect the imagery of being torn by wild beasts to be consistent from phrase to phrase—and it is. A modern update of the King James Bible, the Revised Standard Version, now includes a footnote acknowledging the more authentic translation of the verse.

We could cite many other examples of allegedly Christological prophetic citations, to each of which the rabbis had their answer. On point after point, Christian exegesis was found to be dubious to anyone who could read the Bible for himself in its original language.

OBJECTIONS FROM RABBINIC LITERATURE. In searching the Talmud for support of their case, medieval Christians were on even shakier ground. A theory they advanced depicted rabbinic sources as something like an archaeological dig whose layers had got all mixed up. Concealed in the Talmud were older traditions, originating before Christ, that predicted his coming. These had been either missed or misunderstood or even falsified by rabbis in the Christian era. Relatively recent were those blasphemous passages that Rabbi Yechiel was compelled to explain away at the Paris disputation.

No doubt some unlettered Jews were taken in by this argument. Others could only have been amused or annoyed when Christian clerics took a dip in the murky waters of Talmudic scholarship. In 1541, the Portuguese Cistercian monk Francisco Machado wrote his *Mirror of the New Christians*. That was forty-four years after Portugal's Jews were all forcibly converted to Catholicism. To strengthen the faith of these "New Christians," he tried to show how their own rabbis of old had preached a proto-Christian faith. This was a tough act for Machado, because he knew no Hebrew and relied on translated bits of the midrash and Talmud. His level of perplexity was such that even the titles of rabbinic books confused him. The name of the principal midrashic work on Genesis, *Bereshit Rabbah* (meaning "Great Genesis," aka *Genesis Rabbah*), he took to be a person, "Rabbi Bereshit." He cited another sage by the name of "Midrash." His alleged quotations from rabbinic literature are frequently not to be found where he says they are or, in the formulation he cites, at all.

Other challenges by Christians along the same lines were more plausible. In the Barcelona disputation, Pablo Christiani confronted Nachmanides with midrashic passages that assumed the "servant" in Isaiah 53 was not Israel but the Messiah. The rabbi responded that while one can find stray traditions to that effect, nowhere do these ever convey a belief that the Messiah, scion of King David—as distinct from his forerunner, the Messiah from the stock of Joseph—would die. True, this allegorically depicted servant might be "like a sheep led to the slaughter" (53:7)—but being *led* to the slaughter, ready to die for the cause of the Lord, was different from actually *being* slaughtered. On the contrary, the Talmud stated that the Davidic Messiah, seeing how the Messiah, son of Joseph, has suffered, will ask God for life and God will grant it to him.[27] Isaiah reflected this with his statements that the servant would live, have children, and enjoy success in battle. As Nachmanides argued, whether you take the passage literally or allegorically, as referring to an individual or the collectivity of Israel, there is no crucified Messiah in it.

At the Tortosa disputation, the Christian disputant Geronimo de Santa Fe opened the proceedings by adducing a rabbinic tradition we saw in the last chapter, which seemed to have the biblical prophet Elijah himself as its source. It was taught in the "academy of Elijah" that the world is destined to exist for six thousand years, starting with the creation of Adam and Eve. The last two thousand years were the "days of the Messiah." Looking back from the perspective of 1413, those "days" had commenced more than a thousand years before. The passage then added, "Because of our sins, which are numerous, [the years] that have gone by, have gone by."[28]

Geronimo, intellectually a more formidable figure than Pablo Christiani, argued simply that this teaching of Elijah made it clear the Messiah had already come. Therefore, "Who is he but our Savior?"

The Jewish leader, or *arenga*, Don Vidal ben Benvenista, stood to offer the first reply for his coreligionists. A wealthy man learned in secular subjects and able to address the assembly in Latin, he looked out on the seventy thrones set up for princes of the church, cardinals, bishops, archbishops, and the pope, all dressed in gold, along with a thousand other dignitaries and prominent Christian citizens, seated in a great disputation hall covered in fine embroidered cloths. We may imagine Don Vidal's heart melting within him, as the chronicler Solomon Ibn Verga said of all the Jews standing there that day.

Lamely, the *arenga* tried to argue semantics. If Geronimo was right, then Elijah should have taught more precisely that the Messiah would come "at the end of the four thousand years" or "at the beginning" of the next two-thousand-year epoch. Thus, "the possibility is left open that he will come at the end" of the entire cycle of six thousand years.[29] This was not convincing, apparently, even to Don Vidal, who later converted to Christianity and attained a high office as a result.

Rabbi Joseph Albo, another disputant, got to the heart of the matter. He pointed out that the rabbis who edited the Talmud were not in the habit of presenting material they fundamentally disagreed with. Even if you thought the Jews willfully rejected Christ despite knowing the truth, that he was the Messiah promised in their own Bible, it made little sense to imagine them putting together a carefully edited document like the Talmud that included teachings that implicitly condemned their failure to recognize God's son. For this reason, Albo accepted the traditional meaning of the passage in question, that there were two limits in time to the "days of the Messiah." He could come as soon as the start of the era if the Jews were worthy or as late as the end if they were not.

On the final day of his own disputation, Nachmanides argued along similar lines. Aragon's King James had come to a synagogue in Barcelona to preach a sermon to the Jews. Allowed a reply, Nachmanides explained that the mere fact that his ancestors, living in the first century, had rejected the claim made on Jesus's behalf was enough to seal the case for him. They knew Jesus. They also knew Paul. They knew what the prophets had to say. And they knew what the rabbinic traditions indicated. With all this in mind, they concluded that Jesus was not the Messiah. What arrogance it would be on his part, living 1,200 years later, to contradict them!

OBJECTIONS FROM PHILOSOPHY AND REASON. Ever since Paul unsuccessfully took his case to the synagogues of the Mediterranean world, Jews and Christians had been debating the applicability of the prophetic texts to Jesus. The Jewish-Christian dispute took a new turn with the Christian innovation of ransacking the Talmud for Christological proofs. The Jews found nothing of value in this new arena of combat. A fresh area of debate that they did welcome, also arising in the Middle Ages, drew upon the discourse of philosophy.

The time was ripe for this sort of intellectual jousting, for Jews in Europe and North Africa were themselves debating the role of reason in the exploration of spiritual realities. Spanish Jews, in the more peaceful and cosmopolitan period before 1391, were mad for philosophy—some thought to a fault. It was feared that as young Jews imbibed the spirit of reason, which sought rationalizations for the commandments, they were becoming weaker in the actual practice of Torah. After all, if the commandments were only physical representations of philosophical truths, as some thought, then once you could articulate the truths themselves, maybe you didn't need, let's say, to keep kosher or observe the Sabbath.

Maimonides wrote his *Guide of the Perplexed* in Arabic to meet the needs of learned Jews who had started wondering why, if they had philosophy, they also needed to be practicing, observant Jews. The rationalizing efforts of the Rambam (his acronym) did not meet with universal Jewish approval. Some felt the whole endeavor of explaining Judaism in philosophical terms could lead only to disaffection and heresy. Accordingly, in some Jewish communities the Rambam's books were actually burned. It was in this distressed atmosphere that the text of the Zohar, the Bible of Jewish mysticism, was mysteriously brought to light in the 1280s, its authorship attributed to a rabbinic figure from antiquity, as an alternative and a corrective to the perceived aridity of Maimonidean philosophical speculation.

Even as some Jews argued with one another about philosophy, others argued with Christians. The latter charged that Judaism denied reason, while Jews maintained that the belief in Jesus simply wasn't logical. Here it was possible for the bitterly clashing opponents to argue on equal ground. Unlike in the arena of disputed prophetic or Talmudic passages, there were no arcane Hebrew or Aramaic texts to wrangle over. In the philosophical field, Jews had no special level of access to a species of literature—Talmud, midrash—in which Christians were neophytes. For philosophical debaters, the challenge was to identify first principles, stemming not from revelation, but from reason, on which the two religions could agree—then to measure the differing beliefs of Judaism and Christianity against those premises. Such an application of reason could not prove a religion to be true, but it could show it to be false.

There were two articles of Christian faith that Jews objected to with particular vigor: the Trinity and the Incarnation. In advocating these, Christians asked Jews to embrace beliefs that both contradicted logic and denied certain basic principles about God. Contradictions of that kind, the Jews said, they could not accept.

Such a logic-minded Jew was Hasdai Crescas, chief rabbi of Saragosa, Spain, who belonged to a circle of sages with an interest in showing the failure of Christianity on philosophical grounds. He wrote his *Refutation of the Christian Principles* for an audience of educated Jewish nobles and other men of high standing who possessed the leisure time to delve into recondite areas of reasoned speculation. He wrote that "faith will not force the intellect to believe something which leads to a contradiction." Also, "One cannot imagine that the divine power is able to contradict either the first intelligibles or the derivative principles which have been clearly and absolutely demonstrated"—that is, God will not act in such a way as to deny what we know about His own nature.[30] On the other hand, the Jews had no problem with beliefs that entailed turning the laws of the natural world upside down, as in the story of God's miraculously splitting the Sea of Reeds when the Jews fled Egypt. The Hebrew Bible was full of miracles.

Of the two most problematic Christian dogmas, the Trinity was the lesser of evils. True, the Bible seemed clear enough in stressing God's Oneness, as in the basic statement of Jewish belief, the *Shema*: "Hear, O Israel: the Lord is our God, the Lord is the One and Only."[31] Yet for some Jews, a certain multiplicity in God's nature was not utterly beyond imagining.

The earliest church tended to conceive of God more as a duality, Father and Son, which is the version of the Christian faith the Talmudic rabbis thundered against. The Trinity emerged as a mature doctrine with the Nicene Creed in 325. The Christians that medieval Jews would have known mostly accepted the declaration of the Athanasian Creed: ". . . thus the Father is God, the Son is God, the Holy Spirit is God; and nevertheless there are not three gods, but there is One God." According to a prominent Christian theory, this three-in-one nature corresponded to three divine attributes—power, wisdom, and goodness. For kabbalistic Jews in particular, the objection to the Trinity required careful formulation, since Jewish mysticism thought of God as making Himself accessible to His Creation in a series of unfolding stages, or *sefirot*—Crown, Wisdom, Understanding, Love, Strength, Beauty, Victory, Splendor, Foundation, Kingship—which by the unlearned could easily be mistaken for attributes.

Maimonides, having patience for neither a Christian nor a Jewish theory of attributes, wrote that anyone who claims that three (or ten) can equal one is just spouting words without meaning. His contempt is palpable: "Those who believe that God is One, and that He has many attributes, declare the unity with their lips, and assume plurality in their thoughts. This is like the doctrine of the Christians, who say that He is one and He is three, and that the three are one."[32]

Jews often asked how, if the Trinity corresponded to God's attributes, it made sense to limit Him to only three. For example, what about the attribute of life? Is God not alive? And what about the "substance" of the Being Himself who possesses these attributes, to which the various qualities relate themselves? Counting this way, in the Barcelona disputation Nachmanides declared to his debating opponent, Pablo Christiani, that there must be not a Trinity but a Quinternity—not three divine attributes but five—at which point Pablo's colleagues had to restrain him from responding. They recognized this was not a fruitful line of argumentation to pursue.

Characteristically, the author of *Nitzachon Vetus* cracked wise on the theme. Writing about Psalm 110, he concealed a serious critique in jokes. Christians understood the psalm as depicting the relationship of the Father to the Son: "The Lord [that is, the Father] said unto my lord [that is, the son], Sit at my right hand."[33] The polemicist assumed a straight face and wrote, "I should like to ask you about this matter of sitting. Just how did he sit near his father before he was born? Furthermore, what did he do before he was commanded to sit? Did he lie down or stand? If he stood, how did he stand? Was it in front of his father, behind him, beside him or in the air? Then his father told him, 'Sit at my right hand.' Let me ask you something. Did he sit or not? If you say he did, then you are describing two powers sitting next to each other. If he didn't, then he disobeyed his father's commandment."

The verse seemed to demand one of two impossible interpretations: either that God the Father "sits" or that the Son is a deity with a will of his own. Elsewhere, the author makes his point without recourse to mockery. If both Father and Son are God, then presumably they share the same will. But Psalm 110, taken as Christians understood it, indicates otherwise. So does Jesus's statement in the Gospel of John, "I seek not my own will but the will of him who sent me."[34] Asked the *Nitazchon Vetus*, "Does this mean that they have two wills, so that one wants what the other does not? According to them, the two are one entity, yet [Jesus] says, 'I seek not my own will.' "[35]

More than the conception of God as Father and Son, it was His presumed Incarnation in the person of Jesus that really rankled Jews. Actually it disgusted, revolted, and enraged them. Medieval Jewish polemic literature is full of exclamations at the indignity suffered by the divine nature in being confined in a woman's womb, squeezing through the birth canal, and suffering all the other earthly things little children do and experience. Imagine changing God's soiled swaddling clothes. Christians replied that enduring the human condition was precisely His intention.

There were relatively more serious objections. Nachmanides called the Incarnation the single clearest point of difference between the two faiths—which, however, hardly seems right. The denial of the covenant with Israel, the commandments from Sinai, surely deserves the honor of being called the hardest thing about Christianity for a Jew to accept.

Apart from its being unbefitting to God, Jews insisted that His becoming incarnate was impossible, unsuited to its presumed purpose, and unnecessary.

They said by nature He is incorporeal, immutable, perfectly simple rather than complex. Thus it was *impossible* for him to become a man. The Jews said it was also not imaginable, if God is One, for only one of the three persons of the Trinity to become incarnate. That would mean He is divisible in a way not admitted by the Athanasian Creed, which would turn the theory of multiple "attributes" into a theory of multiple deities.

The purpose of the Incarnation, specifically of death suffered on the cross, was to address the primordial sinful nature of man. Adam and Eve had sinned against the Lord—an infinite crime. This required an atonement or sacrifice of infinite scale, the sacrifice of God's own Son. But the Jews asked how the Crucifixion met this requirement. Only the sacrifice of a God can be called infinite—but a God cannot die. If the sacrifice was not of a God, but of a man or a God-man, then it was not infinite. Thus, the alleged purpose of the terrible event was not met.

Hasdai Crescas asked a related question—the kind that Nachmanides felt that Christians fail to ask because they drank in their Christian principles as unquestioned faith, as if at the maternal breast, never questioning just as children never question why they love their mother. Crescas said, Wasn't there something counterintuitive about one sin, that of Adam and Eve, being forgiven because the guilty party's descendants commit *another* sin? The philosopher was amazed at this: "Even if we posit that God can become incarnate, this redemption is impossible. This is so because disease is cured by the opposite, that is, sin with commandments, rebellion with worship. The curing of disrespect with a great disrespect is curing rebellion with rebellion, and sin with sin."[36]

Anyway, still granting the infiniteness of the sin of the first man and woman, and even granting that it's meaningful to speak of God as having a "Son," there was *no need* to atone for the great sin by God's offering up the incarnate second person of the Trinity. God can forgive any crime, finite or infinite, if He wishes, but Christians made it sound as if He were bound by some law beyond Himself, as if He could not forgive mankind without letting his Son die on the cross. Of course there is no law beyond God.

To every such objection the Jews might raise, Christian philosophers like Thomas Aquinas (1225–1274) had an answer, some more convincing than others. He maintained in great detail that his faith was entirely compatible with reason. For example, to the Jewish challenge that it was unbefitting for God to become flesh, the Christian sage replied that yes, that was true, "it pertains to the dignity of God to be altogether separated from bodies." However, in fact the Son did not turn into flesh but rather, "for the sake of man's salvation, He united it to Himself."[37] God *took on* the physical nature of a man—almost as you might put a sock puppet on your hand and move it about.

And so round and round the philosophers went. There are times when, reading through the reverberating challenges and responses, one feels that what Maimonides said of his Christian opponents applies also to his Jewish compatriots. In the philosophical realm, words go into battle against words, arranged in impenetrable formulations like stone-clad fortresses. Cleverness is prized, but in the end the truth may be obscured rather than clarified. It's hard to say that, on the merits, either side wins the war.

The question of whose arguments you find more convincing may well come down to which coincides with the religious position you favored to begin with. This is the way with philosophy, which is one reason some Jews for millennia have cast a skeptical eye on it. The modern scholar Daniel Lasker wrote a whole book surveying the landscape of philosophical polemics written by medieval Jews against Christianity and concluded that philosophy was not so much the reason they rejected the other religion. Instead, it was a weapon used to defend a position to which the Jewish debaters had already committed themselves. The same judgment, undoubtedly, might be rendered about the arguments of Christian philosophers against Judaism.

WE HAVE RAISED THE QUESTION OF whether Jews, when stating their objections to Christianity, were genuinely explaining their loyalty to the ancestral religion or, on the contrary, offering post facto rationalizations for a commitment that preceded all such logical-sounding discussions.

In the philosophical realm, it was more the latter than the former; but what about Jewish objections based on scriptural and other holy texts? Another modern historian, Jacob Katz, in narrating how Jewish attitudes toward Christianity evolved over the course of the Middle Ages and into the modern era, concluded about Jewish polemics in general that we mustn't "overrate" their importance. Much more significant was the "emotional attachment" Jews felt to Judaism.

This was expressed in the rabbinic traditions about the passionate, sometimes stormy love between God and Israel, a relationship that transcends reason just as the love of husband and wife transcends reason. Indeed, the Lord and His people, the Jews, were often compared to a married couple, husband and wife. The Bible's Song of Solomon, a great love poem suffused with sexuality, was so interpreted by Rashi as an allegorical representation of God's relationship with His bride, Israel: "Let him kiss me with the kisses of his mouth; for your love is better than wine."[38] Rashi taught that this mutual affection was so intense that when the Jews went into exile from the holy land, God went with them and shared all their distresses.[39] Medieval Jewish liturgical poetry repeated this and related themes over and over.

Katz concludes that in the understanding of medieval Jewry, in being true to Torah, the Jew was simply acting out of "his own essential nature."[40] What's fascinating about this is how closely it parallels, in positive rather than harshly negative terms, the medieval Christian theory about why the Jews rejected the offer of Christ's salvation: It was something in their wicked, twisted nature, their perversely stubborn constitution, that drove them to it. Obviously Jews differed with Christians on the question of whether their ancestors recognized Jesus as Messiah, but there is a hint in Jewish thinking in this period that maybe the reasons for not accepting Christianity are secondary to something prerational in the essence of a Jew—his preexisting relationship with the one true God—that explains the defiance of Christian efforts to convert him.

There actually seems to be far more substance to the scripturally based anti-Christian polemics than to the philosophical ones. The more one reads in this genre, the more convinced one becomes that it's awfully hard to make Christian doctrine sit naturally on its presumed foundation, the Hebrew Bible. Yet even the arguments based on prophecies obviously aren't perfectly invulnerable to refutation. Otherwise there would be no Christians, or at least no thoughtful Christians. They would all be Jews. The idea of a Jewish essence that explains the rejection of Christ is an attractive one, and we shall return to it.

Before moving on, however, let us notice how the interest of the question posed in this book is heightened when we consider the changing Jewish evaluation of Christianity as a whole. We began this chapter by noting how the Jewish reaction to the veneration of Jesus evolved from indifference (in regard to Jesus himself when he was alive), to impatient disgust (regarding Paul), to a sometimes vague dismissiveness (in the Talmudic period).

In the Middle Ages, Jews formed very specific and concrete judgments of the opposing religion in its entirety. These were at first predictably negative, finding little to appreciate except for the fact that Christianity introduced gentiles to the Jewish concept of the Messiah. When the real Messiah appeared, they would benefit from having some familiarity with this.

In comments traditionally censored from the original text of his *Mishneh Torah*, Maimonides wrote: "All these matters relating to Jesus of Nazareth . . . only served to clear the way for King Messiah, to prepare the whole world to worship God with one accord, as it is written, 'For then will I turn to the peoples a pure language, that they may all call upon the name of the Lord serve Him with one consent' [Zephaniah 3:9]. Thus the Messianic hope, the Torah, and the commandments have become familiar topics—topics of conversation [among the inhabitants] of far isles and many peoples, uncircumcised of heart and flesh . . . [Hence] when the true King Messiah will appear and succeed, be exalted and lifted up, they will forthwith recant and realize that they have inherited naught but lies from their fathers, that their prophets and forebears led them astray."[41]

This was a strictly utilitarian appraisal of the other faith, which apart from preparing the ground for the universal embrace of the God of Israel was dismissed as "naught but lies." But a slightly earlier sage, the Spanish liturgical poet Rabbi Judah Halevi (c. 1086–1145), prefigured the development of a more positive evaluation. Born in Toledo and experiencing in his lifetime the fierce reconquest of Spain from Muslim control by Christian forces, Halevi was able to cast an informed eye on both Christianity and Islam. He too wrote of the other faiths as serving "to introduce and pave the way for the expected Messiah" but used the metaphor of a tree (the Torah of Moses) bearing seeds and fruit (through the medium of Christianity and Islam):

"God has a secret and wise design concerning us, which should be compared to the wisdom hidden in the seed which falls into the ground, where it undergoes an external transformation into earth, water and dirt, without leaving a trace for him who looks down upon it. It is, however, the seed itself which transforms earth and water into its substance, carries it from one stage to another, until it refines the elements and transfers them into something like itself . . . The original seed produced the tree bearing fruit resembling that from which it had been produced. In the same manner the law of Moses transforms each one who honestly follows it, though it may externally repel him."[42]

Because it came from a seed of the tree of Torah, Christianity, though seemingly repelled by the law of Moses, had the potential of transforming those who came into contact with it. They could in time become fruit of the very same tree that bore Israel.

Halevi, though earlier than Maimonides, went further than he did. Another medieval sage transformed and illuminated the Jewish attitude like a bolt of lightning: Rabbi Menachem ha-Meiri, who lived in Provence, in southern France, and died about 1315. Among Jewish, Christian, and Muslim thinkers, he went further than any ever had done before in articulating a rationale for religious tolerance.

Best known for his Talmud commentary, *Beit ha'Becheirah*, ha-Meiri set forth criteria for determining the characteristics of those cultures that deserve admiration and acceptance. He distinguished between "nations restricted by the ways of religion" (*ummot ha'gedurot b'darchey ha-datot*) and "nations not restricted by the ways of religion."

The former merit a Jew's warm regards however they might diverge theologically from a true conception of God and His ways (that is, from Judaism). Ha-Meiri's dividing line was not based on religious dogma, in which area Christianity with its Trinity and Incarnation falls short, compared to Islam with its rigorous monotheism. Rather, as Professor Moshe Halbertal has written, the difference is "between nations possessed of law and lawless nations, i.e. between barbarism and civilization." There is even a certain sense in which such nations— again despite their errors in dogma—are to be considered under the designation of "Israel."

Of course, this doesn't mean Jews can intermarry even with the most civilized gentiles or breach other walls that God, wishing to set them apart for special responsibilities in the world, established to keep Israel separate from other peoples. But even with such limitations in mind, ha-Meiri's way of thinking still sounds radical from a medieval rabbinic sage.

Yet he constructed his ideology of tolerance on a sound Torah basis. The Talmudic rabbis had formulated a distinction between religious laws and other truths that can be known only through revelation and those that can be discovered through our own powers of reason. The latter could form the basis of non-Jewish religions that promote the values of civilization, lifting gentiles to the heights of human potential—and "this would be entirely sufficient for them, according to the nature of their religions."[43]

Looking around himself at the Christians of Provence, he saw a nation "restricted by the ways of religion," a worldview "entirely sufficient for them." Utterly to be condemned, on the other hand, were those peoples not possessing a religion or possessing a religion that promoted barbarism.

This approach to thinking about Christianity would gain further ground in coming centuries. With it in mind, resolving the question this book asks becomes more urgent. After all, if Christianity really isn't as bad as Maimonides seemed to think, if it possesses not only a narrowly utilitarian value in setting the table for the messianic banquet, but also conveys ultimate truths, why did the Jews turn so decisively away from it? Why must they continue to do so? Modern Jewish thinkers would offer what is, I think, a compelling and satisfying answer to this question.

CHAPTER SEVEN

MODERN TIMES
THE NEVER-ENDING DISPUTATION

The period in Jewish history from the close of the Middle Ages to today is notable for the progressive alienation of a large portion of the people Israel from their traditional faith. In the medieval era, there were defectors to Christianity, but it could be taken for granted that in the absence of coercion to change one's religion, anyone born to Jewish parents would likely continue to identify himself as a believer in and a practitioner of Torah and its commandments. Of course, that's not true today, but the present situation was long in developing. What does this imply about the question this book seeks to answer?

Jews in earlier times spurned the belief in Jesus apparently because they found it incompatible with what they knew, or thought they knew, about God and His relationship to humanity. Since what they knew about God came from Judaism, it would seem to follow that their reasons in the modern period for rejecting Jesus could not be the same ones their medieval forebears would have offered. This, however, overlooks the possibility that the Jews reject Jesus in every age not primarily because of the reasons they give for doing so, but rather from some other cause or purpose of which they may not be consciously aware.

Modernity for European Jews may be dated to the rise of the Protestant Reformation, for Martin Luther's spiritual revolution broke

up the monopoly of the medieval church in the realm of religious doctrine. From then on, the gradual undermining of church authority set
in, and liberty of conscience became more and more the norm in Europe. This had its effect on gentiles—encouraging the questioning of
age-old beliefs, the embracing of ideas that never before had even been
considered—and so did it also upon Jews.

The question of why the Jews rejected Jesus thus becomes more
complicated. Jews were no longer limited to the old two-pronged
choice: remain in the old religion or become a Christian. They could
now choose to be nothing at all. Christianity itself was no longer
monolithic, so that one might reject the Christ of the Catholic Church
while finding a Protestant Christ more palatable. The complexity of
the Jewish dilemma becomes clear when we briefly review the history
of this period, from the career of Martin Luther to the birth of the
world's greatest Protestant nation, the United States.

FROM EARLY IN Luther's campaign against the church, Jews rejoiced
at what they at first took to be a turn by the former German monk in a
remarkably Jewish direction. Luther himself speculated that the refusal
of the Jews to accept Jesus was historically attributable to malfeasance
on the part of the church. If only the Jews were not treated so
abysmally, he reasoned, they would flock to Christianity. In 1523, in a
pamphlet titled *That Jesus Christ Was Born a Jew,* he wrote, "I would advise and beg everybody to deal kindly with the Jews and to instruct
them in the Scriptures; in such a case we could expect them to come
over to us." Why did Luther care? Like Paul and like so many Christians
before, he was still preoccupied with winning over the Jews. The fact of
their rejection of Jesus still disturbed Christian minds, with its hidden
implication that maybe the Jews, from whom Jesus came and who
wrote the scriptural books to which Christians appealed in making
their case for his messiahship, really were right about him all along. No
believing Christian could admit this, even to himself, but it's obvious.

Jews, for their part, mistakenly interpreted Luther's initial warmth
as a sign that he himself was ready to convert to Judaism. As late as 1535,

he was still open enough to engage in a dialogue with three Jewish sages on the interpretation of scriptural references to the Messiah. But by 1543, enraged by the continuing Jewish refusal to accept the offer of becoming Protestants, he turned on the Jews in a fury, asking, "What then shall we Christians do with this damned, rejected race of Jews?" His suggestions included burn their synagogues, tear down Jewish houses, confiscate prayer books and Talmuds, make teaching Judaism a capital offense, restrict Jewish travel rights, put Jews to work as farmers, and if all else failed, "let us drive them out of the country for all time."

The heritage of Protestantism has been a mixed one for the Jews. On the one hand, Luther prepared the way for the planting of new ideas, which eventuated in the first hints of religious tolerance in the eighteenth century, in whose last decades Jews were being freed from the ghettos. (They had been confined there, starting with the Venice ghetto, from the early sixteenth century.) Jewish emancipation in Europe was initiated by Napoleon but came to fruition from the 1860s on. But this new freedom was no boon to Judaism. On the contrary, it resulted in Jewish defections to Christianity, or Christianized forms of Judaism.

Previously, walled in by the ghetto, Jews could hardly imagine joining the non-Jewish society outside. But when that gentile world opened itself up to limited Jewish participation, baptism beckoned as "an entrance ticket to European society." So the poet Heinrich Heine (1797–1856) put it. He purchased his ticket, as did some 250,000 other Jews in the heart of Europe over the course of the nineteenth century. However, to say that these baptized Jews had embraced Jesus Christ would not be entirely accurate. No doubt some were sincere, but many, probably most, were motivated by the hope of material advancement. For these born-Jews, a sincere embrace of Christ would have been asking too much.

The rise of secularism as an alternative framework for interpreting the world meant that religion switching could mean little more than switching jobs or moving from one neighborhood to another. For many upwardly mobile Jews, going to the baptismal font held little of the horror it did for their ancestors. Heine is among the most famous instances of Jews joining the Christian church for purely nonreligious reasons. His cynicism was matched by Heinrich Marx, father of Karl (baptized in 1824 at age six), and Isaac D'Israeli, father of Benjamin (baptized in 1817 at age twelve), the future British prime minister.

A decline in religious consciousness among the most worldly and urbane men and women had another consequence for those Jews who couldn't bring themselves to make a clean break with the religion of their forefathers. Three centuries after Luther's Reformation, there was a Jewish "Reformation" of a sort. In 1818, the first Reform temple was opened, in Hamburg. An entirely German creation, the new Reform movement differed from Luther's rebellion against church authority in that Luther was inarguably a serious character whose challenge to Rome was based on profound theological questions about religious leadership and scriptural interpretation. By contrast, the Jewish "Reformation" was about superficialities—the thesis that there should be organ music in synagogues (a Sabbath violation in Jewish law) as there was in the churches, that there should be Protestant-style sermons, that rabbis should dress up in robes like Protestant ministers. The Reform movement sought to assuage the shame of prosperous Jews who felt pain at the fact that religious services for Jews were not as orderly and decorous as those enjoyed by their Christian neighbors. Christian styles of worship were thus adopted while stopping short of accepting the structure of Christian belief.

The religious options open to Jews were multiplying rapidly. Whereas in medieval Europe there was one form of Christianity you could accept or reject, Protestantism created countless new variations on the theme of Jesus as Messiah. Some forms of Protestantism might, like Luther himself, despair of winning over the Jews. It's easy to see why they would feel unwelcome in Luther's church. However, other churches were far more warmly inclined, if not to Jews per se, then at least toward Christianity's Jewish heritage.

From one such strand of Protestantism there arose a great blessing to the Jews: the founding of the United States. Today, the most earnestly Christian country on earth, as well as the most benevolently inclined toward its Jewish population, and at the same time the most affected by Jewish ideas, the United States presents a problem to Jews. To reject American Christianity seems almost ungrateful.

Perhaps the first thinker to try to explain the Jewishness of America was the revered Reform rabbi Leo Baeck (1873–1956), leader of German Jewry before World War II. A survivor of the Theresienstadt concentration camp, Baeck attributed what is special, and especially Jewish, about America to its Christian heritage.

An amazingly observant and prescient writer, he understood Judaism's daughter religion as being in a constant state of war with her own Jewish soul. In certain periods of Christian history, he explained, the Judaic heritage—what he called "classical" religion—was dominant: an emphasis on ethics, on commandments. In other periods, this Jewish side of Christianity was submerged under a "romantic" tendency that revered not ethical action but emotional experience, that gauzy, swooning sensation of feeling and glorying in being personally "saved." This essentially narcissistic, passive version of religion loves sacred music and wafting incense but can look with indifference on injustice and tyranny. By contrast, the Judaic "classical" countertendency thinks less about the self and more about the wrongs done by human beings and directs a focused passion to setting things right on earth.

In Baeck's retelling of Christian history, the religion of the historical Jesus was classical, while the apostle Paul's was romantic. The romantic and classical tendencies were balanced in the medieval church. With Luther's Reformation, the pendulum swung to the romantic side—which would explain how German Lutheranism could be so indifferent to Nazi violence. In his essay "Romantic Religion," Baeck was already writing on this theme in 1922! But another branch of Protestantism, that of Calvinism, embraced the Judaic/classical paradigm. Here is where America—her Puritan and Baptist roots—comes in. Baeck wrote in 1925:

"This idea did not become an ecclesiastical movement until the time of so-called Baptism, this religious movement from which, together with Calvinism, there was derived . . . almost everything which transformed and reorganized religion and religious thought in England and the United States . . . The Baptist movement represents a real revolution of that which was Jewish within the Church. It strove and gained its world-historical successes at the time of Cromwell in England, and in the states of the Pilgrim fathers."[1]

The Pilgrims and the Founders alike considered themselves as following in the footsteps of ancient Israel. As Abraham Lincoln said, America was the "almost chosen people."

Yet for all that Protestant attitudes toward Jews and Judaism were protean, changing, the resistance of Jews to the Christian idea remained steady. The number of cynical conversions for purposes of social climbing only illustrates this, as does the Jewish "Reformation," which likewise could contemplate no more than an acceptance of Christian window dressing. No matter how much Protestantism renovated and expanded the number of Christian options available to the Jews, the Jewish rejection of Jesus has remained a constant.

AT THE SAME TIME, among Jews committed to traditional Judaism, or at least to membership in the Jewish people, the attitude toward Christianity has been in a process of evolution. From the utter rejection that characterized the position of such leading medieval sages as Maimonides and Nachmanides, we saw the start of a softening in feeling initiated by another influential scholar, Rabbi Menachem ha-Meiri. The warming trend continued in the sixteenth century, proceeding and developing down to our own time. The question before us is thus sharpened, as we'll see.

Ha-Meiri's tolerance and acceptance was confirmed by the foremost authority on Jewish law who ever lived in the Ashkenazic communities of central and Western Europe, Rabbi Moses Isserles (called Rema, 1530–1572). In his contributions to the standard Jewish legal code, the *Shulchan Aruch*, he states that while the Christians of his day (he lived in Krakow, Poland) included idolatrous elements in their worship, "nevertheless their intention is [to worship] the Maker of Heaven and Earth."[2] Among traditional Jews, the *Shulchan Aruch* is still the authoritative guide to Jewish practice. For Ashkenazim, Rema's would be the accepted and binding view: Christians worship the same God that Jews do.

Beyond this somewhat theoretical issue, there was a more stirring question. God has allowed Christianity to flourish—a religion that grew from the root of Judaism. What, if anything, did He intend to accomplish by this?

In the post-Reformation period, rabbinic authorities have given various answers, most concluding that Christianity plays a crucially important role in the world. Rabbi Samson Raphael Hirsch (1808–1888), the greatest exponent of modern German Orthodoxy and a passionate fighter against liberalizing Reform tendencies in his own religion, wrote very clearly about the positive contribution of Christianity. He described the time immediately before the Romans expelled the people Israel from their land, after the destruction of the Second Temple in 70 CE. At that time, Israel "produced an offshoot which *had to* become estranged from it in great measure, *in order* to bring the world—sunk in idol worship, violence, immorality and the degradation of man—at least the tiding of the One Alone, of the brotherhood of all men and of man's superiority over the beast."[3] Note the emphasis (added above in italics) on the positive *necessity* of Christianity's break with the parent religion.

Another towering Torah commentator, Rabbi Naftali Zvi Yehuda Berlin (Russian, called Netziv, 1817–1893), offered a striking exegesis of a verse in Genesis. We've seen that the biblical figure of Esau, the patriarch Jacob's problematic brother, has long been understood by Jews as a type for Rome, by extension for the Roman church and for Christianity in general. In one touching scene in the Bible, Jacob tremblingly prepares for a reunion with Esau after many years of estrangement. As scripture tells the story, when the brothers at last met again, "Esau ran to greet him and they embraced and he fell upon his shoulders."[4]

Netziv wrote: "They both wept. This comes to teach that at this Jacob was roused to love Esau. So it shall be in future generations that when the seed of Esau is roused through a spirit of purity to recognize the seed of Jacob . . . then we too should be roused to recognize Esau for he is our brother."⁵ Living in the age of pogroms, amid vicious anti-Semitic violence to be exceeded only by the Holocaust, Netziv sought to clarify the prophecy encrypted in the Bible's account of the brothers' meeting. In the future, Esau, the church, will recognize Jacob, the people Israel. At that time, Jacob should respond in kind by embracing and recognizing Esau, for "he is our brother."

Yet in all the writings of the greatest rabbis of the modern era, none gave a heartier embrace to Christianity as a brother religion than Jacob Emden, a leading German rabbi who died in the year of the American Revolution (1697–1776). Not shy of controversy, he was among the foremost opponents of the Sabbatian heresy, of which we'll say more in a moment, accusing other rabbis of being secret adherents. Hailed as a "prophet" by a slightly later sage of equal stature, the renowned ultratraditionalist Rabbi Moses Sofer (called Chasam Sofer, 1762–1839), Emden had nothing but praise for Jesus and Paul.

Apparently not concurring with what we learned in chapter 2, that Jesus dismissed the oral Torah while upholding the written, Emden praised "the Nazarene" for bringing "about a double kindness in the world. On one hand, he strengthened the Torah of Moses majestically ... and not one of our Sages spoke out more emphatically concerning the immutability of the Torah. And on the other hand, he did much good for the Gentiles ... by doing away with idolatry and removing the images [of pagan gods] from their midst ... He also bestowed upon them ethical ways, and in this respect he was much more stringent with them than the Torah of Moses." Only "errant scholars" among the Christians, wrote Emden, insist that Jesus intended to displace the Torah and abrogate its commandments among the Jews.⁶

It would be hard to exaggerate what a radical statement this is from a traditional sage, once again a trenchant opponent of those in his time who sought to reform Judaism. Even today, learned Jewish opinion has not yet caught up to him.

ALTHOUGH JEWISH OPINION WAS migrating toward a new appreciation of the positive, if mixed, contribution made by Jesus to human history, this was more a matter of theory than of gut-level emotion. Approaching the present day, we find Jewish sentiment darkening, not least because of the reflection that faith in Jesus apparently did so little to mitigate murderous hatred of Jews in Nazi Germany and elsewhere in Europe during World War II.

In the decades after War World II, and possibly inspired by guilt at having allowed the Holocaust to occur, the Second Vatican Council (1962–1965) granted some limited recognition to Judaism as a legitimate spiritual path and absolved Jews of collective responsibility for the death of Christ. It was an unprecedented moment in the evolution of Christian thinking about Judaism—arguably the beginning of Esau's recognition of Jacob that Netziv had found prophesied in scripture, obligating Jacob's children to prepare themselves similarly to recognize the legitimacy of Esau's religious longing as expressed in Christianity. More recently, in 2002, the Catholic Church went even further in recognizing Judaism's dignity, declaring that the "Jewish messianic wait is not in vain."

But for many Jews, the Holocaust proved to be a sticking point, to say the least. In 1966, the year immediately following the promulgation of Vatican II, the Jewish philosopher Eliezer Berkovits expressed his contempt for what he took to be a pale attempt on the part of Christians to make up for past crimes:

"A straight line leads from the first act of oppression against the Jews and Judaism in the 4th century to the Holocaust in the 20th. In order to pacify the Christian conscience it is said that the Nazis were not Christians. But they were all the children of Christians. They were the fruit of 19 centuries of Christianity—the logical fruit of violence and militancy, oppression and intolerance, hatred and persecution, which dominated European history for the 16 centuries since Constantine the Great."[7]

That's one way of looking at it. Another could not help but notice that the chief architects of Nazism not only were not Christian themselves, but were declared enemies of Christianity. So what if they were the descendants of Christians? Karl Marx was a vile hater of the Jewish people, yet he descended from a long line of rabbinic forebears, including a grandfather and an uncle. Did the fact that Marx was the child of a rabbinic family show that Judaism is also a cause of anti-Semitism?

In the very same year that Berkovits published his screed, the great modern theologian Rabbi Abraham Joshua Heschel pointed the way toward what has emerged very recently as the newest direction in the Jewish evaluation of what Jesus produced. No conservative, to be sure, but rather a friend of all liberal political causes, Heschel pointed out that "Nazism in its very roots was a rebellion against the Bible, against the God of Abraham." Nazi Germany was defeated, but Heschel understood that the same force that animated Hitlerism also was behind a leading ideological force that persisted and drew adherents, including many Jews, with increasing success. This force is called secularism, the will to erase the vestiges of all biblical religion from public life and to limit its practical application in private life, too. "The process of eliminating the Bible from the consciousness of the Western world goes on. It is on the issue of saving the radiance of the Hebrew Bible in the minds of man that Jews and Christians are called upon to work together."[8] A man ahead of his time, he called for a Jewish alliance with Christians against secularism.

However, at the approach of the last decade of the twentieth century, Jewish attitudes in America still followed the line advocated by Eliezer Berkovits. The secular leadership of the country's Jewish community was always launching attacks on prominent Christians for stating their religious beliefs publicly, if those beliefs could in any way be construed as casting Jews or Judaism in a negative light. It somehow came to be that America's most prominent Jewish leaders arose from organizations devoted to fighting anti-Jewish "defamation." The implicit and perilous bargain these groups made with their major donors, in order to appear relevant and justify the funding of budgets in the tens of millions of dollars, required that the groups constantly discover new domestic threats to Jewish safety. Christians, especially Evangelical conservatives, made a convenient target for denunciations.

Antidefamation activists argued that, after all, these Christians had a not-so-secret wish to convert Jews to Christianity. True enough, drawing Jews to Christ has been the shared fantasy of Christians since the very beginnings of the church. In the 1990s, a series of novels, *Left Behind,* made news as they jumped to the top of best-seller lists. The story told by Evangelical Christian authors Tim LaHaye and Jerry B. Jenkins was of the earth's last days, after all the true Christians have been gathered up into the clouds to meet Jesus while the Antichrist prepares to fight the war of Armageddon. In the second installment of the series, *Tribulation Force* (1996), Christian readers thrilled to the depiction of Jews discovering faith in Jesus: "The 144,000 [new converts, a figure derived from New Testament prophecy] would be Jews, 12,000 from each of the original twelve tribes, but they would be gathered from all over the world, a restoration of the dispersion of Jews throughout history. Imagine . . . Jews ministering in their own lands and their own tongues, drawing millions to Jesus the Messiah."[9] In the story, even an Orthodox rabbi—the ultimate prize in the Evangelical imagination—declares Jesus as Messiah on CNN, electrifying Jews around the world.

In the Jewish community, much energy (and money) was expended publicizing the supposed danger of Christian wistfulness at the hope of Jews accepting Christ. Then September 11, 2001, happened.

The day that militant Islam collided with Americans on their own soil was a revolutionary milestone in the development of Jewish attitudes about Christianity. When Heschel wrote of those who would "eliminate the Bible from the consciousness of the Western world," he had Western secularists in mind, not angry Muslims on the other side of the planet. But since 9/11, Jews increasingly have come to understand the threat that Jews and Christians equally face from Islamic radicals who despise the biblical religions and who are far from being content with daydreams about Jews and Christians accepting the teachings of Muhammad.

For the first time in American history, Jews in this country were faced with an imminent danger to their lives, and it was not from Christians. On the contrary, Jewish and Christian fates were tied intimately with each other. Meanwhile, in a singularly important development that seemed to happen almost overnight, those in the Jewish community who care about the security of the ever endangered State of Israel came to perceive that the Jewish nation's best friend in the world was America, specifically because American Evangelical Christians who vote are readers of the Bible from page one. They believe in scripture's promises to the Jews of a holy land. Jewish sentiment toward Christians, seen more and more as allies rather than enemies, has been warming ever since. Heschel was revealed as a prophet.

My reason for trying to summarize five hundred years of Jewish thinking about Christianity in a few pages is to show the general trend and thus to suggest that the answers today to the problems posed in the title of this book cannot be assumed to be the same answers we found in earlier chapters.

For Jewish thinking is obviously tending toward increased acceptance of Christianity as a faith of profound dignity possibly equal to that of Judaism—a friend of the Jews, not an opponent. Yet at the same time, resistance to Jesus himself remains as strong as ever. As one Jewish observer of the American scene, Michael Medved, has noted, the one and only thing Jews all agree on today is that Jesus was not the Messiah. Why is this? If the old theological-textual reasons were sufficient for medieval Jews, they are not anymore. Nowadays, most Jews aren't even aware of the issues—having to do with the Bible, the Talmud, and philosophy—that we discussed in the last chapter.

I shall spend the rest of this chapter detailing some of the reasons, relating to modern times, for the Jewish rejection of Jesus. In the conclusion, however, we'll ask whether there lies behind them all an ultimate reason, laying bare the hidden historical dynamic that has animated these two faiths in conflict for two thousand years.

ANOTHER MESSIANIC DISAPPOINTMENT. The mere existence of the Christian faith would suggest that the ancient prophecies can, with imagination and ingenuity, be construed as lending support to the Christian claim. But the fact that Christianity exists, the fact that many people find it plausible, clearly doesn't prove that the identification of Jesus as Messiah is accurate. The force of this point was and is underlined for Jews when they remember the catastrophe of Sabbatai Zevi.

A seventeenth-century failed messiah, he and his followers also found proofs for his messianic candidacy in the Hebrew prophets. He revealed himself as the Messiah, in the city of Gaza on the coast of Ottoman Palestine, in 1665. Likely he was a manic-depressive, without question mentally ill, undergoing swings from the deepest gloom to the highest exaltation. In the latter moods, he would commit gross violations of Torah law as a kind of sacrament. With remarkable speed, word spread through the Jewish world, and anticipation as far as the European Ashkenazic communities of central Europe was intense. But the excitement, verging on mass hysteria, collapsed when Zevi was imprisoned by the Ottoman sultan and faced with the choice of conversion to Islam or death. In 1666, he became a Muslim.

But the movement he had inspired did not end there, nor did it end with his death, just as the Jesus movement did not end with Jesus's death. On the contrary, believers who could not bear to think that their earlier faith in him was in vain constructed a new religion centered upon the idea that Zevi's conversion, his spiritual death, was part of a necessary process of self-sacrifice that would ultimately result in the redemption of the world. Zevi was the teacher of a new, secret Torah, a new testament, one might say, predicated on the abrogation of the old Torah. From as early as 1683, many Jews followed him and became Muslims, others became Catholics, but only outwardly— retaining their belief in Zevi even as they prostrated themselves in the mosque or the church. Others felt that this self-sacrifice was for the Messiah alone to make. They remained Jews at least in their outward observances, while some violated the Torah in private.

The parallels with Christianity are remarkable. Some Sabbatians taught, as Paul did, that those who continued to cling to the old teaching, the Torah as formerly understood, condemned themselves to spiritual darkness. Other Sabbatians argued that the Jews would be released from the old covenant only upon the Messiah's resurrection and return. It was said that Zevi's apostasy was a "mystery"—much as Christians say of the Crucifixion—whose outline was limned in the Hebrew prophets. The book of Psalms was found to be full of allusions to Zevi, which no one had understood until they were fulfilled. This was the line taken by the Sabbatians Nathan of Gaza and Abraham Cardozo, much as Luke in his Gospel has the resurrected Jesus explaining to his disciples "in all the scriptures the things concerning himself," "open[ing] their minds to understand the scriptures."[10] Like Christians, Sabbatians stressed Isaiah 53, but everywhere they showed how the Bible and the Zohar foretold the details of Zevi's life and suffering. There was a kind of Trinitarian doctrine, with the Godhead being divided into three hypostases—the "Holy Ancient One," the "Holy King," and *Shechinah*, God's Immanent Presence. In time, as happened in the evolution of Christianity, something about the inherent, internal dynamic of this kind of thinking led Sabbatians to the conclusion that their Messiah was not merely a human being, but a divine incarnation: in Sabbatai Zevi, God Himself walked the earth.

The same dynamic led to moral horrors unprecedented in Jewish history, mainly of a sexual nature. The historian Gershom Scholem points out the organic link between messianism and antinomianism— that is, between the belief that the redemption promised in the Bible is already upon us and the will to throw off the ancient covenant of the Torah and its laws. There is a certain logic in this. If the law was appropriate for the preredemption era, then didn't it make sense that now that the world is redeemed, some new way of relating to God should displace the old legal rigors? The most radical Sabbatian would have agreed with Paul when the apostle said, "But now we are discharged from the law, dead to that which held us captive, so that we serve not under the old written code but in the new life of the Spirit."[11]

There is every reason to think that Paul's gentile followers were moral people. When they strayed, he rebuked them severely. But among later Christians there were those—notably in the Gnostic sects—who followed the logic of Paul's antinomian message to a twisted, corrupt end point, taking the form of unfettered sexuality, orgies, and adultery and worse. So it was for centuries after among some Sabbatians, who viewed wife swapping as a holy sacrament. Scholem describes the "primitive abandon such as the Jewish people would scarcely have thought itself capable of after so many centuries of discipline in the Law . . . In the light of what happened there is little to wonder at when we read in the text of rabbinical excommunications dating from the 18th century that the children of the 'believers' were automatically considered bastards [that is, offspring of incestuous or adulterous unions]."[12] One sect of Sabbatians, the Donmeh, persisted until the twentieth century. In Salonika, Greece, they celebrated a yearly "Festival of the Lamb," including an orgiastic observance called "the extinguishing of the lights" deriving from an ancient pagan cult of the "Great Mother."

The horror of Sabbatianism—the grievous disappointment of those of his followers who held fast to Judaism, the apostasy of those who converted to Islam and Christianity to follow the path of the master, the sexual dissolution of those who abandoned the law—formed a trauma that affected the Jewish people long after Sabbatai Zevi was dead. Today, for most Jews his name rings only the vaguest of bells, but in the eighteenth century Jewish communities were convulsed by his legacy. Accusations of crypto-Sabbatianism flew back and forth among community leaders. Certain distinguished rabbis who vehemently denied it of themselves are known now to have been secret believers.

The pain that was generated can only have served as a warning to Jews. Judaism is a messianic faith, assigning great significance to faith in a coming Messiah, but premature messianism—the leap to the belief that the Messiah has already come despite evidence before your eyes that the world remains as before—was poison. It bled Israel of Jews, destroyed Jewish communities, befouled Jewish morals. At least this was the case with the Sabbatian movement. Into the nineteenth century, any European Jew who might have contemplated becoming a follower of the Christian Messiah surely had cause to reflect on this. Did it deter baptisms? How could it not?

THE LIBERAL CRITIQUE OF CHRISTIANITY. One of the fascinating tendrils of Sabbatianism, as Gershom Scholem demonstrates, is liberal Judaism. Many of the same families who were secret devotees of Sabbatai Zevi in the eighteenth century finally lost faith in his imminent return and as a result loosed their grip on religious belief in general. Those same families provided some of the earliest leaders of the Reform movement and of the *Haskalah*, the secular Jewish "Enlightenment."[13] Jewish liberals had their own reasons for rejecting Christ.

To be precise, the liberal case was not so much against Jesus as against the ethical heritage of those who followed him. Medieval Jewish disputants commonly pointed out what they took to be the low moral atmosphere of Christian communities, which, as they saw it, reflected the basic untruth of Christian doctrine. Paul had taught that the moral law of Christ is written on men's hearts.[14] Medieval Jews asked, given what they knew about how Christians behaved, how this could be true.

Jewish liberals were less keen on pressing the point about ultimate religious truth, a concept in which many did not believe anyway. They were more interested in showing how Christianity fell short of an ideal of progressivism, enlightenment, and tolerance. A hint of this may be found in the words of the philosopher Moses Mendelssohn (1729–1786), sometimes celebrated as a father of the *Haskalah*, other times as an exponent of modern liberal orthodoxy. He was traditionally observant, knowledgeable of Jewish classical tradition, and at the same time worldly, cosmopolitan, no less learned in the secular traditions. He famously refused to engage in a disputation against Christianity and posed a challenge to any who might do so in the future.

In 1763, there took place a private discussion between Mendelssohn and some rather ardent Christians, including Johann Casper Lavater, a Swiss theologian. Mendelssohn said more than, evidently, he later thought prudent on the theme of why he could not accept faith in Christ. Lavater subsequently challenged him, in public, to defend his refusal to become a Christian. Mendelssohn wished he had never got into this fix, where, at first consideration, needlessly giving offense seemed the only honorable course for a Jew to take. Instead, he ingeniously replied in a letter to Lavater in which he refused to refute the Christian's faith head-on but resorted to what he evidently saw as Judaism's chief virtue: tolerance. This tolerance, he implied, should have kept Lavater from trying to convert him, as it kept Mendelssohn from trying to undermine Lavater's faith by defending his own. Proselytizing, he wrote, was "completely alien" to Judaism.

But this last point about Jews as missionaries needs to be addressed before we move on. On the contrary, Jews actually have believed in rather aggressive methods of weaning non-Jews from their false value systems—see, for example, Maimonides's alarmingly frank comments on this in his *Mishneh Torah*, which I almost hesitate to quote because they are so aggressive. But the familiar myth of Jewish passivity should really be stamped out. What Maimonides says is that in time to come, in the days of the Messiah when Jewish law rules in the holy land, Jewish courts will be obliged to take into account that "Moses our teacher was commanded by the Almighty to compel all inhabitants of the world to accept the commandments that were enjoined upon the children of Noah"—the seven categories of basic ethical rules obligatory for all mankind. "If one does not accept these laws, he should be executed." Maimonides then gives a crisp exposition of the Noachide laws, based on the Talmud's lengthy discussion.[15]

A sage who lived on the cusp of our modern period, the Italian physician Rabbi Ovadiah Sforno (1470–1550), wrote just as Luther was turning his wrath on the Jews. At ease in and familiar with Christian society in Rome and Bologna, serving at one point as a Hebrew teacher to the German humanist scholar Johann Reuchlin, Sforno explained that being a "kingdom of priests" (Exodus 19:6) means "to instruct all of mankind to call in unison on the Name of the Lord and to serve Him with one accord." His intent was not that all humans convert to Judaism, but rather that they become adherents of the God of Israel as *Gentiles*.[16]

It becomes clear that Mendelssohn, while certainly a committed Jew, was at least on this point more committed to the emerging ideal of liberalism: "If a Confucius or a Solon were to live among our contemporaries, I could, according to my religion, love and admire the great man without succumbing to the ridiculous desire to convert him. Convert a Confucius or a Solon? What for?"[17] His rebuke of Lavater turns upon the assumption that any "good" religion will fully respect the civilized beliefs of others and seek no opportunity to change them. To the extent a Christian was not tolerant in this way, it revealed a weakness in his religious thinking.

So too if a believer in Christ could not muster the appropriate level of enthusiasm for the liberal-progressive project of fixing the world (*tikkum olam*). Jews had always believed that the world would indeed be fixed—when the Messiah comes. To imagine that the process of redemption had advanced further than it really had done was simply more premature messianism of which the Jews ought to have had enough by now. But "enlightened" Jews held Christians at fault for thinking, since their Messiah had already come, the world was satisfactory as it was. Joseph Klausner (1878–1958), historian and Jewish nationalist, who taught Hebrew literature at Hebrew University, wrote that "the Jews can and must march at the head of humanity on the road of personal and social progress, on the road to ethical perfection . . . The Jewish Messianic faith is the seed of progress, which has been planted by Judaism throughout the whole world."[18]

Yet for all that Jewish liberalism departs from timeless Judaism, one has to admit there is a certain inherent moral force to this facet of the liberal view that *is* authentically Jewish. The Hebrew prophets truly are harsh critics of social injustice, even in the present time before the Davidic king emerges—though this doesn't mean they thought social relations could be transformed in their entirety.

Thanks to the prophetic legacy, a Jew is necessarily a social critic, which is why Leo Baeck wrote so scathingly of Christianity's romantic longing for religious experience, its tendency to belittle its own ethical Judaic heritage. For that tendency could result in a high comfort level with injustice: "This self-assurance of the possessing . . . has also often found expression in a tranquil, comfortable, almost smug indifference. Being satisfied with itself, the Church was capable of beholding a great deal without being at all upset . . . One was prepared to overlook and discount and indulge anything: the correct faith was easily satisfied with itself; for 'whoever believes in him is just.'

"A good deal of Church history is the history of all things which neither hurt nor encroached upon this piety, all the outrages and all the baseness which this piety was able to tolerate with an assured and undisturbed soul and an untroubled faith. And a spirit is characterized not only by what it does but, no less, by what it permits, what it forgives, and what it beholds in silence."[19]

When we remember that Baeck wrote these words in the decade

before Hitler came to power in the rabbi's native Germany, where the Lutheran Church would largely bend to the wave of nationalist hatred engulfing the country, we have to admit that Baeck not only spoke in the voice of the prophets, he was something of a prophet himself.

A FIRST-RATE IDEA. Some modern Jews have not so much rejected Jesus as relativized him. If it's true, as F. Scott Fitzgerald wrote in his essay "The Crack-Up," that "the test of a first-rate intelligence is the ability to hold two opposed ideas in the mind at the same time," then early Jewish minds could not have been first-rate. It seemed to premodern Jews (and Christians) that it could not be true that both Jesus and Judaism were aligned with God's intentions. One had to accept or reject the Christian claim for Jesus. If Christ was from God, then it made little sense to continue practicing Judaism.

This seemed unarguable until Franz Rosenzweig (1886–1929) found a way to affirm the truth claims of Judaism and Christianity at once. The young German Jewish man of letters came very close to converting to Christianity himself and conducted a famous epistolary theological and philosophical disputation with his converted Jew-turned-Christian cousin Eugen Rosenstock-Huessy. On July 7, 1913, Rosenstock spent an entire night arguing with Rosenzweig, trying to bring him around, which provoked the other man to plunge deeper into the Christian and Jewish sources, to find a way to grasp what God was getting at in creating Judaism and then bringing Christianity forth from its womb. He accepted the formulation of John's Gospel that "no one comes to the Father but by the Son" (14:6) but reasoned that since he was already *with* the Father by virtue of being a Jew, he had no need for the Son. But a gentile, who was not with the Father by any inherited right to begin with, could come to the Father only by way of Jesus Christ. Thus there were two covenants, one with the Jews, one with everyone else: Judaism "relegates work in the world to the church and acknowledges that the church brings salvation for all heathens, for all time."[20] Much the same position was later adopted by the Catholic Church with Vatican II.

Rosenzweig was an impenetrable writer, whose book *The Star of Redemption* is more revered than read. In an uncharacteristic moment of clarity, he wrote, "Israel can bring the world to God only through Christianity." The Jewish philosopher Will Herberg (1901–1977), an American who taught at Drew University and was the religion editor of *National Review*, considered himself to be a disciple of Rosenzweig in the role of "representing" the master's ideas to readers, but in far more lucid style. Herberg argued that Judaism was not suited to take its message of the One God to the world. It needed an understudy, unrestricted by the bounds of Jewish law, which limited Judaism's appeal to a mass audience: "The restrictive conceptions which dominated [the early Christian] community were such that, had they triumphed, Christianity would have been doomed to remain just another Jewish sect."[21] Here is the very seed of the concept I am driving toward in this book: the blessing to the world that came about through the Jewish rejection of Jesus.

THE NEVER-ENDING DISPUTATION. So far in the modern context, we have touched on three reasons, uniquely related to the post-Reformation world, for the Jewish rejection of Jesus. We'll now turn to a theme with a lineage extending back into antiquity, that of Jewish-Christian polemic. As they did for the fifteen centuries before the modern period, Jews still argue with Christians about prophecy.

If the old theological-textual issues separating Judaism from Christianity are no longer foremost in the minds of most Jews when contemplating the other faith, that doesn't mean that in the minds of all Jews they are relegated to the background. On the contrary, the polemics that went back and forth between rabbis and priests in the Middle Ages are still heard today, in no less urgent tones.

The same prophetic passages are picked over and debated. Luther himself had his favorite texts—Genesis 49:10, 2 Samuel 23, Haggai 2, Daniel 9. The sixteenth-century Jewish polemicist Isaac Troki, whom we met in the last chapter, wrote in his *Hizzuk Emunah* ("Faith Strengthened") about an argument he had with "an eminent disciple of

Martin Luther." Troki made the interesting point that if Luther was right that Roman Catholicism promoted the worship of images, this itself was a proof that the Messiah had not yet come. Isaiah had said in reference to the promised Davidic king, "And the idols he shall utterly abolish."[22] If Jesus was this Messiah, there should be no idols to abolish.

More than three centuries later, Troki still irritated some Christians. An active and effective English Protestant polemicist of the last century, A. Lukyn Williams, composed a two-volume work devoted to answering Troki's arguments, *Christian Evidences for Jewish People* (1911, 1919). Williams also published a scholarly translation of Justin Martyr's *Dialogue with Trypho* (1930) that I have spent some time responding to in this book. And so it goes.

As ever in the polemical genre, prophecies drawn from the Hebrew Bible take center stage. However, modern Christian marketing techniques have never been more sophisticated. In the Middle Ages, churchmen saw the advantage of making their case to the Jews by means of other Jews—deploying spokesmen and debaters who were born-Jews turned Christian. So too today, when this resource has been even more cleverly exploited.

The Christian-funded missionary group Jews for Jesus, founded in San Francisco in 1970 by Baptist minister Martin ("Moishe") Rosen, is only the best-known example of ex-Jews, funded by Christians, reaching out to Jews. Since the 1970s, there has been a surge of such "Jewish Christian" activity, centered around "Messianic Jewish" congregations where Jewish window dressing (prayer shawls, yarmulkes, Yiddish and Hebrew phrases dropped strategically in proselytizing appeals) is adopted to make Jews feel comfortable worshipping Jesus, or so it's hoped, much as nineteenth-century Reform temples adopted Christian incidentals to make Jews of a very different generation and outlook feel at ease.

Missionary activity by "Jewish Christians" focuses, as ever, on extracting the meaning of Hebrew prophetic texts. In 1985, a Jewish countermissionary organization, Jews for Judaism, was founded to answer these "Christian evidences"—as A. Lukyn Williams would have put it.[23] When Messianic Jews hold conventions in hotels, representatives of Jews for Judaism will park themselves in the lobby, where, because they look Jewish, they can count on being proselytized. Scott Hillman, executive director of Jews for Judaism, told of winning over an Israeli-born "Jewish Christian" woman in a Virginia Beach hotel lobby on such an occasion. He explained to her that the famous "virgin" in Isaiah 7:14 ("Behold, a virgin shall conceive, and bear a son"— King James Version), taken by Christians as a reference to the Virgin Mary, isn't a virgin at all. Not having looked closely at the Hebrew before, she was taken aback and exclaimed, *"Mah pitom!"* ("What gives!").[24]

In his dialogue with Justin, the Jew Trypho had made the same point. Justin did not record his response to the challenge. So the basic material remains the same, yet textual arguments today have been honed, achieving new levels of plausibility. If anything, Christian arguments for Jesus are stronger now, backed up by more evidence from ancient sources than ever before.

The most comprehensive example of a recent Christian polemic runs to three volumes (of a projected four), titled *Answering Jewish Objections to Jesus*. The author is a Jew by birth, Michael L. Brown, who as a self-described sixteen-year-old heroin-shooting rock-drumming teen rebel startled his parents by accepting Jesus. That was in 1971, when he couldn't so much as read Hebrew. Today, decorated with a PhD in Near Eastern languages from New York University, Brown heads a ministry school in New York City and speaks around the country at churches, which lionize him as that very rare prize, a Jew turned Christian who knows something about Jewish traditional sources. Actually his book learning is impressive. For thirty years, he has been obsessively searching the Hebrew Bible and the Talmud for proof that Jesus was the Messiah. It's worth a pause here to glance at some of his material, because it is so representative of the stuff—if more packed with erudition—that a Jew is likely to hear even today from missionary-minded Christians.

In the volumes he has published so far, Brown addresses 124 common objections to Jesus. Here are several, with Brown's answer to the objection followed by the obvious Jewish rejoinder.

Objection: "If Jesus is really the Messiah, why isn't there peace on earth?"

Answer: Brown replies that all the famously unfulfilled prophecies (for instance, that the messianic era will be one of peace) apply to the second and final act in Jesus's career, when he returns to earth. This is a convenient and necessary dodge: The Bible itself never speaks of a two-act messianic drama. In the course of making his argument, Brown goes back to the same Talmudic passage that Nachmanides argued over with Pablo Christiani, the one about a two-thousand-year period, the "Days of the Messiah," that seemingly began about 242 CE. Brown wants to use this as a proof, which necessitates moving that date back a couple of centuries, to coincide with the appearance of Jesus—or "Yeshua," as Brown likes to call him. The details needn't detain us, but he does this by rejecting a figure, taken from Daniel 9, for the number of years the Second Temple stood, 420 years, and adjusting that to 600 years. But only eight pages later, we find Brown citing the very same verse in Daniel as if it were authoritative, divine writ. Which is to say, he very much comes from the familiar "heads I win, tails you lose" school of biblical exegesis. Is scripture to be understood in a rigorously literal way or not? Yes, when it can be turned to argumentative advantage—but no when it cannot.

Objection: "Jews don't believe in the Trinity. We believe in one God, not three."

Answer: Brown rejects Maimonides's teaching that God's unity is to be understood as absolute, as in Deuteronomy 6:4, "Hear, O Israel: the Lord our God, the Lord is the One and Only." But two pages later, we find him citing Abraham Ibn Ezra, another medieval Jewish sage, who in his comments on the same verse emphasizes a different point. Brown jumps on this, presenting the "revered" Ibn Ezra as authoritative.[35] Why? Because he is less inconvenient here than Maimonides to a Christian understanding. Again, it's heads I win, tails you lose.

Objection: "If you claim that Jesus is God, then you are guilty of making God into a man. You are an idol worshipper!"

Answer: Brown argues that there is nothing idolatrous in thinking of God's Presence being revealed on earth in a physical, material representation. For instance, the Torah describes how the "glory of the Lord" filled the Tabernacle that the Jews built in the desert after leaving Egypt. Brown asks: How is that different from Jesus? Well, it's different because the Israelites did not worship the Tabernacle. To do so would indeed have been idolatrous.

Objection: "Jews don't believe in a divine Messiah."

Answer: Brown cites Psalm 45, traditionally understood by Jews as being addressed to the future Davidic king. Read literally, verse 7 seems to address the king as "God": "Your throne, God, is forever and ever, the scepter of fairness is the scepter of your kingdom." Must be referring to Jesus, right? No. One has to understand that the psalms were written to be sung by multiple voices in combination, with different voices singing various divisions of verses in a given psalm. This is not unlike modern verse, which can make a poem like *The Waste Land* hard to follow. So a psalm, as here, may begin by addressing the king—"Gird your sword upon [your] thigh, O mighty one" (v. 4)—and then switch voices and ecstatically speak directly to God Himself—"Your throne, God, is forever and ever . . ." The immediate context would also disallow applying Psalm 45 to Jesus. Adjoining verses speak of the king as a mighty warrior and married man, with a "queen stand[ing] erect at your right in the golden jewelry of Ophir" (v. 10). Concerning the very best verse in the whole Hebrew Bible for asserting the divine nature of the Messiah, Daniel's vision of the "son of man, coming with the clouds of heaven . . . all peoples, nations and men of every language worshipped [or bowed] to him" (7:13), Brown admits that even this is "certainly debatable."[26] The Aramaic word translated as "worshipped" can also mean "bowed" or "prostrated," which would connote only reverence for royalty: King David's own wife bowed to him.[27]

Objection: "Nowhere in the Hebrew Bible are we told that we must 'believe in the Messiah.' "

Answer: Suddenly rehabilitating the previously rejected Maimonides, Brown quotes from the *Mishneh Torah* to show that Jews really have traditionally taught, as Christians do, that believing in the Messiah is a religious obligation. Writes Maimonides, "Anyone who does not believe in him, or who does not anticipate his coming, denies not only all the other prophets, but also the Torah [itself] and Moses our Teacher." So now Maimonides is authoritative—but Brown neglects to quote the rest of the passage, which defines the Messiah in terms that unambiguously would exclude Jesus: "The King Messiah is destined to arise and restore the kingdom of David to its former state and original sovereignty. He will rebuild the Temple and gather in the dispersed of Israel. All the ancient laws will be restored in his day as they were before. We will once again offer sacrifices," and so on.[28] From chapter to chapter, medieval Jewish exegetes fall in and out of Brown's favor with such rapidity that it becomes impossible to keep up. He has no criteria for deciding whether a rabbinic teaching is worthy or not other than whether or not it can be used as a support for his case. If it undermines the case for Yeshua, it must be wrong. This is the kind of reasoning that is called "circular."

Objection: "Isaiah 53 cannot refer to Jesus because it says the servant of the Lord was sickly and died of disease."

Answer: Brown contends that the much-disputed Isaiah 53 has brought more lost souls to Yeshua than any other Hebrew biblical passage. My response may seem like hairsplitting, but since Brown insists on a minutely accurate correspondence between prophecy and Jesus's career, the details need to match or else the case for Jesus as Messiah is severely wounded. Here, the passage speaks repeatedly of the servant—identified with the Messiah by some ancient Jewish sources—as a victim of disease. "He was despised and isolated from men, a man of pains and accustomed to *illness* . . . But in truth it was our *ills* that he bore . . . we had regarded him as *diseased*, stricken by God, and afflicted! . . . For he had been removed from the land of the living, an *affliction* upon them that was my people's sin . . . The Lord desired to oppress him and He *afflicted* him" (v. 3–10). Each of the italicized words in this passage has, in Hebrew, the connotation of disease. Brown correctly points out that in other contexts in the Bible, the same verbal roots are occasionally used to describe other forms of suffering—for example, being wounded by an arrow. But when in a single passage the language used by the prophet again and again is one *normally associated* with illness, it's natural to assume that Isaiah is speaking about a sick person, which Jesus was not.

Objection: "Isaiah 53 does not say the servant will rise from the dead."

Answer: Brown observes that Isaiah speaks of the "servant" suffering death but also enjoying long life. The solution, he says, must be that the Messiah will be resurrected. The passage does speak of the servant's being "removed from the land of the living" and "submitting [himself] to his grave like wicked men" (v. 8–9). That sounds like death, if rendered literally and taken out of context. However, from as early as the third century (Babylonian sage Rav Huna), Jewish tradition understood the progression from facing the grave to enjoying health, children, and prosperity—"he will see offspring and live long days and the desire of the Lord will succeed in his hand" (v. 10)—as denoting a recovery from serious illness.[29] Brown is free to insist on his literalistic reading, but then to be consistent he should also agree that his resurrected Messiah will sire children—but this ("he will see offspring") Brown insists on rendering figuratively: "This would mean that the servant of the Lord would see godly, spiritual posterity, true disciples transformed by means of his labors on their behalf."[30] In other words, heads I win, tails you lose.

Objection: "Daniel 9:24 was clearly *not* fulfilled by Jesus."

Answer: Daniel 9:22–27 concerns events that the prophet, who was among the Jewish captives in Babylon, foresaw as occurring in the last "seventy weeks" before the destruction of the Second Temple in 70 CE. The phrase *seventy weeks* is universally agreed to designate seventy periods of 7 years each, or 490 years. The sequence of years begins with the return of Daniel's compatriots to the holy land to rebuild Jerusalem. To make a most complicated argument as simple as possible, the point under dispute turns upon Daniel's statement that after 7 "weeks," followed by another 62 "weeks"—that is, 69, meaning 483 years—"the anointed one will be cut off and will exist no longer." The figure of 483 years is 490 minus 7. So the end point of the period of 69 "weeks" is 7 years before 70 CE—that is, 63 CE. Daniel prophesies that in the very end, the seventieth "week," a foreign power "will destroy the city and Sanctuary," Jerusalem and the Temple. So, concludes

Brown, "this anointed one" whom Daniel refers to—the anointed Messiah, as Brown presumes—"will be killed at some point before 63 CE." This "anointed" must be Jesus, right? No, on the contrary, he can't be Jesus. The anointed one dies *after* the year 63, as verses 25–26 make clear. But Jesus died around the year 30. The "anointed" here cannot be anyone's messiah because neither Jews nor Christians say a messiah died between 63 and 70 CE. To construe the prophecy as pointing to Jesus, Brown is obliged to argue that the 490 years actually took place over a span of 608 years, which stretches credibility and understanding beyond the legal limit. It seems far more likely that, as Daniel himself indicates, these prophecies won't be understood before they are fulfilled. As an angel told the prophet, "The matters are obscured and sealed until the time of the End."[31]

Objection: "Zechariah 12:10 has nothing to do with Jesus."

Answer: Zechariah was among the Jews after Daniel's time who returned to Israel to rebuild the Temple. Among his many highly esoteric statements we find the following, apparently referring to the End time. Says God, "It shall be on that day I will seek to destroy all the nations that come upon Jerusalem. I will pour out upon the house of David and upon the inhabitants of Jerusalem a spirit of grace and supplications. They will look toward Me whom [or "because of whom"] they have stabbed; they will mourn over him as one mourns over an only child . . ."[32] According to Brown, the "only child" must be Jesus, whom the "inhabitants of Jerusalem" stabbed or "pierced." He writes, "So, the Scripture is saying that the Jewish people will be in mourning for one whom they pierced and killed."[33] The problem with construing the verses this way is that even by the New Testament's account, it wasn't the Jews who pierced Jesus with nails and a spear at the Crucifixion; it was the Romans (John 19:34, 37). Again, this may seem like nitpicking, but when polemicists like Brown insist on finding justification for the most fundamental beliefs in apparent throwaway lines in the Hebrew prophets, fastening on to and interpreting scriptural nits, then a Jew can only respond in kind.

Objection: "Jesus fulfilled none of the messianic prophecies!"

Answer: In the tradition of earlier Christian polemicists, Brown replies to this sweeping Jewish objection to Jesus with a lengthy catalog of prophetic verses that Jesus supposedly fulfilled. However, looked at closely, these prophecies almost always include things that not even the Gospels say that Jesus did. Thus, Brown shows from Isaiah 35:5–7 that the Messiah "performed miraculous deeds of deliverance and healing." But the same passage has the Messiah rejuvenating a ravaged physical environment: "The scorched place will become a pond and the parched place a spring of water; the abode where jackals rested will become grassland with reeds and bulrushes" (v. 7). Brown shows from Isaiah 42:4 that distant nations "will long for his teaching." And indeed, many people in countries around the world today seek out Christian teachings. But the very same verse says he will "set justice in the land," meaning the holy land, which Jesus did not do. Brown shows from Isaiah 49:6 that the Messiah will be "a light to the nations." But again in the same verse, the same exalted personality is credited with "restor[ing] the ruins of Israel." Brown thinks that he shows from Zechariah 9:9 that the Messiah will "suffer before his exaltation."[34] Actually, that verse says only that the messianic "king" will be "a humble man riding upon a donkey." Anyway, the next verse has the same messianic personage ruling "from sea to sea" while God eliminates "the bow of warfare" (v. 10)—a description inapplicable to Jesus and his accomplishments. Brown thinks he shows from Psalm 78:2 that the Messiah will speak in parables, as Jesus did. But nothing in the psalm—"I will open my mouth with a parable, I will utter [and explain] riddles from antiquity"—even hints that the parable teller is anyone other than the psalm's author, identified in the previous verse as Asaph, a Levite musician in David's kingdom.[35]

And so on and on. I have devoted considerable space to Brown's replies to Jewish objections to demonstrate an important truth. To everything I've said here, this remarkably smart man would have his own reply. And we could go on arguing, back and forth, ad infinitum. He does prove that it is possible to *construe* the Hebrew prophets as pointing to Jesus. This requires much twisting and turning of their words, but it obviously can be done. I say "obviously" because if the Hebrew Bible could not be manipulated in this way to produce "Christian evidences," if this could not be accomplished to the satisfaction of many people, including many intelligent people, then there would be no Christianity. The fact that there is such a thing as the Christian religion itself indicates that there is enough ambiguity, enough veiled and cryptic language in the prophets, to allow scripture to be so construed.

But the amount of intellectual heavy lifting this requires, the groans of strained interpretations, provides one of the best answers to the question we have set ourselves in this book. The Jews rejected the Christian claim for Jesus in large part because if God wanted them to see the true Messiah in Jesus, if in fact their eternal salvation was dependent on their making this identification, then He would have made it much clearer, far less open to doubt. God is fair, after all. To think that He wants Jews to abandon the Torah and its commandments on the basis of an interpretation of the prophets that seems so arguable, so tenuous—well, that's just very hard to believe.

So perhaps it shouldn't surprise us, incidentally, that for all the efforts of Jews for Jesus and their cohorts, the success of such Jewish-led Christian missionary drives has been modest. This becomes clear when you figure it on a dollars-per-convert basis. As I was writing this book, Jews for Jesus was engaged in a $10 million international campaign called Behold Your God. About a third of the way into a conversionary push expected to hit sixty-six Diaspora cities, the group claimed to have made 448 converts in nineteen cities, though only 31 converts in the United States itself. At that rate, Jews for Jesus could expect to harvest 1,556 new "Jewish Christians," at $6,427 per Jew.

This is assuming that the "Jews" being converted were actually Jewish to begin with—a doubtful proposition. Many of those who attend Jewish-Christian congregational services were born gentiles. This began to dawn on me when I paid a visit to the Messianic synagogue in my area, near Seattle. Congregation Beit Tikvah is led by the earnest and genial Rabbi Hylan Slobodin, who tells me that of the two hundred or so people who attend services at Beit Tikvah, about 2 percent are Jewish—mirroring the Jewish demography of Seattle, he points out.

One of the notable things about those Jews who do get hooked by the "Jewish-Christian" exegesis of the Hebrew prophets is that, like Rabbi Slobodin, almost all come from backgrounds of very minimal Jewish education. This was not so in the past, when pressures threatening one's livelihood, or life itself, induced even Jews who knew a lot about Judaism to be baptized.

Slobodin claims no formal Jewish learning at all ("like the rabbis of old," he says). At one point as we're talking his cell phone rings, playing "Hava Nagila," a Jewish tune often heard at bar mitzvahs. He asks me, "Do you know what that song is?" It's his wife, Rita, calling, and he punctuates his part of the conversation with Yiddish and Hebrew exclamations, the kind you'd learn in an afternoon Hebrew school program, "*Nu? . . . Lo . . . Efo? . . . Ken, ken, ken.*" ("So? . . . No . . . Where? . . . Yes, yes, yes.") When I inquire whether or not any of his congregants ever ask him to *posken* for them—that is, to answer questions having to do with Jewish ethics and law, something rabbis traditionally spend a lot of time doing—he says, "What's that?"

A recent issue of the Evangelical Christian magazine *World* poignantly illustrates how innocent Jewish Christians tend to be. Edited by Marvin Olasky, a Jew who was raised to be an unbeliever by his socialist parents but who subsequently became "born again," the special edition was devoted to exploring the tension between Judaism and Christianity. On the cover, Olasky placed a photo of a decrepit old man wearing phylacteries and a scowl—the archetypal religious Jew in the minds of those who understand Judaism to be only a mummified fossil. A centerpiece feature in the issue listed Jews through the ages who converted to Christianity, with capsule biographies. Those from Europe when it was at its most dangerously anti-Semitic included many who had been educated as Jews, but those from recent years, from America, were almost all individuals who gave up Judaism without ever knowing what they had left behind.[36]

This, curiously, is in contrast with those former Christians one meets today who are converts to traditional Judaism. Before considering Judaism, most of the ones I have talked to were intensely committed to and educated in their Christian faith. These new Jews rejected Jesus because, as Christians, they perceived how imperfectly their own inherited religion sits on its presumed Old Testament base, like a statue that has been placed precariously on the wrong-shaped pedestal. As Christians, they knew too much, understood too well.

A KINGDOM OF PRIESTS

So far, we have discussed a number of the reasons Jews have given for not accepting Jesus as their Messiah. The sheer variety of these is itself striking, even suspicious. If I ask a friend why he chose to act a certain way on a certain occasion, and if he proceeds to give me not one reason but thirty, I'm likely to doubt that he is being entirely frank with me or possibly with himself. This is not to say that our decisions in life, particularly the important ones, can be motivated by only one or two considerations. People are complicated. But the more rationales somebody gives in explaining himself, the more one tends to wonder if something else is going on. Very possibly he was driven by some desire or fear, love or hate, of which even he may not be consciously aware. Alternatively, he may feel that if he were to confess his one and only true motivation, his listener might not find this convincing enough, so he piles on with thirty other possible justifications.

So it is with the Jews and Jesus. You would be right at this point in wondering if any of the reasons we have touched on so far is the real one for the Jewish rejection of Christ, or if maybe only one of these is the ultimate reason while the rest are secondary.

I would like to try to answer this question in a theological, a mystical, and finally a historical way. They all come down to the same ultimate truth. All the reasons we have considered so far are genuine and substantive, but they may not be ultimate.

Theologically, we may put the truth in one word: Sinai. Jews have always considered the meaning of their existence to be summarized in the event before the Mountain of God where they encamped, three months after leaving Egypt, to hear God's commandments. It was the moment of birth for the Jewish people. On that occasion, the Lord introduced himself to the people this way: "You have seen what I did to Egypt, and that I have borne you on wings of eagles and brought you to Me. And now, if you hearken well to Me and observe My covenant, you shall be to Me a kingdom of priests and a holy nation."[1]

The covenant—the commandments—was the reason God brought the Jews to meet Him. There is no other purpose to Jewish existence. There is no other purpose to *human* existence. The Jews have long believed that the universe remains in existence only because they accepted the Torah, which obligated them to be "a kingdom of priests," ministering to other peoples, teaching them about God. The commandments were simply the terms of this relationship with God that Israel now entered into.

To abandon those commandments was to abandon the whole meaning of Jewish existence. To give them up, you had to have an awfully good reason. Jews who ceased to believe in God had a reason. But Christianity had none that was satisfying. Accepting Christ, as his message was preached by Paul, means abrogating the commandments. Beyond the one solitary verse that could be understood as God's promising a new covenant—Jeremiah 31:31, which we have seen that Christians misconstrued—the Hebrew Bible offers no escape clause from the Jewish mission. If God really intended the Jews to regard themselves as "dead" (as Paul put it) to the Sinai covenant, surely He ought to have made this crystal clear, repeated and emphasized it over and over, in that part of scripture that, when Paul came along, the Jews already regarded as authoritative. Paul declared the covenant a "curse" on his own authority. Jews could not accept this. Everything else Christians might argue on behalf of Jesus as Messiah, all the other rhetorical points they lodged in their disputations and pamphlets and polemics and apologetics, falls away before this simple fact. No authentic Messiah would inspire a religion that ended up calling upon the Jews to reject the manifest meaning of Sinai. It is really that simple.

You may ask, If it's so simple, why don't Christians see this problem? An answer was suggested to me, indirectly, by the Reverend Billy Graham. In a newspaper column, the great evangelist was asked a good question. A woman wrote to him saying that she was just now getting interested in the Christian faith and had set herself the task of reading the Bible. She'd started out with Genesis and Exodus and found their narratives stirring, but she got bogged down in Leviticus, with its myriad laws of the Jewish priesthood. Reverend Graham replied with the recommendation that she skip the rest of the Hebrew Bible for now. She should start her reading of the Bible with the New Testament.

It was shrewd advice. Christians see the Sinai covenant as they do because they read the New Testament first. Literally, they tend to read it first in their religious education. And metaphorically, they valorize it above the Hebrew Bible. They begin with the assumptions of the New Testament, which form the lens through which they contemplate the "Old Testament." One of those assumptions is that the "old covenant" is not God's ultimate, overriding directive to the Jews. Paul's substitution of Christ for the Torah, as the focal point of religious experience, colors everything a Christian sees in the Hebrew Bible.

But it doesn't for a Jew, at least not for a Jew who absorbed the Hebrew Bible and *its* assumptions before evaluating the offer of Jesus as Messiah. A Jew reads the Hebrew scriptures first. This was even truer of those who personally heard Jesus or Paul teach than it is today. For a Jew, it is the New Testament that must prove its compatibility with the Hebrew Bible. And on this crucial point, keeping the commandments or abrogating them, it cannot do so.

MYSTICALLY, SINAI ALSO IS the key to our puzzle. The Talmud in its tractate *Avodah Zarah* has a curiously self-deprecating image of the Jewish people. When God brought Israel to Sinai, it is said, they were not His first choice. He had first offered the covenant to every other people on earth, but they all turned it down. So much for the "chosen people"!

A great rabbinic sage of the modern period, Judah Loew (called Maharal, died 1609), explained what this really means. He was the leader of the Prague Jewish community (and the legendary creator of the *golem*, a humanoid whom he made to live by inscribing God's name on the creature's forehead). Does the Talmud mean us to understand that God literally went from country to country like a Mormon missionary? No, instead the Talmud intends to convey an esoteric truth: "The meaning is that He examined their character, to see if they possessed a predisposition to the Torah, and did not find it in them, and this constituted their refusal."[2]

From this we are not to draw any conclusion about Jewish superiority: Remember, the Talmudic source text is precisely the one that knocks Jewish pride down a lot of notches by telling Jews they were really the last chosen. Rather, what Maharal conveys is the mystic uniqueness of the Jewish essence or nature. There is something distinct about the Jewish soul.

What this has to do with the rejection of Christianity was made clear by the Jewish thinker who, more than any other, is still read by Christians for inspiration. Martin Buber (1878–1965) was, like his contemporary Leo Baeck, a leader of the German Jewish community before World War II. He was called on to debate increasingly Nazified Christians in modern-day disputations. On one occasion in 1930, he addressed a group of German missionaries to the Jews in Stuttgart. He spoke to them about what he regarded as the uniqueness of the Jewish soul that accounted for the fact that he and other Jews were not lining up to accept Jesus.

Like Maharal, Buber saw the special essence of the Jewish soul as having preexisted Sinai: "It is the soul which approached Sinai, and there received what it did receive." Appreciable only from within Judaism, the Jewish soul was unique in two ways. First, by its nature it sees God as at once "beyond the grasp of man, and yet . . . present in an immediate relationship with these human beings who are absolutely incommensurable with him." Second, also by nature the Jewish soul feels the worlds, in a remarkably visceral way, as unredeemed: "He feels this lack of redemption against his skin, he tastes it on his tongue, the burden of the unredeemed world lies on him. Because of this almost physical knowledge of his, he cannot concede that the redemption has taken place, he knows that it has not."

Taken together, these "foci of the Jewish soul" tend to rule out an acceptance of Jesus as Messiah. The first precludes a belief in the Incarnation, God walking as a man on earth, a foreign concept that violates what the Jew knows about the transcendent yet immediately present God. The second precludes the Christian opinion that the Messiah has already come to redeem the world.

Nor is it only religiously observant or knowledgeable Jews who feel these things as surely as you feel anything that brushes your skin or touches your tongue: "These two foci of the Jewish soul continue to exist for the 'secularized' Jew too, insofar as he has not lost his soul."³ This is precisely because they preexist Sinai. The Jews brought these "foci" with them to God's Mountain. Because of this twofold essence of the Jewish soul, in the presence of Jesus worship, with rare exceptions, "secular" and "religious" Jews alike feel the same reaction, the same refusal, the same instinctive turning away. In a word: No.

IF THE TALMUD, Maharal, and Martin Buber are right, does this mean that the Jewish essence is, at its heart, merely a negation? Does it not serve a positive, constructive purpose? The answer is found in history, the history of Judaism and of Christianity.

The Jewish rejection of Jesus was the founding act of Western civilization. Had the Jews welcomed the Christian message, at any stage prior to the crucial council of Jerusalem at which Peter and James accepted Paul's belief that it was time to drop Jewish law from the requirements placed on Christians, the Jesus movement would have remained a Jewish sect with all the handicaps that implies. Unlike Christianity, and also unlike Islam, Judaism was never intended or suited to be a mass religion. Had the Jews embraced the Gospel of Jesus Christ in greater numbers, there would be no Christian Europe.

When Islam, that other daughter faith of Judaism, arose in the seventh century, its armies would have confronted a Europe that was a spiritual vacuum, which Muhammad's teachings would likely have filled. The book that the Muslim prophet composed, the Koran, would still include, as it does today, its occasional admiring references to Jesus as a Jewish prophet. The Christian faith would never have spread across the Atlantic Ocean to the Americas. The history of the United States as we know it, among other things, would be unthinkable.

If the historian Rodney Stark is correct in attributing the progress of Western science to the belief system of the Bible, then our world would be a poorer, less scientifically advanced one, not unlike the Muslim nations today would be, were it not for the technology they import from the nations of Europe and North America, cultures nourished on the Bible.

I am speculating here that it was the essence of the Jewish soul, and the fact that Jews read the Hebrew Bible before contemplating the doctrines of the New Testament, that more than anything else accounts for that civilization-creating act, the rejection of Christ. All the other reasons given by the Jews over the centuries helped them explain to themselves why they had done this thing that continued to distress and appall their Christian neighbors.

But I think we can crystallize even further the reasons for the Jewish rejection of Christ—if we try to look at it from God's perspective.

Recall His introduction to the Sinai covenant: "And now, if you hearken well to Me and observe My covenant, you shall be to Me a kingdom of priests and a holy nation." As we noted in the last chapter, the sixteenth-century scholar Rabbi Ovadiah Sforno summarized the Jewish understanding of the verse as a call, a mission, to share God with other peoples: "to instruct all of mankind to call in unison on the Name of the Lord and to serve Him with one accord." Being a "kingdom of priests" means ministering to others in a priestly role, for who can claim to be a priest if he has no congregation? God's instruction to the Jews at the moment of the revelation of the Torah was to serve the congregation of humanity, bringing the knowledge of the Lord to them.

It would seem the Christian church now plays the role of congregation, as the Muslim *umma* also does, with the Jews serving in the ministerial position. Christians and Muslims alike know of the God of Abraham only because they met Him in the Bible. Except the priests and the congregants don't always realize that they are playing this role—though sometimes a religious personality arises who does see this picture clearly. One such figure, another Italian sage, the rabbi and mystic Elijah Benamozegh (1823–1900), wrote that in the phrase *kingdom of priests* we find Judaism's universal mission: "For inasmuch as priests are ordained only for the sake of the laity, the priesthood of Jews presupposes a mankind in whose service the Jews have been placed by Providence . . . Israel calls the Lord *its* God because in worshipping Him it worships the God which it has been called upon to make known to all men."[4]

But it was not God's intention that all the congregation serve Him in the same way: "Unlike Paul, we do not say of this Providence that it knows neither Jews nor Greeks, for that implies an inadmissible leveling of differences, a suppression of all nationality. We affirm, rather, that Providence recognizes equally Jews, Greeks, and Barbarians—in a word, all races and peoples, who ought to be perceived as one though without losing their individual identity."[5]

It served God's purposes that there be a unique religion, acknowledging Him, for the people who spread out from Europe. It was not Judaism. It departs from Judaism in many ways. But in revering the God of Israel, it contains the seeds for an ultimate reunification of the peoples in God's service. Someday, as the prophet Zechariah proclaimed and as Jews traditionally affirm three times daily in the prayer *Alenu*, "The Lord will be King over all the land; on that day the Lord will be One and His Name will be One."[6]

We may wonder at the need for a tension, sometimes a very painful one, between the two faiths. For centuries, Jews and Christians reviled each other. But however unpleasant, this too was indispensable to God's plan. There must be a priesthood and there must be a laity. Attempts to reduce the level of tension have often led to disaster. Moses Mendelssohn sought to evade the confrontation with Christianity. He valued tolerance more than truth. And four of his six children became Christians. His grandson Felix Mendelssohn became the greatest composer of Christian music of his time. In this family, the priesthood evaporated into the congregation.

The Jewish rejection of Christ made possible the sublime culture of Europe in which Felix Mendelssohn flourished, as well as the sublime politics of America whose blessings we enjoy. This act, initiated in 30 CE, which goes on and is reaffirmed daily by millions of Jews who live among fellow citizens who would be ecstatic to see them join the church, makes possible our lives as we know them. For that, thank the Jews.

ACKNOWLEDGMENTS

Not everyone who has been of help to me in writing this book will necessarily want to be acknowledged as having done so. This is because not everyone, including not every Jew, shares my certainty that now is the time to open a discussion with Christians about the reasons for the Jewish rejection of Jesus. I respect their dissenting viewpoint, even as I disagree with it. Rather than try to distinguish those who do share my perspective from those who don't, I will only note that nothing I say here should be understood as an indication of what opinion anyone mentioned happens to hold.

I owe much gratitude to Rabbis Daniel Lapin, Jacob Neusner, David Berger, and Meir Soloveichik, for their inspiration, instruction, friendship, and generosity. My editor, Adam Bellow, watched out for my best interests in every way, most notably in providing the clearest and wisest guidance in developing and improving this book at every stage. He was ably assisted, as I was, by Jenny Choi and Dan Feder. Other editors encouraged the development of ideas that appear in this book but that were printed elsewhere in various earlier forms: Michael Potemra of *National Review*; J. J. Goldberg, Oren Rawls, and Daniel Treiman of the *Forward*; Laura Sheahen and Rebecca Phillips of Beliefnet; Susan Brenneman of the *Los Angeles Times*; and Lee Moriwaki of the *Seattle Times*. As in previous books, I have often relied on the translations and elucidations of classical Jewish texts from the team of scholars at Artscroll, that most amazing of Jewish publishing companies. My agent and dear friend, Milly Marmur, has believed in me from the start. Gavriel Sanders and Paula Fredriksen offered valuable suggestions early on. Michael and Diane Medved, Alex Abrams, Mark

Miller, and Bennett Schneir are wonderful friends and sources of insight, and have been so not only as I was writing this book but over the years and over the decades. In my work, I have depended on the kindness of other incredibly generous and supportive friends who provided not only good company but office space without which I don't know what I would have done: Rabbi Lapin, Paul and Michele Isherwood, Bruce Chapman, and Jay Richards.

My father, Paul Kaye, has been a source of every type of support for as long as I can remember. My children, Ezra and Naomi, are lights in my life. Above all, my loving and beloved wife, Nika, creates a home full of sweetness, stimulation, comfort, and good cheer.

NOTES

INTRODUCTION. THANK THE JEWS

1   Isa. 45:3.
2   B. Ketubot 111a.
3   Acts 13:46.

1. BEFORE CHRIST

1   Luke 4:22.
2   Ibid. 4:28.
3   Matt. 7:28–29.
4   Luke 6:30.
5   Matt. 12:14.
6   Mark 3:6.
7   John 5:16.
8   Jer. 8:11, 15.
9   *Jewish Antiquities*, 18:58–59.
10   Josephus, *Jewish War* 2:165.
11   Ibid.
12   Josephus, *Jewish Antiquities* 18:12–15.
13   See B. Sotah 20a, 22b.
14   Deut. 18:15.
15   *Jewish War* 2:261–63.
16   The figure of four hundred is from Acts 5:36; Josephus tells the story of Theudas in *Antiquities* 20:97–99.
17   John 5:46–47.
18   Sifra on Lev. 25:1.
19   Where sages are on record as disagreeing with one another, it is assumed that

there is truth in all their opinions. God communicates paradoxical truths through such seemingly contradictory statements.

20   M. Shabbat 7:2.
21   M. Avot 3:14.
22   Genesis Rabbah 1:1.
23   *Jewish War* 1:154ff.
24   Deut. 4:15–16.
25   Ibid. 5:7, 9.
26   Ibid. 4:24.
27   Ibid. 6:15.
28   Ibid. 29:19.
29   Ibid. 4:35.
30   Ibid. 4:39.
31   Ibid. 32:39.
32   Ibid. 6:4.
33   Ibid. 6:5–6.
34   Deut. 4:5–6.
35   Ibid. 4:40.
36   Ibid. 6:2.
37   Ibid. 8:6.
38   Ibid. 11:8.
39   Ibid. 11:1.
40   Ibid. 5:10.
41   Ibid. 29:13–14.
42   Ibid. 4:2.
43   Ibid. 13:1.
44   Ibid. 30:11–14; also see Sanders, *Jesus and Judaism*, pp. 190–91.
45   Ibid. 13:2–6; cf. the promise of a true prophet, 18:15, like Moses; but not his equal, 34:10.
46   Ibid. 32:21.
47   Ibid. 30:2, 4–5.
48   Ibid. 30:6, 8.
49   1 Chron. 16:15, 17.
50   Ps. 111:9.
51   Ibid. 105:8–9.
52   Ibid. 1:1–2.
53   Ibid. 19:8, 11.
54   Ibid. 119:47–48, 97, 27.
55   Jer. 7:22–23.
56   Isa. 1:11, 13.
57   Ibid. 1:15.

58   Isa. 45:1.

59   Hab. 3:13.

60   Dan. 9:26.

61   Gen. 17:14; Exod. 12:15ff., 31:14; Lev. 7:20ff., 18:29, 22:3, 23:29; Num. 19:20. It is ironic that Christians apply Daniel 9:26 to their savior.

62   Gen. 49:10.

63   2 Sam. 7:12–16.

64   Micah 5:1–4.

65   Isa. 2:2–4.

66   Ezek. 36:24–27, 33.

67   Ibid. 41:1–2, 7–8.

68   Ibid. 37:28.

69   Ibid. 37:21–26.

70   Amos 3:7.

71   Jer. 31:30–32.

72   Ibid. 31:35–36.

73   Ezek. 11:17–20.

74   Isa. 1:17.

75   Jer. 17:21.

76   Ezek. 18:6.

77   Mal. 2:11–12.

78   Zech. 14:16.

79   Mal. 3:22.

80   Dan. 11:14.

81   Ps. 146:3.

82   Num. 23:19

2. FIRST ENCOUNTER

1   *Antiquities* 18:63–64.

2   An allusion to Jesus in a version of the *Jewish War* preserved in Old Church Slavonic is even more dubious than the one in the *Antiquities*.

3   Isa. 1:21.

4   Jer. 3:1–2.

5   Y. Shabbat 15d.

6   See John 7, and see Vermes, *Jesus the Jew*, pp. 52–57.

7   *Antiquities* 18:118.

8   Mark 3:6.

9   Matt. 14:21, 15:38.

10   John 7:31, 12:19.

11 Matt. 8:28.

12 Luke 10:13–15.

13 Mark 13:9.

14 John 8:59, 10:31.

15 John 19:6.

16 Matt. 10:32–33.

17 Luke 10:16.

18 John 3:18.

19 Vermes, *Jesus the Jew*, p. 22.

20 Jaynes, *The Origin of Consciousness in the Breakdown of the Bicameral Mind*, pp. 232–33.

21 Matt. 4:24.

22 Mark 5:1–13.

23 Matt. 12:24.

24 B. Baba Metzia 86a.

25 M. Avot 5:6.

26 B. Berachot 6a.

27 Ibid.

28 B. Shabbat 67a.

29 *Antiquities* 8:46–47.

30 B. Pesachim 112b.

31 M. Taanit 3:8.

32 M. Sotah 9:15.

33 Luke 24:19; Matt. 11:20; Acts 2:22.

34 B. Berachot 34b.

35 Ibid. 33a.

36 B. Megillah 7b.

37 M. Sotah 9:15.

38 Wilson, *Our Father Abraham: Jewish Roots of the Christian Faith*, p. 40.

39 Sanders, *Jesus and Judaism*, p. 55.

40 Matt. 5:17–19.

41 I heard this explanation from Rabbi Daniel Lapin.

42 John 5:8, 10.

43 Ibid. 9:16.

44 See M. Shabbat 14:3, Yoma 8:6.

45 M. Shabbat 7:2.

46 Mark 3:23, Matt. 12:1.

47 B. Berachot 6a, a *tannaitic* teaching of about the same vintage as the Mishnah.

48 Matt. 6:6.

49 M. Yoma 8:1.

50 Matt. 6:17.

51   M. Berachot 3:1.

52   Matt. 8:22, Luke 9:60.

53   Matt. 17:26–27.

54   Mark 7:8; also Matt. 15:9.

55   M. Shabbat 19:2.

56   John 7:23.

57   Matt. 15:7, 9

58   Luke 11:46

59   Matt. 7:28–29; also see Mark 1:22, 11:18; Luke 4:32.

60   M. Avot 2:14; the derivation of the word *apicuros* is debated in rabbinic literature.

61   Matt. 16:16–17.

62   Matt. 26:64; Luke 22:70.

63   Mark 14:62.

64   John 4:25–26.

65   *Jewish War* 6:312.

66   Vermes, *Jesus the Jew*, p. 132.

67   Ibid., p. 134.

68   John 18:36.

69   Matt. 16:28; see also Matt. 24:34; Mark 14:30; Luke 9:27, 10:9.

70   See Fredriksen, *Jesus of Nazareth*, p. 89.

71   Luke 17:20–21, 21:27.

72   Deut. 13:2–4, 18:22.

73   Nor is the problem solved by Luke's alternative genealogy tracing Jesus's forebears back to David.

74   John 7:42.

75   Matt. 1:23; citing Isa. 7:14.

76   Matt. 1:18.

77   Matt. 2:18, citing Jer. 31:14.

78   Matt. 2:15.

79   Matt. 2:23.

80   Isa. 11:1.

81   Wilson, *Jesus: A Life*, p. xvi.

82   2 Cor. 4:4; Col. 1:15.

83   Matt. 28:19.

84   See Vermes, *Jesus the Jew*, pp. 192–213, for an extensive discussion on which I've relied here.

85   Mark 3:11, Matt. 14:33.

86   John 11:30–31; in a similar vein, see 5:18, 14:9–10.

87   2 Sam. 7:14.

88   Ps. 2:7.

89   Ps. 86:9, 72:11.

90   Dan. 7:13–14.

91   Gen. 33:3.

92   Matt. 24:30; also see 26:64; Mark 13:26, 14:62; Luke 21:27.

93   Matt. 24:34.

3. FATAL ATTRACTION

1   John 19:6.

2   Matt. 27:24–25.

3   Deut. 21:22–23.

4   B. Sanhedrin 43a; also see Sanhedrin 107b and Sotah 47a.

5   Deut. 13:7ff.

6   M. Sanhedrin 6:4; the other sages are quoted as slightly disagreeing with Rabbi Eliezer, saying that only a blasphemer and an idolater are hung from such a cross after being stoned. By tradition, the practice in this case would follow the sages.

7   Josephus, *Jewish War* 1:88.

8   Fredriksen, *Jesus of Nazareth*, p. 254.

9   B. Shabbat 15a; John 19:31.

10   Matt. 26:64; Dan. 7:13.

11   So the affirmation appears in Mark 14:62; in other Gospel versions, Jesus's reply is ambiguous.

12   2 Sam. 7:14.

13   M. Sanhedrin 7:5.

14   B. Sanhedrin 43a, 107b.

15   B. Shabbat 104b, where Jesus is called "Ben Stada." R. Travers Herford writes, "There can be no reasonable doubt that the 'Jeshu' [Jesus] who is variously called Ben Stada and Ben Pandira is the historical Jesus, the founder of Christianity."

16   B. Sanhedrin 106a.

17   See Goldstein, *Jesus in the Jewish Tradition*, pp. 148–54.

18   Matt. 21:9.

19   Ibid. 21:4–5.

20   Isa. 62:11; Zech. 9:9.

21   Zech. 9:10.

22   Matt. 27:1, 22–23.

23   Matt. 13:14–15.

24   Isa. 6:9ff.

25   John 12:37–40.

26 Luke 22:37; also see Mark 15:28.

27 Isa. 53:3–5.

28 Ibid. 53:11–12.

29 Ibid. 49:3.

30 Ibid. 44:1.

31 Ibid. 44:2.

32 Jacob, the third patriarch, son of Isaac and grandson of Abraham, was also called Israel and gave his name to the people Israel. For the name "Jeshurun," see Deut. 32:15; 33:5, 26.

33 Isa. 53:7.

34 Ps. 44:23, 8.

35 Isa. 53:10.

36 Ps. 22:19; see Matt. 27:35, Mark 15:24, Luke 23:34, John 19:24.

37 John 19:37, citing Zech. 12:10.

38 John 19:36.

39 Zech. 12:10.

40 B. Sukkah 52a.

41 B. Sanhedrin 98b.

42 Obadiah 1:18; see B. Baba Batra 123b.

43 Luke 24:44–46.

44 Hosea 6:1–2.

4. A NEW RELIGION

1 Acts 8:1.

2 See Acts 5:1–11.

3 Quoted in Eusebius, *History of the Church* 2:23; Hegesippus's works are mostly lost except for fragments preserved in other books, notably Eusebius's.

4 This is the convincing view set forth by P. Travers Herford in his classic book *Christianity in Talmud and Midrash*.

5 See Alon, *The Jews in Their Land in the Talmudic Age,* pp. 298–300.

6 Ibid. 13:45.

7 Ibid. 18:6.

8 Ibid. 14:19.

9 2 Cor. 11:24–25.

10 Acts 28:25–28.

11 Ibid. 13:46.

12 Ibid. 18:6.

13 Acts 22:3.

14 Ibid. 23:6, 24:14.

15 Gal. 1:14.

16 Phil. 3:5–6.

17 B. Berachot 16b.

18 Maccoby, *The Mythmaker: Paul and the Invention of Christianity*, p. 96.

19 Ibid., p. 70. For a telling example of how Paul's Hebrew illiteracy shaped his understanding of the Bible, which in turn informed the Christian understanding, see Sanders, *Paul and Palestinian Judaism*, p. 137.

20 Acts 4:13.

21 1 Thes. 4:16–17.

22 Gal. 2:12.

23 Acts 15:5.

24 Ibid. 15:12.

25 Eccl. 9:7, 12:13.

26 M. Sanhedrin 10:1.

27 E. P. Sanders makes this all clear in his book *Paul and Palestinian Judaism*.

28 Acts 9:18–22.

29 Ibid. 18:28.

30 Ibid. 17:2–5.

31 Acts 8:26–35, referring to Isa. 53:7.

32 M. Avot 1:16.

33 Acts 18:12–15.

34 1 Cor. 8:6.

35 Gen. 1:26.

36 Genesis Rabbah 8:11, B. Chagigah 16a.

37 Acts 13:45, 50; see also 17:5.

38 Ibid. 15:1.

39 Ps. 9:18; the discussion is presented in B. Sandhedrin 105a.

40 See Maimondes, *Mishneh Torah, Hilchot Melachim* 8:11.

41 The Talmud finds all seven categories of moral precepts encoded in a single verse in the Bible's story of the creation of Adam: "And the Lord God commanded the man, saying, 'Of every tree of the garden you may freely eat' " (Gen. 2:16). See B. Sanhedrin 56b. While these rabbinic teachings were recorded in the Talmud centuries after Paul died, they surely originated long before. The rabbis were not isolated from the gentile world. It is inconceivable that by Paul's time they had still failed to reflect on what awaited their fellow men, apart from their fellow Jews, in the afterlife.

42 Ps. 105:8–9, 111:9; 1 Chron. 16:15, 17.

43 Acts 21:21, 27–28.

44 Rom. 2:29.

45 Lev. 12:3.

46 Col. 2:22.

47 Rom. 4:31.

48 Ibid. 7:7.

49 Ibid. 7:19.

50 Ibid. 7:6.

51 Ibid. 10:4.

52 Ibid. 14:14.

53 I Cor. 9:20, 22.

54 Ps. 111:9.

55 Hab. 2:4. See B. Makkot 23b–24a, cf. Gal. 3:11, also Heb. 10:38, which deploys the same verse.

56 Moore, *Judaism in the First Centuries of the Christian Era: The Age of the Tannaim*, vol. 3, pp. 150–51.

57 Gal. 3:10.

58 See B. Sanhedrin 81a.

59 Ps. 103:10.

60 Ibid. 143:2.

61 I Chr. 21:13.

62 Heb. 9:22.

63 I Kings 8:47–50.

64 Sanders, *Paul and Palestinian Judaism*, p. 443.

65 Gal. 3:13.

66 Rom. 7:19.

67 Remember that where the Hebrew Bible speaks of God's "Torah," the Greek Bible that Paul read misleadingly translated that word as "the Law." It does not mean "law," with all that word conveys of hidebound stuffiness, but rather "teaching."

68 For similar expressions in the same book, see Ps. 1:2; 19:8, 11; 34:12–15; 37:31; 94:12; 147:20.

69 Deut. 20:19.

70 Ex. 15:25.

71 I heard this explanation of the image of Marah and its waters from Rabbi Daniel Lapin.

72 Gal. 3:14.

73 Quoted in Maccoby, *The Mythmaker: Paul and the Invention of Christianity*, p. 182.

74 B. Berachot 28b.

75 Frend, *The Early Church*, p. 36.

76 B. Shabbat 116a.

77 B. Yoma 39b.

78 Of course, Christians have taken the opposite view—that the portents and the destruction were due not to the acceptance of Christianity by some Jews, but

to the death of Jesus at the instigation of his fellow Jews. Eusebius (c. 260–339 CE) writes in his *History of the Church* that God, for inscrutable reasons, granted the Jews a forty years' stay of execution before bringing the Roman whirlwind. The martyrdom of James, Jesus's brother, at Jewish hands was the last straw.

79 Lamentations Rabbah 1:1.

5. AFTER CHRIST, BEFORE CONSTANTINE

1 Eusebius, *History of the Church* 4:5.

2 See Frend, *The Early Church*, p. 24.

3 For an extended discussion of the issue at hand, in which Johnson is quoted, see Stark, *The Rise of Christianity: A Sociologist Reconsiders History*, pp. 49–71.

4 *History of the Church* 4:18.

5 Justin Martyr, *Dialogue with Trypho* 1:1.

6 Ibid. 34:3.

7 Amos 5:21.

8 Ibid. 5:23.

9 Eze. 20:25.

10 Ibid. 20:21.

11 Ibid. 13:3.

12 *Dialogue with Trypho* 57:1.

13 Ibid. 142:1.

14 See Marcel Simon's outstanding book, which I've made much use of here, *Verus Israel: A Study of the Relations Between Christians and Jews in the Roman Empire AD 135–425*, pp. 173–77, 197–98.

15 *Jewish Antiquities* 19:8; cf. Acts 12:19–23.

16 Num. 23:19.

17 J. Taanit 65b; the following rabbinic citations are found in Herford's classic *Christianity in Talmud and Midrash*.

18 Exodus Rabbah 29:5.

19 See B. Shabbat 116a, 152a; B. Avodah Zarah 17b.

20 B. Avodah Zarah 4a.

21 Deut. 23:18; B. Avodah Zarah 16b–17a. The verse from Deuteronomy has to do with the prohibition of bringing, as an offering to the Temple, money that had been given to a prostitute for her services. See Herford, *Christianity in Talmud and Midrash*, pp. 138–43.

22 I heard this about Eve and the Serpent from Rabbi Daniel Lapin.

23 *Dialogue with Trypho* 56:23 on Gen. 19:24.

24 Gen. 4:23.

25 *Dialogue with Trypho* 52:2 on Gen. 1:26.

26 Gen. 1:27.

27 For accounts of Ishmael, Yochanan, and other sages in their encounters with *minim*, see B. Sanhedrin 38b–39b.

28 Genesis Rabbah 8:8.

29 *History of the Church* 1:4.

30 Barnabas 10:6.

31 Genesis Rabbah 64:4.

32 Gen. 19:3.

33 Genesis Rabbah 48:12.

34 Ibid. 46:2.

35 B. Shabbat 151b.

36 B. Niddah 61b.

37 I heard this explanation from Rabbi Daniel Lapin.

38 See the opening of the midrashic work Sifra, which gives Rabbi Ishmael's thirteen rules of exegesis.

39 Exodus Rabbah 47:1.

40 B. Sanhedrin 97b.

41 Ibid. 97a.

42 Deut. 30:1–10.

43 B. Shabbat 118b, citing Isa. 56:4, 7.

44 B. Sanhedrin 98a, citing Isa. 60:21, 59:16, 48:11.

45 For the origins of the Jesus tradition with Rabbi Eliezer, see Herford's classic study, invaluable to me in completing this book, *Christianity in Talmud and Midrash*, p. 352. For use of the name Ben Stada and Ben Pandira as referring to Jesus, see Herford, pp. 37ff.

46 In the *Mishneh Torah*, a shockingly frank discussion of Jesus appears in the also censored eleventh chapter "Hilchot Melachim."

47 B. Shabbat 104b.

48 B. Sanhedrin 106a.

49 The story is given in B. Sanhedrin 107b.

50 B. Sanhedrin 43a.

51 B. Gittin 56b–57a.

52 J. Nedarim 3:10.

53 See Neusner, *Judaism and Christianity in the Age of Constantine*, from which I've drawn heavily here.

54 Matt. 15:9.

55 See, for example, Genesis Rabbah 44:15–17.

56 Quoted in Neusner, p. 64.

1   Maccoby, *Judaism on Trial*, p. 158.

2   Ibid., pp. 169–70.

3   Ibid., p. 182.

4   Quoted from the outstanding annotated translation in Berger, *The Jewish-Christian Debate in the High Middle Ages*, p. 169.

5   Ibid., p. 48.

6   Talmage, ed., *Disputation and Dialogue: Readings in the Jewish-Christian Encounter*, pp. 119–23.

7   Berger, "The Jewish-Christian Debate in the High Middle Ages," in *Essential Papers on Judaism and Christianity in Conflict*, ed. Cohen, p. 497.

8   Maimonides, *Mishneh Torah*, "Hilchot Melachim" 11:1.

9   Isa. 60:21.

10   Maccoby, op. cit., p. 121.

11   Ibid., p. 118.

12   Talmage, op. cit., pp. 30–31.

13   See Talmage, "R. David Kimchi as Polemicist," in *Hebrew Union College Annual* 37 (1967).

14   From the "Epistle to Yemen," in Twersky, *A Maimonides Reader*, p. 441.

15   Berger, op. cit., pp. 107–8.

16   Maccoby, op. cit., p. 105.

17   Berger, op. cit., p. 90.

18   Isa. 53:3–5.

19   See Shereshevsky, "Rashi's and Christian Interpretations," *Jewish Quarterly Review* 61 (1970), p. 77.

20   Rashi on Isa. 53:3.

21   Ibid. on Isa. 53:1.

22   Ibid. on Isa. 53:4.

23   Isa. 52:9–10.

24   Ibid. 54:1; see Ibn Ezra on 52:13.

25   Kimchi, op. cit., p. 55.

26   Berger, op. cit., p. 90.

27   B. Sukkak 52a.

28   B. Avodah Zarah 9a; B. Sanhedrin 97a.

29   Maccoby, op. cit., p. 174.

30   Crescas, *The Refutation of Christian Principles*, trans. Lasker, p. 27.

31   Deut. 6:4.

32   Maimonides, *Guide of the Perplexed*, trans. Friedlander, p. 67.

33   Ps. 110:1.

34   John 5:30.

35   Berger, op. cit., pp. 163–4, 198.

36   Crescas, op. cit., p. 35.

37   Quoted in Lasker, *Jewish Philosophical Polemics Against Christianity in the Middle Ages*, p. 111.

38   Song of Solomon 1:2.

39   Rashi on Deut. 30:3.

40   Katz, *Exclusiveness and Tolerance: Studies in Jewish-Gentile Relations in Medieval & Modern Times*, pp. 21–22.

41   Translation in Twersky, *A Maimonides Reader*, 226–27.

42   Halevi, *The Kuzari*, translated by Hirschfeld, pp. 226–27.

43   See Katz, op. cit., pp. 115–21.

7. MODERN TIMES

1   Baeck, "Judaism in the Church," in *Jewish Perspectives on Christianity*, ed. Rothschild, pp. 104–5.

2   Shulchan Aruch, "Orach Chaim" 156:1.

3   Hirsch, *The Nineteen Letters*, p. 126.

4   Gen. 33:4.

5   Netziv on Gen. 33:4.

6   See Falk, *Journal of Ecumenical Studies* 19:1 (1982), pp. 105–11.

7   Berkovits, "Judaism in the Post-Christian Era," *Judaism* 15 (1966), pp. 74–84.

8   Heschel, "No Religion Is an Island," *Union Seminary Quarterly Review* 21 (1966), pp. 117–33.

9   LaHaye and Jenkins, *Tribulation Force*, pp. 366–67.

10   Luke 24:27, 45.

11   Rom. 7:6.

12   Scholem, *The Messianic Idea in Judaism*, p. 113.

13   Ibid., p. 140.

14   Rom. 2:15.

15   Maimonides, *Mishneh Torah*, "Hilchot Melachim" 8:10, 9:1.

16   That is, as Noachides, guided in their lives by the seven fundamental moral imperatives associated with the descendants of Noah (all humanity) and outlined in the Talmud's tractate Sanhedrin.

17   Mendelssohn, *Jerusalem and Other Jewish Writings*, trans. and ed. Jospe, pp. 113–12.

18   Klauser, *The Messianic Idea in Judaism*, pp. 519–31.

19   Baeck, "Romantic Religion," in op. cit., p. 85.

20   Quoted in Rothschild, ed., *Jewish Perspectives on Christianity*, pp. 170–71.

21   Ibid., p. 246.

22   Isa. 2:18; see Talmage, ed., *Disputation and Dialogue*, p. 15.

23   As with Williams, on the Jewish side we also find serious scholars setting aside their professorial reserve to author hard-hitting polemics. Brooklyn College professor David Berger, a contemporary star in the study of medieval Jewish polemic literature and translator of the anonymous *Nitzachon Vetus*, also wrote a punchy, concise pamphlet for Jews for Judaism, *Jews and "Jewish Christianity": A Jewish Response to the Missionary Challenge* (2002).

24   Quoted in "Countering Christian Missionaries and Messianists," *Forward*, August 8, 2003.

25   Brown, *Answering Jewish Objections to Jesus*, vol. 2: *Theological Objections*, p. 6.

26   Ibid., p. 217.

27   I Kings 1:16.

28   Maimonides, *Mishneh Torah*, "Hilchot Melachim" 11:1.

29   B. Berachot 5a.

30   Brown, *Answering Jewish Objections to Jesus*, vol. 3: *Messianic Prophecy Objections*, p. 84.

31   Dan. 12:9.

32   Zech. 12:9–10.

33   Brown, op. cit., p. 151.

34   Ibid., pp. 153–54, 160.

35   I Chronicles 16:5.

36   *World*, March 2, 2002.

CONCLUSION

1   Ex. 19:4–5.

2   Quoted in Katz, *Exclusiveness and Tolerance*, p. 141.

3   Buber, *Israel and the World*, pp. 28–40.

4   Benamozegh, *Israel and Humanity*, pp. 139–40.

5   Ibid., p. 133.

6   Zech. 14:9.

BIBLIOGRAPHY

JEWISH TRADITIONAL SOURCES

Targum Onkelos
Mishnah
Sifra
Jerusalem Talmud
Babylonian Talmud
Genesis Rabbah
Exodus Rabbah
Lamentations Rabbah
Pirke d'Rabbi Eliezer
Mishneh Torah
Shulchan Aruch

JEWISH MEDIEVAL AND LATER COMMENTATORS

Rashi
Radak
Rambam
Ramban
Ibn Ezra
Sforno
Netziv
Samson Raphael Hirsch

SOURCES IN ENGLISH

Abrams, Elliott. 1997. *Faith or Fear: How Jews Can Survive in a Christian America*. New York: Free Press.

Ahlstrom, Sydney E. 1975. *A Religious History of the American People*, vol. 2. Garden City, N.Y.: Image Books.

Alon, Gedaliah. 1996. *The Jewish in Their Land in the Talmudic Age*. Translated and edited by Gershon Levi. Cambridge, Mass.: Harvard University Press.

Armstrong, Karen. 1996. *Jerusalem: One City, Three Faiths*. New York: Knopf.

Becker, A. H., and A. Y. Reed, editors. 2003. *The Ways That Never Parted: Jews and Christians in Late Antiquity and the Early Middle Ages*. Tübingen, Germany: Mohr-Siebeck.

Benamozegh, Elijah. 1995. *Israel and Humanity*. Translated and edited by Maxwell Luria. New York: Paulist Press.

Berger, David, translator and editor. 1979. *The Jewish-Christian Debate in the High Middle Ages*. Philadelphia: Jewish Publication Society.

Berkovits, Eliezer. 1966. "Judaism in the Post-Christian Era." *Judaism* 15:74–84.

Bokser, Ben Zion. 1954. *From the World of the Cabbalah: The Philosophy of Rabbi Judah Loew of Prague*. New York: Philosophical Library.

Braude, William G., translator. 1959. *The Midrash on Psalms*. New Haven, Conn.: Yale University Press.

Brown, Michael L. 2000, 2001, 2003. *Answering Jewish Objections to Jesus*. 3 vols. Grand Rapids, Mich.: Baker Books.

Buber, Martin. 1948. *Israel and the World*. New York: Schocken.

Chilton, Bruce. 2000. *Rabbi Jesus: An Intimate Biography*. New York: Doubleday.

Cohen, Jeremy, editor. 1991. *Essential Papers on Judaism and Christianity in Conflict: From Late Antiquity to the Reformation*. New York: New York University Press.

Crescas, Hasdai. 1992. *The Refutation of the Christian Principles*. Translated by Daniel J. Lasker. Albany, N.Y.: State University of New York Press.

Dinnerstein, Leonard. 1994. *Anti-Semitism in America*. New York: Oxford University Press.

Eusebius. 1965. *The History of the Church*. Translated by G. A. Williamson. London: Penguin.

Falk, Harvey. 1982. "Rabbi Jacob Emden's Views on Christianity." *Journal of Ecumenical Studies* 19, no. 1: 105–111.

Fredriksen, Paula. 1999. *Jesus of Nazareth: King of the Jews*. New York: Knopf.

Frend, W. H. C. 1965. *The Early Church*. Philadelphia: Fortress Press.

Friedlander, M., editor and translator. 1873. *The Commentary of Ibn Ezra on Isaiah*, vol. 1. New York: Philipp Feldheim.

Gibbon, Edward. 1994. *The History of the Decline and Fall of the Roman Empire*. 3 vols. London: Penguin.

Goldstein, Morris. 1950. *Jesus in the Jewish Tradition*. New York: Macmillan.

Halbertal, Moshe. 2000. " 'Ones Possessed by Religion': Religious Tolerance in the Teachings of the Me'iri." *The Edah Journal* 1:1.

Halevi, Judah. 1964. *The Kuzari*. Translated by Hartwig Hirschfeld. New York: Schocken.

Harris-Shapiro, Carol. 1999. *Messianic Judaism: A Rabbi's Journey Through Religious Change in America*. Boston: Beacon Press.

Herford, R. Travers. 1975. *Christianity in Talmud and Midrash*. New York: Ktav Publishing House.

Heschel, Abraham Joshua. 1966. "No Religion Is an Island." *Union Seminary Quarterly Review* 21:117–133.

Hirsch, S. R. 1996. *The Nineteen Letters*. Translated by Joseph Elias. Jerusalem: Feldheim Publishers.

Jaynes, Julian. 1976. *The Origin of Consciousness in the Breakdown of the Bicameral Mind*. Boston: Houghton Mifflin.

Johnson, Paul. 1987. *A History of the Jews*. New York: Harper & Row.

Josephus. 1965. *Jewish Antiquities*, books 18–19. Translated by Louis H. Feldman. Cambridge, Mass.: Harvard University Press.

———. 1981. *The Jewish War*. Translated by G. A. Williamson. London: Penguin.

Justin Martyr. 1930. *The Dialogue with Trypho*. Translated by A. Lukyn Williams. New York: Macmillan.

Katz, Jacob. 1961. *Exclusiveness and Tolerance: Studies in Jewish-Gentile Relations in Medieval & Modern Times*. West Orange, N.J.: Berhman House.

Kimhi, Joseph. 1972. *The Book of the Covenant*. Translated by Frank Talmage. Toronto: Pontifical Institute of Mediaeval Studies.

Klauser, Joseph. 1955. *The Messianic Idea in Judaism*. New York: Macmillan.

LaHaye, Tim, and Jerry B. Jenkins. 1996. *Tribulation Force*. Wheaton, Ill.: Tyndale House.

———. 1995. *Left Behind: A Novel of the Earth's Last Days*. Wheaton, Ill.: Tyndale House Publishers.

Lasker, Daniel J. 1977. *Jewish Philosophical Polemics Against Christianity in the Middle Ages*. New York: Ktav Publishing House.

Maccoby, Hyam. 1986. *The Mythmaker: Paul and the Invention of Christianity*. San Francisco: HarperSanFrancisco.

———, editor and translator. 1982. *Judaism on Trial: Jewish-Christian Disputations in the Middle Ages*. London: Littman Library of Jewish Civilization.

MacMullen, Ramsay. 1984. *Christianizing the Roman Empire: AD 100–400*. New Haven, Conn.: Yale University Press.

Maimonides. 1956. *The Guide of the Perplexed*. Translated by M. Friedlander. Reprint. New York: Dover.

Mendelssohn, Moses. 1969. *Jerusalem and Other Jewish Writings*. Translated and edited by A. Jospe. New York: Schocken.

Menocal, Maria Rosa. 2002. *The Ornament of the World: How Muslims, Jews, and Christians Created a Culture of Tolerance in Medieval Spain*. Boston: Little, Brown.

Moore, George Foot. 1927, 1930. *Judaism in the First Centuries of the Christian Era: The Age of the Tannaim*. 3 vols. Cambridge, Mass.: Harvard University Press.

Murphy-O'Connor, Jerome. 1992. *The Holy Land: An Archaeological Guide from Earliest Times to 1700*. Oxford: Oxford University Press.

Neusner, Jacob. 1987. *Judaism and Christianity in the Age of Constantine: History, Messiah, Israel, and the Initial Confrontation*. Chicago: University of Chicago Press.

Pagels, Elaine. 1979. *The Gnostic Gospels*. New York: Vintage.

Podhoretz, Norman. 2002. *The Prophets*. New York: Free Press.

Rothschild, Fritz, editor. 1996. *Jewish Perspectives on Christianity*. New York: Continuum.

Sanders, E. P. 1977. *Paul and Palestinian Judaism*. Philadelphia: Fortress Press.

———. *Jesus and Judaism*. 1985. Philadelphia: Fortress Press.

Scholem, Gershom. 1971. *The Messianic Idea in Judaism: And Other Essays on Jewish Spirituality*. New York: Schocken.

———. 1946. *Major Trends in Jewish Mysticism*. New York: Schocken.

Shereshevsky, Esra. 1970. "Rashi's and Christian Intepretations." *Jewish Quarterly Review* 61:76–86.

Siker, Jeffrey S. 1991. *Disinheriting the Jews: Abraham in Early Christian Controversy*. Louisville, Ky.: Westminster/John Knox Press.

Simon, Marcel. 1996. *Verus Israel: A Study of the Relations Between Christians and Jews in the Roman Empire, AD 135–425*. London: Littman Library of Jewish Civilization.

Stark, Rodney. 1996. *The Rise of Christianity: A Sociologist Reconsiders History*. Princeton, N.J.: Princeton University Press.

———. 2003. *For the Glory of God: How Monotheism Led to Reformations, Science, Witchhunts, and the End of Slavery*. Princeton, N.J.: Princeton University Press.

Talmage, Frank. 1975. *Disputation and Dialogue: Readings in the Jewish-Christian Encounter*. New York: Ktav Publishing House.

———. 1967. "R. David Kimhi as Polemicist." *Hebrew Union College Annual* 38:213–35.

Twersky, Isadore. 1972. *A Maimonides Reader*. New York: Behrman House.

Vermes, Geza. 1981. *Jesus the Jew: A Historian's Reading of the Gospels*. Philadelphia: Fortress Press.

———. 1997. *The Complete Dead Sea Scrolls in English*. New York: Penguin.

———. 2000. *The Changing Faces of Jesus*. New York: Penguin Compass.

Wilson, A. N. 1997. *Paul: The Mind of the Apostle*. New York: Norton.

———. *Jesus: A Life*. 1992. New York: Norton.

Wilson, Marvin R. 1989. *Our Father Abraham: Jewish Roots of the Christian Faith*. Grand Rapids, Mich.: Wm. B. Eerdmans Publishing Co.

Winner, Lauren F. 2002. *Girl Meets God: On the Path to a Spiritual Life*. Chapel Hill, N.C.: Algonquin Books.

INDEX